CW01163059

ADVANCES IN GROUP PROCESSES

ADVANCES IN GROUP PROCESSES

Series Coeditors: Edward J. Lawler and Shane R. Thye

Recent Volumes:

Volumes 1–17:	Edited by Edward J. Lawler
Volume 18:	Edited by Edward J. Lawler and Shane R. Thye
Volume 19:	Group Cohesion, Trust and Solidarity – Edited by Edward J. Lawler and Shane R. Thye
Volume 20:	Power and Status – Edited by Shane R. Thye and John Skvoretz
Volume 21:	Theory and Research on Human Emotions – Edited by Jonathan H. Turner
Volume 22:	Social Identification in Groups – Edited by Shane R. Thye and Edward J. Lawler
Volume 23:	Social Psychology of the Workplace – Edited by Shane R. Thye and Edward J. Lawler
Volume 24:	Social Psychology of Gender – Edited by Shelley J. Correll
Volume 25:	Justice – Edited by Karen A. Hegtvedt and Jody Clay-Warner
Volume 26:	Altruism and Prosocial Behavior in Groups – Edited by Shane R. Thye and Edward J. Lawler
Volume 27:	Edited by Shane R. Thye and Edward J. Lawler
Volume 28:	Edited by Shane R. Thye and Edward J. Lawler
Volume 29:	Edited by Will Kalkhoff, Shane R. Thye and Edward J. Lawler
Volume 30:	Thirtieth Anniversary Edition – Edited by Shane R. Thye and Edward J. Lawler
Volume 31:	Edited by Shane R. Thye and Edward J. Lawler
Volume 32:	Edited by Shane R. Thye and Edward J. Lawler
Volume 33:	Edited by Shane R. Thye and Edward J. Lawler
Volume 34:	Edited by Shane R. Thye and Edward J. Lawler

EDITORIAL ADVISORY BOARD

Stephan Bernard
Indiana University, USA

Jessica Collett
University of Notre Dame, USA

Karen Hegtvedt
Emory University, USA

Michael Hogg
Claremont Graduate University, USA

Will Kalkhoff
Kent State University, USA

David Melamed
University of South Carolina, USA

Jane Sell
Texas A&M University, USA

# ADVANCES IN GROUP PROCESSES

EDITED BY

SHANE R. THYE
University of South Carolina, USA

EDWARD J. LAWLER
Cornell University, USA

emerald PUBLISHING

United Kingdom – North America – Japan
India – Malaysia – China

Emerald Publishing Limited
Howard House, Wagon Lane, Bingley BD16 1WA, UK

First edition 2018

Copyright © 2018 Emerald Publishing Limited

Reprints and permissions service
Contact: permissions@emeraldinsight.com

No part of this book may be reproduced, stored in a retrieval system, transmitted in any form or by any means electronic, mechanical, photocopying, recording or otherwise without either the prior written permission of the publisher or a licence permitting restricted copying issued in the UK by The Copyright Licensing Agency and in the USA by The Copyright Clearance Center. Any opinions expressed in the chapters are those of the authors. Whilst Emerald makes every effort to ensure the quality and accuracy of its content, Emerald makes no representation implied or otherwise, as to the chapters' suitability and application and disclaims any warranties, express or implied, to their use.

British Library Cataloguing in Publication Data
A catalogue record for this book is available from the British Library

ISBN: 978-1-78769-014-1 (Print)
ISBN: 978-1-78769-013-4 (Online)
ISBN: 978-1-78769-015-8 (EPub)

ISSN: 0882-6145

Printed and bound by CPI Group (UK) Ltd, Croydon, CR0 4YY

ISOQAR certified Management System, awarded to Emerald for adherence to Environmental standard ISO 14001:2004.

Certificate Number 1985
ISO 14001

INVESTOR IN PEOPLE

CONTENTS

List of Contributors	ix
Preface	xi

"Can a Girl's Best Friend be Born in a Lab?" The Role of Ritual in Production Process Conservatism *Jaekyung Ha, Renée Gosline and Ezra Zuckerman Sivan*	*1*
Accelerometers as a Methodological Tool in Group Processes Research *Christin L. Munsch and Elizabeth S. Zack*	*29*
Modeling Small Group Status and Power Dynamics Using Vocal Accommodation *Joseph Dippong and Will Kalkhoff*	*51*
Identity Theory Paradigm Integration: Assessing the Role of Prominence and Salience in the Verification and Self-Esteem Relationship *Kelly L. Markowski and Richard T. Serpe*	*75*
Occupational Status, Impression Formation, and Criminal Sanctioning: A Vignette Experiment *Amy Kroska and Marshall R. Schmidt*	*103*
Understanding White Americans' Perceptions of "Reverse" Discrimination: An Application of a New Theory of Status Dissonance *Deena A. Isom Scott*	*129*
When do We Feel Responsible for Other People's Behavior and Attitudes? *Vanessa K. Bohns, Daniel A. Newark and Erica J. Boothby*	*159*
Expectations and Coordination in Small Groups *Antonio D. Sirianni*	*181*
Index	*209*

LIST OF CONTRIBUTORS

Vanessa K. Bohns	Department of Organizational Behavior, Cornell University, NY, USA
Erica J. Boothby	Department of Psychology, Cornell University, NY, USA
Joseph Dippong	Department of Sociology, University of North Carolina at Charlotte, NC, USA
Renée Gosline	Sloan School of Management, MIT, MA, USA
Jaekyung Ha	Strategy and Organisation Department, EMLYON Business School, Écully, France
Will Kalkhoff	Department of Sociology, Kent State University, OH, USA
Amy Kroska	Department of Sociology, University of Oklahoma, OK, USA
Kelly L. Markowski	Department of Sociology, Kent State University, OH, USA
Christin L. Munsch	Department of Sociology, University of Connecticut, CT, USA
Daniel A. Newark	Department of Management, HEC Paris, France
Marshall R. Schmidt	Department of Sociology, University of Oklahoma, OK, USA
Deena A. Isom Scott	Department of Criminology and Criminal Justice and African American Studies Program, University of South Carolina, SC, USA
Richard T. Serpe	Department of Sociology, Kent State University, OH, USA
Antonio D. Sirianni	Department of Sociology, Cornell University, NY, USA

Elizabeth S. Zack	Department of Sociology, Indiana University, IN, USA
Ezra Zuckerman Sivan	Sloan School of Management, MIT, MA, USA

PREFACE

Advances in Group Processes is a peer-reviewed annual volume that publishes theoretical analyses, reviews, and theory-based empirical chapters on group phenomena. The series adopts a broad conception of "group processes." This includes work on groups ranging from the very small to the very large, and on classic and contemporary topics, such as status, power, trust, justice, conflict, social influence, identity, decision-making, intergroup relations, and social networks. Previous contributors have included scholars from diverse fields, including sociology, psychology, political science, economics, business, philosophy, computer science, mathematics, and organizational behavior.

Several years ago, we added an editorial board to the series to broaden the review process and draw upon the expertise of some of the top scholars in the discipline. That board consists of Steve Benard, Jessica Collett, Karen Hegtvedt, Michael Hogg, Will Kalkhoff, David Melamed, and Jane Sell. This group of scholars has made the series better, and we are grateful for their service, guidance, and advice.

The volume opens with a paper that addresses a topic probably somewhat novel for the readers of *Advances*. "Can a Girl's Best Friend Be Born in a Lab?" The Role of Ritual in Production Process Conservatism" by Jaekyung Ha, Renée Gosline, and Ezra Zuckerman Sivan aims to understand why consumers often prefer goods that are manufactured in a traditional manner rather than those created using new technologies and practices, even when the latter are of higher quality. This question is posed in the context of a widespread preference for traditionally mined diamonds (as engagement or wedding rings) over diamonds created in a laboratory. This preference is termed "production process conservatism" and is examined using two experiments involving online and student MBA samples. The results indicate that women do prefer traditionally mined diamonds and that this process is mediated by the perceived risk associated with the ritualism of the event. This chapter yields provocative insights into fundamental sociological processes as they relate to macro-consumer behavior.

The next two chapters address issues within the realm of measurement. First, Christin L. Munsch and Elizabeth S. Zack present "Accelerometers as a Methodological Tool in Group Processes." They review the literature in a variety of disciplines that use accelerometers — a device used to measure force due to gravity or a change in speed or direction. They present data from four unique experiments that address the reliability, validity, and sociological relevance of accelerometers for use in the study of aggression. They convincingly demonstrate the utility of these tools for sociological research and social sciences more generally. The next chapter "Modeling Small Group Status and Power Dynamics Using Vocal Accommodation" by Joseph Dippong and Will Kalkhoff offers insights into the development of status and dominance hierarchies. They first review the literature that links patterns of vocal accommodation in the paraverbal range of the voice to the emergence of status and dominance hierarchies in small groups. This measure of voice variability is discussed in the context of two theoretical traditions: the communication accommodation theory and the expectation states research program. They find that vocal accommodation is consistently linked to viewer perceptions of dominance, but not perceptions of prestige. This chapter will certainly interest scholars interested in communication theory, small group structures, social influence, and debate strategy.

The next three papers address theoretical and empirical issues regarding status and identity. The first paper "Identity Theory Paradigm Integration: Assessing the Role of Prominence and Salience in the Verification and Self-esteem Relationship" by Kelly L. Markowski and Richard T. Serpe integrates the structural and perceptual control programs of the structural identity theory. Examining data on the parent spouse identities, they test the direct impacts of salience, prominence, and nonverification on the authenticity, efficacy, and worth as indicators of self-esteem. They find significant interactions among the three independent variables as they impact authenticity, efficacy, and worth. Overall, this paper represents an important integration of two important research programs in the identity domain and suggests key directions for future research. Next, Amy Kroska and Marshall R. Schmidt examine the antecedents of criminal sentencing recommendations in "Occupational Status, Impression Formation, and Criminal Sanctioning: A Vignette Experiment." Specifically, they examine the effects of an offender's occupational status (white- vs blue- or pink-collar) and crime label (overcharging vs robbery) on recommended criminal sentences. Using predictions from the affect control theory, they find that white-collar offenders and those who commit robbery receive higher recommended sentences, and that these effects are mediated by perceptions of crime seriousness. In the final paper of the trio, Deena A. Isom Scott examines reverse discrimination in "Understanding White Americans' Perceptions of 'Reverse' Discrimination: An Application of a New Theory of Status Dissonance." Using the Pew Research Center's Racial Attitudes in America Survey III, she develops and tests a theory that addresses why it is that some White Americans perceive an anti-White racial bias and reverse discrimination. The theoretical and empirical analysis yields provocative insights into the causes and consequences of perceived social inequality.

The final two papers address issues of influence and cooperation in groups. A relatively unexplored phenomenon is examined in "When Do We Feel Responsible for Other People's Behavior and Attitudes?" by Vanessa K. Bohns, Daniel A. Newark and Erica Boothby. For many years, sociologists and psychologists have explored how the social environment produces social influence processes such as conformity, persuasion, and obedience. However, the focus of this past research has been primarily on the target of social influence or characteristics of the influencer. This paper asks a new question – how accurately do people assess their own influence over another person's attitudes and behaviors. In this sense, the paper addresses an important yet unexplored facet of social influence. The final paper explores whether or not rules for expectation formation directly improve coordination. In "Expectations and Coordination in Small Groups," Antonio D. Sirianni uses agent-based simulations to examine how empirically observed expectation-generating rules produce group coordination. The results indicate that expectations about one another often produce suboptimal levels of coordination. Theoretically, the paper adopts a game theoretic notion of interaction to the e-state structuralism model of hierarchy formation. This paper should be of particular interest to scholars focused on coordination or cooperation, status structures, game theory, or behavioral economics.

Shane Thye
Edward J. Lawler
Series and Volume Coeditors

"CAN A GIRL'S BEST FRIEND BE BORN IN A LAB?" THE ROLE OF RITUAL IN PRODUCTION PROCESS CONSERVATISM

Jaekyung Ha, Renée Gosline and Ezra Zuckerman Sivan

ABSTRACT

Purpose — *In this paper, we aim to understand why consumers often prefer products made using traditional practices even when products made using new practices are not of lower quality. We argue that this resistance, which we call "production process conservatism," is heightened when the product is used in the performance of a social ritual.*

Methodology — *We develop this argument in the context of diamond jewelry, as consumers have generally been resistant to diamonds that are produced in laboratories, i.e., lab-created diamonds. Hypotheses were tested using experiments conducted with an online sample (Experiment 1) and with an MBA student sample (Experiment 2).*

Findings — *In Experiment 1, we find that married female respondents significantly prefer mined diamonds to lab-created diamonds when they are used as part of an engagement gift as opposed to a more routine gift. In Experiment 2, we find the same effect among women; in addition, the perceived risk associated with the ritual is found to mediate this production process conservatism.*

Social Implications — *This paper contributes to the understanding of a macrosocial phenomenon — acceptance of an innovation — by examining microinteractive processes in groups.*

Originality/value of Paper — *This paper develops an original theory that when individuals deviate from traditional aspects of rituals, they risk signaling a lack of commitment or cultural competence to the group even when such aspects are not explicitly stated.*

Keywords: Ritual; social valuation; public knowledge; production process; lab-created diamonds; technological innovation

INTRODUCTION

Why do consumers care about production processes — namely, where, how, and by whom a product has been made — at some times but not at other times? One obvious consideration is that different production processes potentially lead to different products, as in the cases of nouvelle cuisine (Rao, Monin, & Durand, 2003) and grass-fed meat (Weber, Heinze, & DeSoucey, 2008). Thus, in some instances, consumers may regard production processes as proxies for the product quality. Moreover, even when the difference in the product quality is difficult to verify, consumers may *perceive* a difference and act accordingly; that is, consumers may be willing to pay a premium for certain production processes under the assumption that such processes indicate the differential quality, even when the quality of the product is indistinguishable or physically identical (e.g., Carroll & Swaminathan, 2000; Frake, 2017; Newman & Bloom, 2012).

However, it is puzzling why people often have preferences for production processes — in particular, "traditional" practices — when alternative processes are more efficient or produce higher-quality products (Hahl, 2016; Negro, Hannan, & Rao, 2011; Rao et al., 2003; Simons & Roberts, 2008). In these cases, the reasons for such preferences are unclear. Under what conditions will consumers be conservative with regard to their evaluation of production processes? In other words, when will they be reluctant to accept the very same product when it is produced by a new production process — a phenomenon we call "production process conservatism"? The existing literature does not provide a clear answer to this question. Several studies acknowledge that "domains" (Podolny & Hill-Popper, 2004), "tastes for popularity" (Lieberson, 2000; Lieberson & Lynn, 2003), or "audience type" (Goldberg, Hannan, & Kovács, 2015; Pontikes, 2012) vary in terms of the extent to which certain dimensions of value — including the production process — are salient. However, the following question remains: Why does such salience vary, and why are production processes sometimes regarded as defining features of an item?

In this paper, we argue that the salience of the production process varies depending on the social context, and we suggest that consumers will be concerned about deviation from traditional production processes when the products in question are used in socially consequential rituals. A ritual is a group process in which members of the group conform to the "conventions that set up visible public definitions" (Douglas & Isherwood, 1979, p. 65). Rituals use symbols to create public knowledge and coordinate people's expectations (Chwe, 2003;

Douglas & Isherwood, 1979; Durkheim, 1976). When people perform rituals, they intend to express appropriate messages to other members of the group about their social relationships (Caplow, 1984; Swidler, 2003). If performers deviate from the rules, they risk inadvertently signaling that they are either incapable of doing or unmotivated to do what is necessary to maintain or strengthen said relationships (Chwe, 2003; Schelling, 1980). Thus, especially when the ritual has *high stakes* (i.e., when the outcome of a ritual is intended to be highly consequential to the parties involved), the parties will tend to signal competence and commitment by conforming to the rules and practicing general conservatism (cf. Zuckerman, 1999).

This paper presents a test of this mechanism by focusing on a case in which the production process is not explicitly prescribed as a rule; however, the high-stakes nature of the ritual will make consumers conservative with regard to buying products that are made using a new process. The specific case is diamond jewelry. Although diamonds have long been used in various forms of jewelry, a special segment of diamond jewelry — engagement rings — is associated with the widespread ritual of engagement and marriage (Brinig, 1990; Epstein, 1982a; Kunz, 1973; Rothman, 1987). In the United States (and many other Western countries), clear conventional social expectations surround engagement rings — for example, the ring's appearance, the finger on which it should be worn, and the amount of money men should spend on it (Bowers, 2015; Spar, 2006). The production process has not been explicitly regarded as a feature of the ritual rules, because diamonds are used to be produced exclusively through mining; therefore, an explicit rule regarding the production process was unnecessary. However, diamonds can now be produced synthetically in laboratories (called "lab-created diamonds" or "synthetic diamonds"). These diamonds have exactly the same chemical, physical, and optical characteristics as mined diamonds, and they are available at lower prices (Markoff, 2015). The advent of an alternative production process thus poses a question to ritual performers: Should the production process be regarded as part of the ritual rules? Is it problematic if the diamond was born in a lab? We aim to show that the answer is yes for people who are knowledgeable about the ritual and are motivated to perform it well.

The rest of the paper proceeds as follows. We first develop a theoretical framework that clarifies the logic of rituals and suggest why traditional practices associated with rituals might be maintained even when no codified rules proscribe change. We then focus on the case of mined vs lab-created diamonds. We briefly review the ritual of giving and receiving diamond engagement rings in the United States and summarize the production processes for mined diamonds and lab-created diamonds. We then test our hypotheses in a series of experiments. We conclude by discussing general implications.

THEORETICAL FRAMEWORK
Why Do People Follow Ritual Rules?

Rituals are a specific form of interpersonal interaction found in various social settings, from shaking hands (Goffman, 1955) to rites of passage (Turner, 1995) to communal religious events (Durkheim, 1976). Rituals generally enable performers to either create or reinforce an institutionalized role relationship in their social group (Collins, 2014). The successful accomplishment of a ritual affirms that the performer is capable of and committed to a particular role and the relationships associated with it.

To communicate a clear message to relevant audiences, rituals play by a set of symbolic rules. A performer's observance of ritual rules serves as the primary basis of an audience's evaluation of said performer. Thus, people follow ritual rules to avoid being evaluated negatively by an audience. For instance, by participating in rituals, performers show their economic competence (Barnett, 1938) and publicize their social status and mutual obligations (Malinowski, 1920). If a performer does not follow ritual rules, his or her message risks being misunderstood and perhaps being cast in a negative light.

In many cases, ritual rules include specifications regarding artifacts or commodities (Douglas & Isherwood, 1979). For example, in the Western Christian culture, people often wear black suits to funerals to express their condolences, and the Americans present each other with wrapped gifts at Christmas. In these examples, "black suits" and "Christmas gifts" are ritual products that are prescribed by each ritual's rules (Caplow, 1984). If an individual performs a ritual without following these rules, he risks not properly publicizing his capability and commitment to a social role. For example, if a person wears a colorful dress to an American funeral, she risks being considered rude, regardless of her true intentions. Disobeying the rules of funeral rituals may impair her relationship with others, particularly the family of the deceased, and weaken her social status relative to others who dress appropriately. Similarly, consider a case in which an American man wants to marry a woman but does not follow the conventional rules of giving her an engagement ring. The risk is that his audience, including his would-be fiancée, will downgrade its evaluation of his cultural competence or commitment compared with that of other men. It could even cause his proposal to be rejected.

The upshot is that when the stakes are high, any given ritual performer will tend to not deviate from ritual rules, thereby reinforcing the primacy of ritual rules for subsequent performers. That is, once established and widely observed, a ritual rule can acquire great social weight, even when there is no functional reason for it (Centola, Willer, & Macy, 2005; Chwe, 2003; Correll et al., 2017; Swidler, 2003). Accordingly, such rules can vary widely across social contexts, and there are social boundaries that separate groups of people who abide by the same ritual rules (Collins, 2014). Whereas mourners may wear black in the Western culture, white is worn at traditional Korean funerals. Obviously, color itself has no functional purpose at a funeral, but following what is known to be the rule in each culture is important. Color thus works as a focal point (Schelling, 1980) or a conventional equilibrium (Elster, 1989) from which no individual can benefit by unilaterally deviating. The more important the ritual is in establishing or reinforcing relationships, the riskier a potential failed outcome is and the more we can expect a ritual performer to abide by ritual rules.

Sensitivity to the Stakes: When Are Ritual Rules Important to Follow?
Ritual rules do not have the same importance in all cases. This variation may stem from two main sources: (1) situational factors in which the level of stakes varies and (2) differences in individuals' capabilities to recognize ritual rules and their sensitivity to them. In this section, we elaborate on these points by noting variation in both ritual types and individual role assignment.

As noted, rituals may facilitate the creation of a new role relationship or reinforce an existing one. In general, the stakes are higher in the former case, because entering a new phase typically entails a greater effort than maintaining the status quo. According to Turner (1995), in the former case, rituals are intervening *liminal* periods between one stable stage, in which an individual's status (reflected by her relationships to others) is stable, and another stable stage. During these periods, the characteristics of ritual performers are subject to close scrutiny. Assessments tend to be more relaxed when relationships are already established.

To illustrate this difference, consider the ritual of handshaking when individuals greet one another in the American business culture. Proper observance of this ritual is clearly more important when two executives meet for the first time than when they meet the second time (and, as they continue their relationship, they will be more likely to dispense with the ritual altogether). Similarly, compare giving a gift as part of a high-stakes ritual such as an engagement proposal, with giving a gift as part of a (relatively) low-stakes ritual such as a birthday. The former case carries much higher risk because this ritual is designed to disrupt the status quo and create a new role relationship. A relationship may be damaged by a poor performance of the gift-giving ritual on someone's birthday, but a relationship is much less likely to survive if the ritual relates to progressing from boyfriend–girlfriend status to marriage.

Consider now how a ritual may be more critical to some roles than others. For example, if anyone should wear black to a funeral, this will be especially true for close family members. By contrast, because much less is at stake for other participants, they can observe the rule at a lower level of compliance (e.g., wearing a gray skirt). Relatedly, the stakes may vary depending on the pre-existing social roles among ritual performers. For example, suppose an employee invites his boss over for a Thanksgiving dinner. The employee would be expected to ensure that all the elements of a traditional Thanksgiving dinner were present more than his boss would if the roles were reversed.

Why Do People Care about Implicit Ritual Rules?
Let us now return to the case at hand and clarify why ritual performers might prefer conservative practices, even when they do not constitute an explicit dimension of ritual rules. In particular, we focus on consumers' acceptance

(or lack thereof) of new production processes in rituals, even when (1) no explicit rule dictates the use of a particular production process and (2) the new production process offers clear benefits (in the form of either a lower price for a given quality or higher quality for a given price). These conditions provide a conservative context to examine the presence of ritual rules and thus help us calibrate the extent of "production process conservatism" that is driven by rituals.

We argue that consumers should be conservative, even with regard to dimensions that are not explicitly prescribed as ritual rules, as long as they have good reason to assume that the other people might regard these dimensions as ritual rules (Chwe, 2003; Correll et al., 2017). Insofar, as other people might regard a certain dimension as a ritual rule, a person risks triggering a negative reaction when he or she deviates from such "rules." In other words, when the stakes are sufficiently high, the performer's personal belief – whether *he* thinks a certain thing is (or should be) a ritual – is overridden by his interpretation of the public belief – what *others* think is (or should be) a ritual rule. Thus, the presumption that potential audiences *might* regard a particular practice as a ritual rule is a sufficient condition for a ritual performer's preference for a conservative practice.

Consider production processes as a dimension of ritual rules, which are the focus of this paper. When production processes are part of the ritual rules (such as Halal or Kosher food), alternative production processes, regardless of how technologically advanced or efficient they are, cannot be accepted as long as the ritual rule proscribes any alternative to the traditional production process. But the implications are unclear when product has historically been produced in only one way such that alternative production processes were unimaginable before. In this case, the advent of a new production process raises the unprecedented question of whether it *is* or *is not* included in the ritual rules. Moreover, if the alternative production process provides clear advantages, a dilemma arises. On one hand, if the production process is not included in the ritual rules, choosing a new production process will not harm the performance of rituals and promises benefits. On the other hand, if the production process is an important part of the ritual, choosing the new production process risks a negative outcome: the failure of the ritual.

We argue that the latter consideration should weigh heavily in a high-stakes ritual context. In this paper, we can hold constant the coupling of the production process with the product, and we vary the extent to which the product is used in a high-stakes ritual context or a low-stakes ritual context. We expect that when the stakes are high, consumers will be conservative about the production process and abide by traditional practices, even when the process may not pertain to a ritual rule and when consumers must forgo a clear advantage. Throughout this paper, we call the conservative preference – in particular, with regard to production process – in ritual contexts the "ritual effect" and aim to both capture its presence and provide an explanation for the underlying mechanism of such an effect. Support for our prediction will provide conservative evidence showing that consumers abide by ritual rules. Our theory leads to the following set of hypotheses.

H1. When products are associated with a high-stakes ritual, people are less accepting of new alternative production processes, even when the production process is not explicitly proscribed and new production processes provide clear advantages.

H2. The perceived level of risk mediates the ritual effect in generating production process conservatism.

SETTING: THE PRODUCTION PROCESS OF DIAMONDS

Diamonds and Engagement Rituals

Diamond rings were not considered to be a prerequisite for betrothal by most of the American brides and grooms until the early twentieth century (Brinig, 1990; Epstein, 1982b). The practice of giving and receiving diamond rings in the process of engagement is believed to be traceable to the successful efforts of De Beers and its marketing agency. Along with the famous slogan of "A Diamond is Forever," De Beers successfully invented the image of a diamond ring as an expression of everlasting love (Epstein, 1982b). As a result, diamond rings became virtually synonymous with engagement among the Americans; by 1965, more than 80% of all brides in the United States received a diamond engagement ring, and the diamond ring is still widely regarded as an inseparable part of courtship and engagement (Bowers, 2015; Brinig, 1990; Kunz, 1973; O'Rourke, 2007; Rothman, 1987).

As the giving and receiving of an engagement ring has become a widespread ritual associated with marriage, conventional social expectations − or "ritual rules" − have emerged about how to perform this practice. For instance, general expectations have developed about the ring's appearance, the finger on which it should be worn, and the amount of money men should spend on it (Bowers, 2015; Spar, 2006). The performance of this ritual practice was partly evaluated by the features of diamonds, commonly known as the "4Cs" − color, cut, clarity, and carats. Developed and standardized by the Gemological Institute of America (GIA) in the 1950s, the 4Cs are a widely adopted measure of quality in the diamond industry; diamonds are highly valued when they are larger, when they are nearly or absolutely colorless, when they have fewer inclusions (i.e., imperfections), and when they have a balanced cut that allows the maximum reflection of light (Scott & Yelowitz, 2010).

Mined Diamonds and the Diamond Pipeline

Diamonds have a particular processing and distribution structure, often called the diamond pipeline that distinguishes them from other materials and natural resources. Because the specific features of the diamond-production process have made a significant contribution to the historical image of the end product, we will briefly explain the full process.

Historically, gem-quality diamonds have been sourced from nature, mostly from the underground mines. Diamonds are formed deep in the earth when carbon is subjected to high pressure and high temperature. *Kimberlite*, a type of volcanic rock, is known to be the major source of diamonds. In the exploration stage, producers attempt to find these kimberlite pipes and perform a geological analysis of minerals to find a diamond-bearing kimberlite and assess whether the kimberlite is a commercially viable source of diamonds. The production of rough diamonds is a highly concentrated industry in terms of both the country of origin and the number of firms involved (Even-Zohar, 2007, pp. 166–168).

A long history of cartel behavior, led by De Beers, has characterized the distribution of rough diamonds. Rough diamond stones are purchased by either small traders or the diamond trading company (DTC), which is the distribution arm of De Beers. Rough diamonds are sorted based on various characteristics that determine their value when they are processed, and they are sold either through the *sightholder* system, tenders, or spot sales. In the processing stage, diamonds are cut and polished from rough stones into finished gems. This stage of the process is highly labor intensive and competitive, and thousands of small players populate this segment of the diamond industry. In the preparation for jewelry manufacturing, finished stones may be graded by organizations such as the GIA. Finally, these polished diamonds are made into diamond jewelry. Diamond jewelry manufacturers tend to be located close to the end market. The United States is the single largest diamond consumer market, consuming roughly half of the world's polished diamonds (Even-Zohar, 2007).

Technological Innovation in the Production Process of Diamonds

Although it has been possible to synthetically produce diamonds since the 1950s, the technology to produce gem-quality diamonds in a cost-effective manner emerged only in the past decade (Markoff, 2015). The production process for lab-created diamonds stands in stark contrast to that of mined diamonds, which are created by geological processes. Whereas mined diamonds rely on natural resources and specialized labor around the globe, lab-created diamonds are based on the technology. Lab-made gemstone diamonds are mostly created using one of two methods. The high pressure-high temperature (HPHT) method replicates the natural geological process. General Electric used this method when it first introduced gem-quality lab-created diamonds in 1970 (Olson, 2000). In the first stage of this process, small seed diamonds are placed into a machine and are covered with a mixture of catalyst metal and graphite powders. The machine replicates the natural geological process, increasing temperatures up to 2,500°C and pressure up to 60,000 atmospheres. With the second method, chemical vapor deposition (CVD), manufacturers create diamond crystals in a low-pressure environment using carbon-bearing gases. This process involves depositing a carbon vapor onto a substrate to grow the stones (Isberg et al., 2002; Spear & Dismukes, 1994).

These lab-created diamonds are different from inexpensive diamond alternatives such as cubic zirconium or moissanite, which bear some visual resemblance to diamonds but have completely different molecular structures. In contrast, lab-created diamonds are chemically, physically, and optically equivalent to mined diamonds. In other words, colorless lab-created diamond gemstones can be made identical to naturally occurring mined diamonds of high quality. However, the market share of lab-created diamonds is very small in the gemstone market. Whereas lab-created diamonds accounted for more than 90% of industrial diamond consumption (Olson, 2000), lab-created diamonds were estimated to represent only 0.01% of the volume of US diamond gemstones sales in 2010 (Bain and Company, 2011, p. 75).

EMPIRICAL EVIDENCE

We designed a series of experiments to test our hypotheses. For Pretests 1 and 2 and Study 1, we recruited participants through Amazon Mechanical Turk (AMT), an online website where researchers can recruit subjects by offering a monetary reward upon task completion. AMT has been found to provide a reliable pool of subjects and to serve as a useful resource for experimental research (Mason & Suri, 2012; Paolacci, Chandler, & Ipeirotis, 2010). However, because the salience of the engagement ritual may be sensitive to respondents' age and life stage, in Study 2, we test our theory using MBA students. For Study 2, we conducted an experiment as a course credit for Master of Business Administration (MBA) students at a private university in the northeastern United States.

Pretests 1 and 2: Expected Market Value for Products Made Using a Non-traditional Production Process

Pretests 1 and 2 sought to confirm a few assumptions that underlie the test of our theory in the main study. First, we wished to confirm that diamonds are associated with rituals. Second, we aimed to establish that people care about the production process of diamonds when the objective measure of quality is identical and the ways in which their evaluations are translated into price discounts.

Method

A total of 232[1] were recruited through AMT, and they completed a short survey for US$0.25. Subjects who had graduated from high school and lived in the United States were eligible for our survey. At the beginning of the survey, subjects were told a cover story, i.e., that the survey aimed to determine how to display and value items to develop an online game and that participants would be given questions on various items. Pretest 1 was conducted as a between-subject design whereby participants were randomly assigned to a survey for either a mined diamond condition or a lab-created diamond condition.

The survey consists of our main questions, questions that supply relevant information, and filler questions designed to disguise the survey's true purpose.

To provide relevant information to the subjects, the survey asked a series of questions that subjects had to read and understand. For example, they were told that "color, cut, carat, and clarity, widely known as the 4Cs, are the standard ways of evaluating a diamond" and were asked, "If you were buying a diamond, which would you think is the most important?" Subjects were also given information about alternative production processes – lab-created diamonds – through these questions. The answers to these questions were not necessarily important for our research purpose; the goal was to provide respondents with relevant knowledge. The survey also included a few filler questions that were unrelated to our research question to make the survey flow more naturally and to make the cover story more credible.

In the main questions, we first asked how much a diamond was associated with special occasions on the 5-point scale. Later, subjects were given descriptions of two diamonds whose objective quality was (almost) the same but that were different in dimensions unrelated to quality such as shape and the date polished. Whereas the basic idea was to provide two items that were identical except for their production processes, to avoid a demand effect, we made slight adjustments in the diamonds' properties such that the production process differences were not explicit (see Fig. 1). Subjects were then asked how much they would expect a lab-created diamond to sell for if a mined diamond was sold for

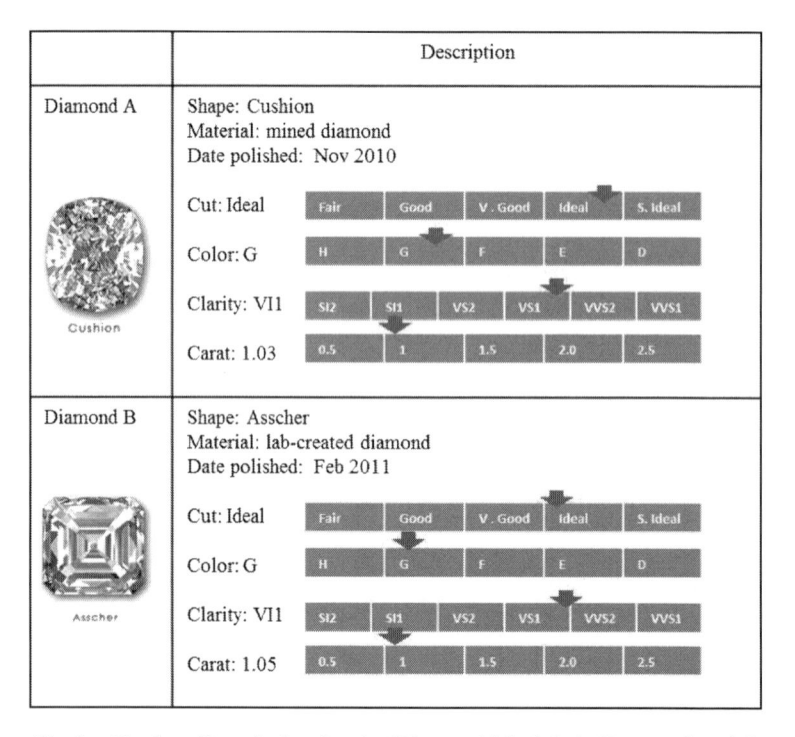

	Description
Diamond A (Cushion)	Shape: Cushion Material: mined diamond Date polished: Nov 2010 Cut: Ideal [Fair / Good / V. Good / **Ideal** / S. Ideal] Color: G [H / **G** / F / E / D] Clarity: VI1 [SI2 / SI1 / VS2 / **VS1** / VVS2 / VVS1] Carat: 1.03 [0.5 / **1** / 1.5 / 2.0 / 2.5]
Diamond B (Asscher)	Shape: Asscher Material: lab-created diamond Date polished: Feb 2011 Cut: Ideal [Fair / Good / V. Good / **Ideal** / S. Ideal] Color: G [H / **G** / F / E / D] Clarity: VI1 [SI2 / SI1 / VS2 / **VS1** / VVS2 / VVS1] Carat: 1.05 [0.5 / **1** / 1.5 / 2.0 / 2.5]

Fig. 1. Product Description for the Diamond Module in Pretests 1 and 2.

10,000 dollars. To check the effect of our adjustments of diamond properties, we counterbalanced those differences.

Although we intended a subtle manipulation to avoid a demand effect, one unavoidable downside was that we could not determine how many of the subjects were actually paying attention to the production process and how their level of attention would influence the result. To clarify subjects' thinking when they revealed their price expectations for lab-created diamonds, Pretest 2 replicated and extended Pretest 1. A total of 319 additional subjects were recruited from AMT. In addition to the questions asked in Pretest 1, these participants were asked the main reason for their price expectations after they submitted their expected prices for lab-created diamonds.

Results and Discussion

Pretest 1 and Pretest 2 present two findings. First, with respect to the first question about the extent to which diamonds are associated with special occasions, the mean response was 1.52 (1 = very strong association and 5 = no association at all; $N = 232$; 95% confidence interval [1.42, 1.62]). This result shows that diamonds are a good example of a ritual product. Second, we find that the subjects cared about the production process independent of the quality and that they expected significantly lower prices for a lab-created diamonds. Compared with US$10,000 for a mined diamond, subjects expected to pay US$8,399 for a lab-created diamond of the same quality ($N = 213$),[2] which indicates a significant difference given that the 95% confidence interval ranged from US$7,973 to US$8,825. Additionally, because no significant difference existed in price expectations with the counterbalance, we can conclude that the pairs of quality measure in our product descriptions were successfully manipulated to represent diamonds of the same quality with slight differences.

Surprisingly, however, a significant percentage of subjects (25.4%) expected even higher prices for lab-created diamonds. Because we planted a subtle manipulation to avoid a demand effect, a considerable number of subjects might have focused on properties rather than the production process and formed their price expectations based on their assessment of such properties.

Pretest 2 confirmed that subjects who focused on the production process expected significantly lower prices for lab-created diamonds. After the expected price question, subjects were asked a follow-up question: "What was your main reason for thinking that Diamond B would sell for a lower [a higher, an equal] price?" Approximately 48% of the subjects answered that they focused on the

Table 1. T-test of Expected Price by Attention to the Production Process (Without Outliers).

The production process is [...]	N	Mean	SE	95% CI	
[...] not the main reason for the price expectation	167	9,791.81	128.45	9,538.20	10,045.42
[...] the main reason for the price expectation	152	7,075.21	168.28	6,742.72	7,407.71

production process. As summarized in Table 1, these subjects expected a significant price discount for the alternative production process (mean = US$7,075.21, $N = 152$, SE = 168.28), compared to other subjects who said the production process was not the main reason for their price expectations (mean = US$9,791.81, $N = 167$, SE = 128.45). The difference between these two groups is statistically significant ($t(317) = 12.97$, $p < 0.001$).

Experiment 1: Ritual and Production Process Conservatism

Experiment 1 is designed to test H1. This experiment includes four important features. First, we test the effect of high-stakes rituals by comparing the same gift-giving behavior in two different social contexts. In particular, we compare two scenarios: (1) a man giving diamond jewelry to his girlfriend purely as a gift and (2) a man giving diamond jewelry to his girlfriend as a part of an engagement ritual. Whereas gift-giving often involves both attention to rules and the performer's identity statements (Camerer, 1988; Mauss, 2006), greater risk is involved when gift-giving is performed as part of a ritual (especially one with high stakes) than when it has no explicit ritual implications. Second, subjects were made to understand that although the naked eye cannot distinguish lab-created diamonds from mined diamonds, they can be distinguished with certificates. This allowed us to test for acceptance of the production process *per se* rather than the ability of a new production process to "pass" as a traditional process. Third, instead of asking the expected price, we asked about subjects' behavioral choices in the form of advice for a friend, which should be more effective in tapping into consumers' lived experience, as subjects were primed for actual involvement. Fourth, when choosing between the two diamonds, subjects were told that they could trade production processes for a larger diamond, i.e., for the same price, they could get a larger diamond when they chose a lab-created diamond than when they choose a mined diamond, providing an incentive to choose the nontraditional production process. Our main dependent variable investigates the extent to which the subjects were willing to move to the nonconventional production process across social settings.

Method

A total of 642 subjects were recruited through AMT, and they completed a survey for US$0.25 each (64% females, average age = 30.8). The survey was constructed as a between-subjects experiment, in which each subject was randomly assigned to either a ritual setting or a nonritual setting. To avoid a demand effect, subjects were told a cover story at the beginning of the survey: The purpose of the survey was to develop an online shopping game, and they would be asked questions about one of the items, which they then found out was diamonds. In practice, all the subjects were given questions about diamonds.

In the ritual setting, subjects were told to imagine an engagement context, in which they ultimately had to give an advice to an imaginary friend who was buying diamond jewelry for *an engagement gift*. In the nonritual setting, subjects were told to imagine that they were giving advice about a diamond jewelry purchase to a friend who was buying *a gift*. The description of this imaginary friend was identical in both settings, i.e., "a 32-year-old male friend who lives in Chicago and who has been in a serious relationship with his girlfriend for 2 years."

Similar to our previous experiments, we used questions that the subjects had to read and understand to provide relevant background knowledge for the experiment. For example, in a series of questions, the subjects read that it is now technically possible to grow diamonds in laboratories and that these lab-created diamonds have the exact same chemical, physical, and optical characteristics as mined diamonds; they also read that even though a mined diamond and a lab-created diamond are identical in 4C measures and indistinguishable to the naked eye, lab-created diamonds are laser-inscribed with an identity name and number that are declared in their certifications.

After the subjects were given information on lab diamonds through this series of questions, they were asked whether a lab-created diamond should sell for the same price, a higher price or a lower price than a mined diamond. In the next section, the subjects were given a description of the specific design and profile of the "mined" diamond that the friend chose to buy. This description was identical in both conditions. Finally, in our key question, subjects were told that the jeweler told the friend that the exact jewelry could also be made with a lab-created diamond and that if he chose to make it with a lab-created diamond, he could obtain a larger diamond for the same price. The subjects were then asked if they "would recommend that he buy a mined diamond (henceforth, "Mined Diamonds")"; they "would recommend that he buy a lab-created diamond (henceforth, "Lab-created Diamonds")"; or their "recommendation would depend on how big the lab-created diamond is (henceforth, "It Depends")." The order of these choices was counterbalanced. Starting with a mined diamond and determining respondents' willingness to change increases the external validity, with the traditional production process acting as the conventional equilibrium and the acceptance of a new production process requiring additional knowledge and an active effort.

Results

Our key question for the dependent variable, "Which one would you recommend that your friend buy?", is measured using a multiple-choice question with three possible answers. The results are summarized in Fig. 2. We approached testing *H1* in two ways. First, as a direct test, we compared respondents' willingness to recommend a mined diamond across conditions using the Mann–Whitney *U* test, a nonparametric test that is suitable for ordinal but not normally distributed dependent variables (Mann & Whitney, 1947). However, we did not find a significantly higher preference for a mined diamond in the engagement condition than in the gift-giving condition ($U/mn = 0.48$, $z = 0.91$, $p = 0.36$). The respondents in the engagement condition ($N = 319$, mean = 1.96) did not show a higher preference for a mined diamond than did the respondents randomly assigned to the gift-giving condition ($N = 323$, mean = 1.90). We then ran a series of *t*-tests of

% of choice by social context
(all respondents)

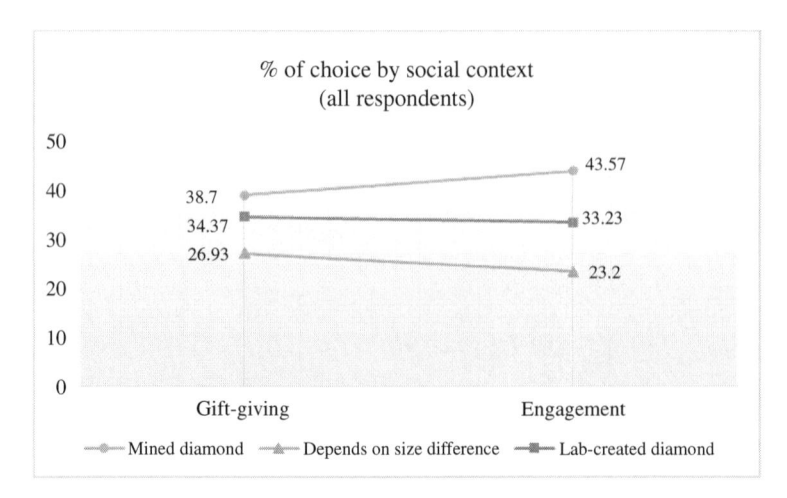

- Mined diamond: Gift-giving 38.7, Engagement 43.57
- Depends on size difference: Gift-giving 26.93, Engagement 23.2
- Lab-created diamond: Gift-giving 34.37, Engagement 33.23

Fig. 2. Experiment 1: The Effect of the Ritual Context (All Respondents).

proportions between the choices of the same diamond across conditions. When the percentage is compared across conditions, neither the proportions recommending a mined diamond (43.57% vs 38.70%, $p = 0.22$ (two-tailed)) nor the proportions recommending a lab-created diamond (33.23% vs 34.37%, $p = 0.8$ (two-tailed)) are statistically significant, although the directions are consistent with our predictions.

Second, in a supplementary approach, we ran a chi-square goodness-of-fit test to show the distributions of diamond choices in *each* social context. In the engagement condition, we find that the frequencies of "mined diamonds" and "lab-created diamonds" are significantly different from random chance (Pearson $\chi^2(1) = 4.44$, $p < 0.05$), with a higher frequency in the former category, whereas in the gift-giving condition, the two categories do not show such significant differences (Pearson $\chi^2(1) = 0.83$, $p = 0.36$). Overall, although the contrast shown in the second approach is aligned with our prediction, we do not find sufficient support for *H1*.

Post hoc analysis. We then ran a series of post hoc analyses to pursue specific objectives. First, because the ritual effect in production process conservatism was suggestive but not strong (as discussed above), we investigated whether certain demographic groups show more salient ritual effects than others. As discussed in the theory section, depending on each respondent's social role in the real world, they might be differently attuned to the importance – or even the existence – of a potential ritual rule. In particular, given that conventional gender roles exist and that people may be more knowledgeable about ritual rules when they experience them, we suspected that gender and marital status might affect the respondents' sensitivity to the production process of diamonds in engagement rituals. Second, we aimed to address the potential argument that stronger preferences for mined diamonds in a ritual setting stem from the giver's increased willingness to buy whatever is more expensive rather than his attention to the production process. To address this possibility, we included price expectations as a control variable and investigated the extent to which this "price signal" works in parallel with the ritual effect.

Since the dependent variable includes three categories, for the sake of simplicity in interpretation, we first tested whether the respondent displays a strict preference for a mined diamond by combining "Lab-created Diamonds" and "It Depends" (coded 0), as opposed to "Mined diamonds" (coded 1).[3]

Tables 2 summarizes the regression results. Model 1 is the baseline model that introduces the control variables. The results show that price expectations are a strong predictor of one's preference for a mined diamond. Compared with when respondents expected a mined diamond to be more expensive (reference category), the odds of recommending a mined diamond decreased when they expected a lab-created diamond to be more expensive ($b = -2.43, p < 0.05$) or when they expected the price to be equal ($b = -2.35, p < 0.001$). Additionally, older respondents – the fourth age quantile – were more likely to recommend a mined diamond ($b = 0.72, p < 0.01$).

Model 2 adds the main independent variable: the ritual context. However, although the coefficient is in the expected direction, there was no significant evidence of a ritual effect ($b = 0.23, p = 0.17$). In Model 3, we added interaction terms – marital status and the engagement condition. The results suggest that the ritual effect was present among married respondents (reference category; $b = 0.67, p < 0.05$); the odds of recommending a mined diamond increased by 95% [exp(0.67) − 1], suggesting a significant ritual effect in this group. To further rule out the "price signal" explanation, in Model 4, we limited the sample to respondents who expected a mined diamond to be more expensive (87% of the respondents). The results show that a preference for mined diamonds among currently married respondents holds. Finally, in Models 5 and 6, we explored whether gender moderates the observed ritual effect. To avoid the difficulty of interpreting three-way interaction effects, we conducted separate analyses for female respondents (Model 5) and male respondents (Model 6). Models 5 and 6 show that the ritual effect is driven by female respondents who are currently married (Model 5: $b = 0.80, p < 0.05$).

We further conducted a multinomial logistic regression analysis, treating the three choices of the dependent variable as categorical. The results are summarized in Table 3. Model 1 shows that in the ritual condition, married females are 2.46 [exp(0.90)] times more likely to choose "Mined Diamonds" than "It Depends," but there was no statistically significant difference by the social context in respondents' likelihood of choosing "Lab-created Diamonds" over "It Depends" ($b = 0.44, p = 0.25$). This pattern held when we limited the sample to respondents who expected a mined diamond to be more expensive (Model 2, $b = 1.01, p < 0.01$) or when we limited the sample to female respondents (Model 3, $b = 1.14, p < 0.01$).

In sum, although Experiment 1 does not provide direct support for *H1* in the overall sample, we found that the subsample of married women showed production process conservatism. Fig. 3 shows that strong production process

Table 2. Experiment 1: Logistic Regression Analysis (DV: Recommend "Mined Diamonds").

	Model 1	Model 2	Model 3	Model 4	Model 5	Model 6
Ritual		0.23	0.67*	0.67*	0.80*	0.40
		(0.17)	(0.28)	(0.28)	(0.34)	(0.52)
Price expectation (*Ref*: mined, expensive)						
Lab-created, expensive	−2.43*	−2.44*	−2.44*		−2.38*	Omitted
	(1.05)	(1.05)	(1.05)		(1.06)	
Same	−2.35***	−2.35***	−2.35***		−1.94***	−3.19**
	(0.48)	(0.48)	(0.48)		(0.55)	(1.03)
Female	0.02	0.02	0.04	0		
	(0.18)	(0.18)	(0.18)	(0.18)		
Marital status (*Ref*: married)						
Widowed	−0.10	−0.23	−0.47	−0.43	−0.57	Omitted
	(1.45)	(1.45)	(1.45)	(1.45)	(1.45)	
Divorced	−0.52	−0.50	−0.2	−0.17	−0.48	0.63
	(0.36)	(0.36)	(0.47)	(0.47)	(0.57)	(0.96)
Separated	−2.10⁺	−2.10⁺	−14.29	−13.93	−14.34	Omitted
	(1.08)	(1.08)	(666.35)	(562.59)	(786.11)	
Never married	−0.15	−0.16	0.18	0.15	0.32	−0.05
	(0.21)	(0.21)	(0.27)	(0.27)	(0.33)	(0.49)
Marital status × ritual						
Widowed × ritual			Omitted	Omitted	Omitted	Omitted
Divorced × ritual			−0.64	−0.62	−0.2	−2.17
			(0.71)	(0.72)	(0.84)	(1.55)
Separated × ritual			12.76	12.43	13.11	Omitted
			(666.35)	(562.59)	(786.11)	
Never married × ritual			−0.73*	−0.67⁺	−0.92*	−0.43
			(0.36)	(0.37)	(0.45)	(0.64)
Age (*Ref*: 2nd quantile)						
1st Quantile	0.13	0.12	0.12	0.1	−0.19	0.58
	(0.25)	(0.25)	(0.25)	(0.25)	(0.33)	(0.39)
3rd Quantile	0.19	0.17	0.13	0.18	0.07	0.18
	(0.25)	(0.25)	(0.25)	(0.25)	(0.32)	(0.39)
4th Quantile	0.72**	0.72**	0.69*	0.62*	0.52	0.89⁺
	(0.27)	(0.27)	(0.28)	(0.28)	(0.34)	(0.50)
Constant	−0.28	−0.39	−0.58*	−0.55⁺	−0.49	−0.54
	(0.25)	(0.26)	(0.28)	(0.29)	(0.32)	(0.48)
Log likelihood	−399.62	−398.67	−395.88	−375.64	−255.61	−136.23
Pseudo R^2	0.08	0.08	0.09	0.03	0.08	0.11
N	642	642	642	560	409	229

Notes: *$p < 0.05$; **$p < 0.01$; ***$p < 0.001$ (two-tailed test).
Coefficients are omitted when there is no variance in the dependent variable for the category.

Table 3. Multinomial Regression Analysis (DV Reference Category: "It Depends").

	Model 1 Mined	Model 1 Lab-created	Model 2 Mined	Model 2 Lab-created	Model 3 Mined	Model 3 Lab-created
Ritual	0.90**	0.44	1.01**	0.66	1.14**	0.63
	(0.35)	(0.38)	(0.36)	(0.42)	(0.43)	(0.47)
Price expectation (*Ref*: mined, expensive)						
Lab-created, expensive	−2.03+	0.69			−2.11+	0.46
	(1.13)	(0.64)			(1.14)	(0.67)
Same	−1.89***	0.72*			−1.62**	0.57
	(0.52)	(0.31)			(0.60)	(0.41)
Female	−0.21	−0.43+	−0.18	−0.31		
	(0.22)	(0.23)	(0.23)	(0.25)		
Marital status (*Ref*: married)						
Widowed	−1.25	−13.48	−1.28	−13.54	−1.51	−15.03
	(1.46)	(771.86)	(1.46)	(755.86)	(1.47)	(1472.43)
Divorced	0.16	0.66	0.24	0.78	−0.08	0.73
	(0.60)	(0.63)	(0.60)	(0.64)	(0.71)	(0.70)
Separated	−13.12	1.28	−12.96	1.40	−14.61	0.88
	(546.11)	(1.19)	(522.37)	(1.19)	(1153.59)	(1.27)
Never married	0.41	0.43	0.42	0.56	0.28	−0.09
	(0.32)	(0.33)	(0.33)	(0.36)	(0.38)	(0.41)
Marital status × ritual						
Widowed × ritual	Omitted	Omitted	Omitted	Omitted	Omitted	Omitted
Divorced × ritual	−0.58	−0.01	−0.82	−0.45	0.41	0.62
	(0.95)	(0.97)	(0.95)	(1.00)	(1.34)	(1.33)
Separated × ritual	11.33	−1.79	11.68	−1.02	13.07	−1.44
	(546.11)	(1.61)	(522.37)	(1.74)	(1153.59)	(1.94)
Never married × ritual	−0.99*	−0.50	−1.02*	−0.68	−1.14*	−0.34
	(0.44)	(0.47)	(0.46)	(0.52)	(0.55)	(0.60)
Age (*Ref*: 2nd quantile)						
1st Quantile	−0.17	−0.54+	−0.09	−0.36	−0.30	−0.24
	(0.30)	(0.30)	(0.31)	(0.33)	(0.38)	(0.39)
3rd Quantile	0.15	0.03	0.2	0.04	0.15	0.14
	(0.31)	(0.30)	(0.32)	(0.34)	(0.39)	(0.40)
4th Quantile	0.54	−0.27	0.55	−0.14	0.43	−0.17
	(0.34)	(0.36)	(0.35)	(0.39)	(0.41)	(0.44)
Constant	0.29	0.28	0.18	−0.01	0.15	−0.11
	(0.34)	(0.35)	(0.34)	(0.38)	(0.37)	(0.38)
Log likelihood	−642.07		−578.58		−411.91	
Pseudo R^2	0.07		0.02		0.07	
N	642		560		409	

Notes: *$p<0.05$, **$p<0.01$, ***$p<0.001$ (two-tailed test).
Coefficients are omitted when there is no variance in the dependent variable for the category.

% of choice by social context
(married women)

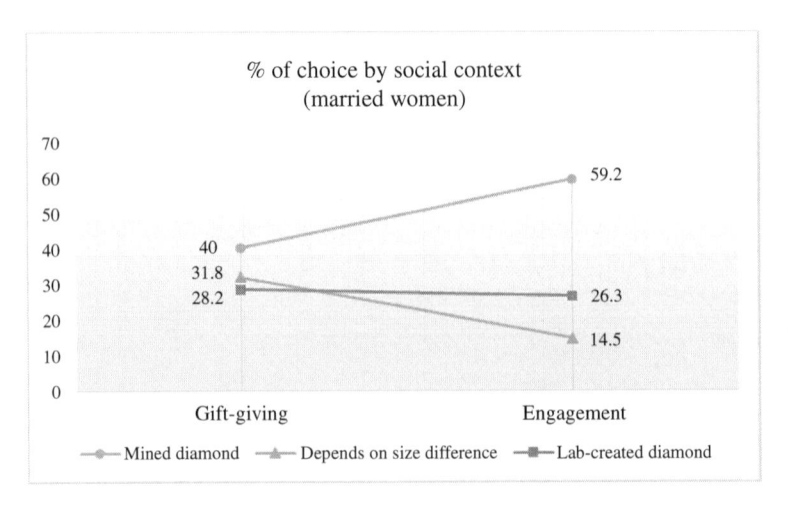

	Gift-giving	Engagement
Mined diamond	40	59.2
Depends on size difference	31.8	14.5
Lab-created diamond	28.2	26.3

Fig. 3. Experiment 1: The Effect of the Ritual Context (Married Women).

conservatism exists among married women in this sample ($N = 161$). Two sample tests of proportions show that preference for a mined diamond is significantly higher in the engagement condition (59.2% vs 40.0%, $p < 0.05$ (two-tailed)), providing support for our theory.

As discussed earlier, marital status and gender likely produce significant variance in respondents' knowledge and sensitivity to the risks associated with the engagement ritual, and our post hoc analysis finds them to be important preconditions to exhibiting production process conservatism. However, the following question remains: Why might married women be the most sensitive to engagement rituals in choosing production processes? These results invite additional testing of the mechanism.

Experiment 2: Perceived Risk as a Mechanism of the Ritual Effect

The goal of Experiment 2 is twofold. First, this study seeks to test whether the perceived risks associated with a ritual are the mediating factor that generates production process conservatism, as suggested in *H2*. Whereas Experiment 1 indicated that the ritual effect is limited to a subgroup of the sample, building on this finding, we aim to test whether the sensitivity to the perceived risk explains the ritual effect observed in the subgroup. The second goal of this study is to test our theory among a different population – MBA students. Although the engagement ritual is widely known to most of the people in society, as indicated by the Mturk subjects, the ritual effect we may observe in the real world is largely enacted by those who are currently involved in the engagement ritual. To increase the external validity of our empirical test, we conducted Experiment 2 as course credit for MBA students at a private university in the northeastern United States. Because we changed the sample pool from AMT participants to MBA students, we start by identifying the presence of a ritual effect. Due to the size of the class, the sample size in Experiment 2 is smaller than that in Experiment 1.

Method
A total of 82 respondents completed the experiment (50% females, average age = 28.5). The procedure was largely similar to that used for Experiment 1, with three differences. First, when respondents reached the question about their recommendation, they were asked to answer on a 5-point scale ranging from 1 = "strongly recommend a mined diamond" to 5 = "strongly recommend a lab-created diamond." Second, if they recommended a lab-created diamond, they were given a follow-up question that asked the main reason for their recommendation; if their recommendation was not based on obtaining a bigger diamond, they were asked to fill in an open-ended blank. This open-ended option allowed respondents to list other reasons for choosing to recommend a lab-created diamond besides its bigger size (e.g., environmental consciousness or a preference for advanced technology) and revealed whether the salience of such reasons varied by the social context. Third, and most importantly, after they reported their recommendations, the respondents were given a battery of questions regarding their perceptions of a diamond purchase on a five-point scale (a higher value indicating stronger agreement). "If she is not satisfied with this [ring/necklace], it will lead to problems in their relationship" directly measured the perceived level of risk, and this statement was used to test the mediating effect proposed in *H2*. We also included multiple filler questions.

Results
The first step involved identifying the existence of a ritual effect in this sample of MBA students. Overall, we did not find a ritual effect in production process conservatism in the overall sample. Although the mean was higher in the gift-giving condition ($M_{\text{gift-giving}}(N = 36) = 2.86$ vs $M_{\text{ritual}}(N = 46) = 2.52$), the difference was not statistically significant ($t(80) = 1.35$, $p = 0.18$, two-tailed test). Among the 21 respondents who leaned toward recommending lab-created diamonds (11 in the gift-giving condition and 10 in the engagement condition), 18 reported that the bigger diamond was the main reason for their recommendation, and 3 said that the other reason informed their recommendation, although they did not specify that reason in the text. The mean difference between the two conditions remained statistically nonsignificant when those three respondents were excluded.

Building on the post hoc analysis in Experiment 1, we further examined subsample variations by employing a regression approach (OLS). In short, we found support for the existence of a ritual effect − i.e., preference for a traditional practice in the ritual context − among female respondents. Table 4 summarizes the results when we added interaction terms to the baseline model (Model 1). Because respondents were either married or never married in this sample, marital status was measured with a dichotomous variable. Model 2 adds the interaction term with gender and the engagement condition, and Model 3 adds the interaction term with marital status and the engagement

Table 4. Experiment 2: OLS Regression Analysis.

	Model 1	Model 2	Model 3	Model 4
Ritual	−0.31	0.24	−0.04	0.29
	(0.26)	(0.38)	(0.44)	(0.47)
Female	0.49+	1.04**	0.52+	1.03*
	(0.27)	(0.39)	(0.28)	(0.39)
Female × ritual		−1.01+		−0.98+
		(0.52)		(0.55)
Never married	−0.00	0.1	0.24	0.16
	(0.28)	(0.28)	(0.42)	(0.42)
Never married × ritual			−0.43	−0.12
			(0.55)	(0.57)
Constant	2.58***	2.29***	2.4***	2.17***
	(0.28)	(0.33)	(0.37)	(0.38)
R^2	0.07	0.11	0.07	0.11
N	79	79	79	79

Note: +$p < 0.1$; *$p < 0.05$; **$p < 0.01$; ***$p < 0.001$ (two-tailed test).

condition, each to the baseline model. Although Model 2 shows that female respondents had a slight preference for mined diamonds in the engagement condition ($b = -1.01$, $p < 0.1$), in Model 3, marital status did not play a role in producing a ritual effect. The ritual effect among women found in Model 2 held in the full model (Model 4). In a t-test, women were significantly less accepting of a lab-created diamond in the engagement condition ($M_{\text{gift-giving}}(N = 19) = 3.32$ vs $M_{\text{ritual}}(N = 22) = 2.54$, $t(30) = 2.06$, $p < 0.05$ (two-tailed test)).

These results bear some similarities and dissimilarities with those of Experiment 1. In both experiments, we observed a preference for mined diamonds over lab-created diamonds in the engagement condition only among a subgroup of the samples – in particular, women. However, marital status was an important factor in Experiment 1, but not in Experiment 2. Although such dissimilarities may be attributable to the different populations from which our samples were drawn, determining the reason for these differences is beyond the scope of this study. Thus, we proceed to test the mediating effect of perceived risk as a direct mechanism for those who exhibited production process conservatism, which is the primary goal of Study 2.

Next, we tested *H2* using subjects' responses to the statement "If she is not satisfied with this [ring/necklace], it will lead to problems in their relationship" as a measure of the perceived risk associated with their recommendations, following Preacher and Hayes (2008). This approach is superior to the traditional Sobel (1982) test for mediation, which assumes a normal distribution of variables. Based on bootstrapping with 5,000 iterations, we estimated the indirect effects via perceived risk. Table 5 shows the moderated mediation (Muller, Judd, & Yzerbyt, 2005). Model 1 shows production process conservatism in the

Table 5. Experiment 2: Moderated Mediation.

	Model 1 DV: Recommendation	Model 2 DV: Perceived Risk	Model 3 DV: Recommendation
Ritual	0.17	−0.38	0.054
	(0.36)	(0.33)	(0.35)
Female	1.00**	−0.58+	0.83*
	(0.37)	(0.35)	(0.37)
Female × ritual	−0.94+	1.10*	−0.62
	(0.50)	(0.46)	(0.50)
Perceived risk			−0.29*
			(0.12)
Constant	2.31***	2.69***	3.10***
	(0.28)	(0.26)	(0.42)
R^2	0.11	0.08	0.17
N	80	80	80

Note: $+p<0.1$; $*p<0.05$; $**p<0.01$; $***p<0.001$ (two-tailed test).

ritual condition (i.e., ritual effect) among women, as discussed above ($b = -0.94$, $p < 0.1$), although females are generally more open to lab-created diamonds ($b = 1.0$, $p < 0.01$). Model 2 establishes the second step, in which female respondents perceive a significantly higher level of risk in the engagement condition ($b = 1.1$, $p < 0.05$). Notably, male respondents show no differences in perceived risks across conditions ($b = -0.38$, $p = 0.25$). Model 3 shows that this perceived risk significantly affects the dependent variable ($b = -0.29$, $p < 0.05$), whereas the effect of the ritual context among women significantly decreases ($b = -0.62$, $p = 0.22$). The 95% bias-corrected confidence interval for the size of the indirect effect excluded zero (-0.73, -0.02). Overall, this result shows mixed support for *H2*. We again did not find the ritual effect in the general population. However, for the subsample who exhibited production process conservatism in the ritual condition, the result supports our proposed theory in *H2* that sensitivity to the perceived risk mediated such preference. In sum, as explained above, our results show moderated mediation.

GENERAL DISCUSSION

The issue of why the same objective conditions are often very differently perceived and evaluated has been a longstanding and important puzzle for social scientists (Salganik & Watts, 2008; Sgourev & Althuizen, 2017; Zuckerman, 2012). In most of the cases in which products made via different production processes are differently valued in the market, consumers have generally been assumed to use the production process as a proxy for quality, whether the quality difference is explicit or implicit. Nonetheless, we still see a few examples in which consumers care about the production process even when the process does not affect the quality of end product. Why do people care about production processes (independent of quality) at some times but not at other times? In other words, when are traditional practices in demand and why?

In this study, we make a theoretical contribution by clarifying how such variations may derive from the social context. We theorize that rituals constitute one driver of "production process conservatism" when the ritual performer's social role, socioeconomic status or social relationships are enacted in a larger group context. To avoid negative social outcomes from a failed ritual, ritual performers must pay extra attention to ritual rules. We developed our argument in the case of diamonds; new and more efficient production processes have recently become available, but diamonds have traditionally been formed underground and extracted from mines. The contrast between a mined diamond and a lab-created diamond provides an excellent setting for our research question, as the advent of a new production process brings uncertainty in terms of what, precisely, the ritual rules prescribe. Thus, we focus on whether consumers care about a traditional production process, even when the production process is only *possibly* part of the ritual rules.

However, our empirical evidence has limitations and leaves some questions unanswered. Although we find support for our prediction in certain subsamples, the effect was not found in the entire sample. On one hand, this may be partially attributable to the conservative nature of our own research question and to the research design. As mentioned above, we used a case in which the production process is an implicit ritual rule rather than an explicit one. Therefore, production process conservatism might have only been relevant to respondents who were able to recognize it as an implicit ritual rule. In addition, in our experimental design, the ritual effect was tested against a control group – the gift-giving condition – that also involved risks of exhibiting low capability and commitment, though to a lesser degree. Thus, the effect that we found is based on the strength of ritual implications across contexts, not on the existence (or lack) of ritual implications altogether. We expect that if a certain practice is more explicitly understood as a ritual rule and the contrast between a ritual condition and a nonritual condition is stronger, the effect will be stronger and more pervasive.

On the other hand, our finding, i.e. production process conservatism in the ritual condition among a subgroup, raises another question. Experiment 2 shows the mechanism to be perceived risk, as hypothesized. But why should (married) women be more knowledgeable and sensitive to such risks than men? Although we did not have a priori predictions about this, our findings suggest possible interpretations based on the gendered nature of social roles and the risks in performing engagement rituals. Conventionally, men are responsible for choosing the ring, and women wear the ring. At first glance, men seem to have more risk in the engagement ritual, because they present the ring as part of a marriage proposal. However, women face another type of risk; because they are the ones who wear the ring, they take on the role of representing the couple's capability and commitment to any larger group in which they are members. In other words, whereas men's high stakes are temporary, the ring has a lasting impact on women. Our evidence suggests that for general respondents (i.e., those who are not likely to be purchasing or receiving a diamond ring at the time of the survey), women are more sensitive than men to their personal stakes.

Our research speaks to various lines of ongoing research. First, our theory of "production process conservatism" joins a broader institutional approach that investigates the question of "why certain practices persist" (e.g., DiMaggio & Powell, 1983; Zucker, 1977). Our study applies the logic of an "institutionalizing" process at the individual level and thus explains the persistence of a particular cultural practice. Just as organizations seek legitimacy for their own survival, individuals pay attention to "what is considered right" by *others* to obtain social approval. This view is in line with a broader literature in economic sociology that claims that individuals conform to other people's opinions (Centola et al., 2005) or a public signal of status (Benjamin & Podolny, 1999; Clark, Clark, & Polborn, 2006; for a review see Correll et al., 2017). We contribute to this literature by suggesting the minimally sufficient conditions for an institutionalizing process related to a ritual. In particular, we have shown that a production process for diamonds can be institutionalized in a ritual context, even when (1) it is not an explicit part of the rules; (2) it is not immediately distinguishable ex post (unless the violator confesses); and (3) it does not generate different quality. Moreover, our study highlights that such institutionalizing power can even trump economic benefits – i.e., in ritual contexts, individuals even forgo a "bigger size" for the sake of conformity to institutionalizing pressures.

Additionally, our analysis joins the literature on technological innovation with a body of research that shows cultural norms as constraints on economic activities (Turco, 2012; Zelizer, 1979, 2010). Our study suggests why technological innovations may not always be accepted in the market, even when they provide a clear benefit (in the form of economic efficiency or higher quality). Whereas existing innovation research largely answers this question by focusing on the trajectory of technology itself (e.g., Arthur, 1990; Cusumano, Mylonadis, & Rosenbloom, 1992; David, 1985; Liebowitz & Margolis, 1995) or organizational resistance (e.g., Strang & Macy, 2001; Tripsas, 2009; Westphal, Gulati, & Shortell, 1997), this paper focuses on the importance of cultural norms in limiting the demand for a technological innovation (cf. Hahl, 2016). A shared cultural understanding often sorts items into two dichotomous categories – what is "accepted" and what is "not accepted" (Douglas, 2002). When such norms are in play, people deem their commitments to certain cultural values to be absolute and inviolable, and they are unwilling to trade off sacred values – i.e., the observance of rules of engagement – with secular ones – e.g., a "larger size" (Fiske & Tetlock, 1997; Tetlock, 2003). However, an innovation that does not fit today's cultural norms will not necessarily be permanently rejected (e.g., Murray, 2010). When a new production process is coupled with new supporting logics, it may appeal to market participants and integrate into group processes. In our case, the sellers and innovators of lab-created diamonds have attempted to introduce the norms of labor ethics, environmental sustainability, and transparency to advocate for lab-created diamonds rather than traditionally mined diamonds (Markoff, 2015). These logics may gain more popularity among market participants, and, if so, we expect that the traditional boundaries of "what is acceptable" will become blurred and that the rules for the engagement ritual will find a new equilibrium.

NOTES

1. The pretest had two additional conditions — "wine" and "Wagyu beef" — as other examples of items that have objective measures of quality and different production processes, with 402 additional respondents. Although the results are consistent with the diamond condition — the participants expect to pay less for the alternative production process — we omit the detailed procedure and the results for brevity.

2. Because the survey asked participants to reveal their expected prices in an open question, the answers varied considerably, including some insincere outliers. Whereas we must exclude values in the analysis that are more than 2 standard deviations from the mean to produce a more reliable result, the inclusion of outliers does not change the overall interpretation of the data.

3. Admittedly, the nature of the dependent variable is a limitation of the current regression approach. One may consider ordinal logit, but it would not be appropriate to do so in this case because we had asked respondents' recommendations in three ways, with no assumptions about the distance between the choices. We further conducted a multinomial analysis that treats the dependent variable as categorical with no natural ordering. To avoid this issue in the dependent variable, we collected the dependent measure in the form of a discrete variable in Experiment 2.

ACKNOWLEDGMENTS

We thank the participants in the MIT-Harvard Economic Sociology Seminar, the MIT Economic Sociology Working Group, and participants at the American Sociological Association conference session and at the American Management Association conference session for their helpful comments. We also thank myriad informants and interviewees in the diamond industry.

REFERENCES

Arthur, W. B. (1990). Positive feedbacks in the economy. *Scientific American*, *262*(2), 92–99.

Bain and Company. (2011). *The global diamond industry: Lifting the veil of mystery*. Antwerp: Bain and Company.

Barnett, H. G. (1938). The nature of the potlatch. *American Anthropologist*, *40*(3), 349–358.

Benjamin, B. A., & Podolny, J. M. (1999). Status, quality, and social order in the California wine industry. *Administrative Science Quarterly*, *44*(3), 563–589.

Bowers, A. (2015). Category expectations, category spanning, and market outcomes. In G. Gavetti & W. Ocasio (Eds.), *Cognition and strategy* (Vol. 32, pp. 241–276). Bingley: Emerald Publishing.

Brinig, M. F. (1990). Rings and promises. *Journal of Law, Economics, and Organization*, *6*(1), 203–215.

Camerer, C. (1988). Gifts as economic signals and social symbols. *American Journal of Sociology*, *94*, S180–S214.

Caplow, T. (1984). Rule enforcement without visible means: Christmas gift giving in Middletown. *American Journal of Sociology*, *89*(6), 1306–1323.

Carroll, G. R., & Swaminathan, A. (2000). Why the microbrewery movement? Organizational dynamics of resource partitioning in the U.S. brewing industry. *American Journal of Sociology*, *106*(3), 715–762.

Centola, D., Willer, R., & Macy, M. (2005). The emperor's dilemma: A computational model of self-enforcing norms. *American Journal of Sociology*, *110*(4), 1009–1040.

Chwe, M. S.-Y. (2003). *Rational ritual: Culture, coordination, and common knowledge*. Princeton, NJ: Princeton University Press.

Clark, C. R., Clark, S., & Polborn, M. K. (2006). Coordination and status influence. *Rationality and Society*, *18*(3), 367–391.

Collins, R. (2014). *Interaction ritual chains*. Princeton, NJ: Princeton University Press.

Correll, S. J., Ridgeway, C. L., Zuckerman, E. W., Jank, S., Jordan-Bloch, S., & Nakagawa, S. (2017). It's the conventional thought that counts. *American Sociological Review, 82*(2), 297–327.

Cusumano, M. A., Mylonadis, Y., & Rosenbloom, R. S. (1992). Strategic maneuvering and mass-market dynamics: The triumph of VHS over beta. *Business History Review, 66*(01), 51–94.

David, P. A. (1985). Clio and the economics of QWERTY. *American Economic Review, 75*(2), 332–337.

DiMaggio, P. J., & Powell, W. W. (1983). The iron cage revisited: Institutional isomorphism and collective rationality in organizational fields. *American Sociological Review, 48*(2), 147–160.

Douglas, M. (2002[1966]). *Purity and danger: An analysis of concept of pollution and taboo*. London: Routledge.

Douglas, M., & Isherwood, B. C. (1979). *The world of goods*. London: Routledge.

Durkheim, E. (1976). *The elementary forms of the religious life*. London: Routledge.

Elster, J. (1989). *Nuts and bolts for the social sciences*. Cambridge: Cambridge University Press.

Epstein, E. J. (1982a). Have you ever tried to sell a diamond? *Atlantic Monthly*, February 23–34.

Epstein, E. J. (1982b). *The rise and fall of diamonds: The shattering of a brilliant illusion*. New York, NY: Simon & Schuster.

Even-Zohar, C. (2007). *From mine to mistress: Corporate strategies and government policies in the international diamond industry*. London: Mining Communications Limited.

Fiske, A. P., & Tetlock, P. E. (1997). Taboo trade-offs: Reactions to transactions that transgress the spheres of justice. *Political Psychology, 18*(2), 255–297.

Frake, J. (2017). Selling out: The inauthenticity discount in the craft beer industry. *Management Science, 63*(11), 3930–3943.

Goffman, E. (1955). On face-work: An analysis of ritual elements in social interaction. *Psychiatry, 18*(3), 213–231.

Goldberg, A., Hannan, M. T., & Kovács, B. (2015). What does it mean to span cultural boundaries? *American Sociological Review, 81*(2), 215–241.

Hahl, O. (2016). Turning back the clock in baseball: The increased prominence of extrinsic rewards and demand for authenticity. *Organization Science, 27*(4), 929–953.

Isberg, J., Hammersberg, J., Johansson, E., Wikström, T., Twitchen, D. J., Whitehead, A. J., ... Scarsbrook, G. A. (2002). High carrier mobility in single-crystal plasma-deposited diamond. *Science, 297*(5587), 1670–1672.

Kunz, G. F. (1973). *Rings for the finger*. New York, NY: Dover Publications.

Lieberson, S. (2000). *A matter of taste: How names, fashions, and culture change*. New Haven, CT: Yale University Press.

Lieberson, S., & Lynn, F. B. (2003). Popularity as taste. *Onoma, 38*, 235–276.

Liebowitz, S. J., & Margolis, S. E. (1995). Path dependence, lock-in, and history. *SSRN Electronic Journal, 11*(1), 205–226.

Malinowski, B. (1920). Kula: the circulating exchange of valuables in the archipelagoes of eastern New Guinea. *Management, 20*, 97–105.

Mann, H. B., & Whitney, D. R. (1947). On a test of whether one of two random variables is stochastically larger than the other. *Annals of Mathematical Statistics, 18*(1), 50–60.

Markoff, J. (2015). Borrowing from solar and chip tech to make diamonds faster and cheaper. *The New York Times*. Retrieved from http://www.nytimes.com/2015/11/12/science/borrowing-from-solar-and-chip-tech-to-make-diamonds-faster-and-cheaper.html

Mason, W., & Suri, S. (2012). Conducting behavioral research on Amazon's Mechanical Turk. *Behavior Research Methods, 44*(1), 1–23.

Mauss, M. (2006). *The gift: The form and reason for exchange in archaic societies*. London: Routledge.

Muller, D., Judd, C. M., & Yzerbyt, V. Y. (2005). When moderation is mediated and mediation is moderated. *Journal of Personality and Social Psychology, 89*(6), 852–863.

Murray, F. (2010). The oncomouse that roared: Hybrid exchange strategies as a source of distinction at the boundary of overlapping institutions. *American Journal of Sociology, 116*(2), 341–388.

Negro, G., Hannan, M. T., & Rao, H. (2011). Category reinterpretation and defection: Modernism and tradition in Italian winemaking. *Organization Science, 22*(6), 1449–1463.

Newman, G. E., & Bloom, P. (2012). Art and authenticity: The importance of originals in judgments of value. *Journal of Experimental Psychology. General*, *141*(3), 558–569.
Olson, D. W. (2000). Diamond industrial. In *Minerals yearbook*. Reston, VA: US Geological Survey.
O'Rourke, M. (2007). Diamonds are a girl's worst friend. *Slate*. Retrieved from http://www.slate.com/articles/news_and_politics/weddings/2007/06/diamonds_are_a_girls_worst_friend.html
Paolacci, G., Chandler, J., & Ipeirotis, P. (2010). Running experiments on amazon mechanical Turk. *Judgment and Decision Making*, *5*(5), 411–419.
Podolny, J. M., & Hill-Popper, M. (2004). Hedonic and transcendent conceptions of value. *Industrial and Corporate Change*, *13*(1), 91–116.
Pontikes, E. G. (2012). Two sides of the same coin. *Administrative Science Quarterly*, *57*(1), 81–118.
Preacher, K. J., & Hayes, A. F. (2008). Asymptotic and resampling strategies for assessing and comparing indirect effects in multiple mediator models. *Behavior Research Methods*, *40*(3), 879–891.
Rao, H., Monin, P., & Durand, R. (2003). Institutional change in toque Ville: Nouvelle cuisine as an identity movement in French gastronomy. *American Journal of Sociology*, *108*(4), 795–843.
Rothman, E. K. (1987). *Hands and hearts: A history of courtship in America*. Cambridge, MA: Harvard University Press.
Salganik, M. J., & Watts, D. J. (2008). Leading the herd astray: An experimental study of self-fulfilling prophecies in an artificial cultural market. *Social Psychology Quarterly*, *71*(4), 338–355.
Schelling, T. C. (1980). *The strategy of conflict*. Cambridge, MA: Harvard University Press.
Scott, F., & Yelowitz, A. (2010). Pricing anomalies in the market for diamonds: Evidence of conformist behavior. *Economic Inquiry*, *48*(2), 353–368.
Sgourev, S. V., & Althuizen, N. (2017). Is it a masterpiece? Social construction and objective constraint in the evaluation of excellence. *Social Psychology Quarterly*, *80*(4), 289–309.
Simons, T., & Roberts, P. W. (2008). Local and non-local pre-founding experience and new organizational form penetration: The case of the Israeli wine industry. *Administrative Science Quarterly*, *53*(2), 235–265.
Sobel, M. E. (1982). Asymptotic confidence intervals for indirect effects in structural equation models. *Sociological Methodology*, *13*, 290–312.
Spar, D. L. (2006). Markets: Continuity and change in the international diamond market. *Journal of Economic Perspectives*, *20*(3), 195–208.
Spear, K. E., & Dismukes, J. P. (1994). *Synthetic diamond: Emerging CVD science and technology* (Vol. 25). New York, NY: Wiley.
Strang, D., & Macy, M. W. (2001). In search of excellence: Fads, success stories, and adaptive emulation. *American Journal of Sociology*, *107*(1), 147–182.
Swidler, A. (2003). *Talk of love: How culture matters*. Chicago, IL: University of Chicago Press.
Tetlock, P. E. (2003). Thinking the unthinkable: Sacred values and taboo cognitions. *Trends in Cognitive Sciences*, *7*(7), 320–324.
Tripsas, M. (2009). Technology, identity, and inertia through the lens of the digital photography company. *Organization Science*, *20*(2), 441–460.
Turco, C. (2012). Difficult decoupling: Employee resistance to the commercialization of personal settings. *American Journal of Sociology*, *118*(2), 380–419.
Turner, V. W. (1995[1969]). *The ritual process: Structure and anti-structure*. New York, NY: Aldine.
Weber, K., Heinze, K. L., & DeSoucey, M. (2008). Forage for thought: Mobilizing codes in the movement for grass-fed meat and dairy products. *Administrative Science Quarterly*, *53*(3), 529–567.
Westphal, J. D., Gulati, R., & Shortell, S. M. (1997). Customization or conformity? An institutional and network perspective on the content and consequences of TQM adoption. *Administrative Science Quarterly*, *42*(2), 366–394.
Zelizer, V. A. (1979). *Morals and markets: The development of life insurance in the United States*. New York, NY: Columbia University Press.
Zelizer, V. A. (2010). *Economic lives: How culture shapes the economy*. Princeton, NJ: Princeton University Press.

Zucker, L. G. (1977). The role of institutionalization in cultural persistence. *American Sociological Review*, *42*(5), 726–743.
Zuckerman, E. W. (1999). The categorical imperative: Securities Analysts and the illegitimacy discount. *American Journal of Sociology*, *104* (5):1398–1438.
Zuckerman, E. W. (2012). Construction, concentration, and (dis) continuities in social valuations. *Annual Review of Sociology*, *38*(1), 223–245.

ACCELEROMETERS AS A METHODOLOGICAL TOOL IN GROUP PROCESSES RESEARCH

Christin L. Munsch and Elizabeth S. Zack*

ABSTRACT

Purpose – *An accelerometer is a device that measures force due to gravity or a change in speed or direction of travel. This paper describes accelerometers and their application in other disciplines and, by way of an example, explores the utility of accelerometers for studying aggression. We end with a discussion of additional ways accelerometers might be used in group processes research.*

Methodology – *We first review the use of accelerometers in other disciplines. We then present the results of four studies that demonstrate the use of accelerometers to measure aggression. Study 1 establishes the measure's concurrent validity. Study 2 concerns its stability and representative reliability. Study 3 seeks to establish the measure's predictive validity by associating it with an existing measure. Study 4 demonstrates the ability of accelerometers to address a sociological research question.*

Findings – *In Studies 1 and 2, we find that accelerometers can be used to differentiate between distinct levels of aggression. In Study 3, we find that men's average peak acceleration correlates with a previously validated measure of aggression. Study 4 uses accelerometers to reproduce a well-established finding in the aggression literature.*

Practical Implications – *We conclude that accelerometers are a flexible tool for group processes' researchers and social scientists more broadly. Our*

---

*Both authors contributed equally to this work.

findings should prove useful to social scientists interested in measuring aggression or in employing accelerometers in their work.

Keywords: Accelerometers; behavioral measures; methods; aggression; average peak acceleration; masculinity threat

Over the past decade, accelerometers have become ubiquitous in daily life. In smart phones and tablets, accelerometer data are used to present landscape or portrait views of the screen depending on the way the device is held. Accelerometers in laptops detect sudden free fall and turn the hard drive off to protect it from damage. Wearable activity trackers use accelerometers to count users' steps and assess sleep quality; and accelerometers in cars detect rapid deceleration and signal airbag deployment. Despite their prevalence, however, few social scientists have explored the use of accelerometers to measure social phenomena. In this paper, we explore how accelerometers − a tool used by researchers in other disciplines − can be used by social scientists and we use aggression as an example case to demonstrate their utility in the study of interpersonal and group processes.

We begin by explaining what accelerometers are and review accelerometer research in other disciplines. Next, we detail previous measures of aggression and their shortcomings. By way of an example, we then present the results of four studies that establish average peak acceleration, an accelerometer-generated measure of aggression, as valid and reliable. Study 1 establishes the measure's concurrent validity. Study 2 concerns its stability and representative reliability. Study 3 seeks to establish the measure's predictive validity by associating it with an existing measure. Study 4 demonstrates the ability of accelerometers to address a specific research question. Together, these studies demonstrate the utility of accelerometers in observing and assessing aggression in laboratory settings. Simultaneously, we hope to begin a conversation about the use of accelerometers in social science research more broadly. Thus, we also discuss additional ways accelerometers might be used, placing emphasis on their application in group processes research. We end with a discussion of the unique limitations and challenges of working with accelerometers.

WHAT IS AN ACCELEROMETER? DEFINITION AND CONSIDERATIONS

An accelerometer is a device that measures force due to gravity or a change in speed or direction of travel. These forces are readily apparent in everyday life − for example, the feeling of being pressed against your seat belt when coming to a stop or pressed to the ground while riding in an elevator. Though the size and means of detection vary by device, all accelerometers operate in a similar manner. An object is held elastically to a frame so that it can flex as the device moves. As the device accelerates, the object flexes against the direction of acceleration. The degree of flex is then detected via electronic, magnetic, or mechanical means.

Typical accelerometers are made up of one, two, or three planes of activity. One-axis accelerometers assess vertical or horizontal movement; two-axis accelerometers assess vertical and horizontal movement; three-axis accelerometers assess the vertical, horizontal, and forward−backward movement.[1] We refer to these axes, respectively, as the x-, y-, and z-axes. The number of axes needed is determined by the application for which the accelerometer is used, although three-axis accelerometers are becoming standard as technology costs decrease. For example, airbag deployment requires two-axis models, while screen presentation requires three-axis models.

In addition to the number of axes, researchers must consider their desired range of measurement (measured in units of equivalent earth gravity or "g") and sampling frequency. A $\pm 1g$ accelerometer can measure small vibrations on a tabletop, a $\pm 2g$ accelerometer can measure the motion of a car or plane. For social scientists interested in using accelerometers in the ways outlined in this paper, a $\pm 1.5g$ device will suffice. The sampling frequency refers to the number of measurements the device takes in a given period of time. Vehicular acceleration can be measured at relatively low frequencies (e.g., one measurement per second) since acceleration change is slow. Conversely, a vibrating object, which rapidly changes direction of acceleration, requires a much higher sampling frequency (e.g., 500 measurements per second). Social behavior can be assessed with a tri-axial accelerometer that takes approximately 20 samples per second; however, higher sampling frequencies allow researchers to detect more subtle behaviors (Kools, 2012).

Commercially available accelerometers come with software that allows researchers to collect and store data in spreadsheet form. Data from one tri-axial accelerometer typically contain four columns. The first column denotes the time; the next three columns report acceleration along the x-, y- and z-axes. If the device measures acceleration 20 times per second, 30 s of data will contain approximately 600 rows of data. Some devices directly interface with a computer. Others store the data to be downloaded later.

PREVIOUS RESEARCH USING ACCELEROMETERS

Burton McCollum and Orville Peters are credited with developing the first accelerometer in 1923. Shortly thereafter, accelerometers were regularly used to conduct airplane drop tests and to calculate torque and rotational speed in steam turbines and engines (Walter, 1999). Today, accelerometers serve similar purposes. Accelerometers are used to verify the aerodynamic performance of airplanes, to test landing systems, and to evaluate crash survivability (e.g., Liu, Guo, Bai, Sun, & Mou, 2015). Engineers conduct vibration tests using accelerometers to assess the structural health of bridges (e.g., Lynch, Wang, Loh, & Yi, 2006; Whelan, Gangone, Janoyan, & Jha, 2009), and accelerometers attached to fire hydrants, valves, and pipes detect leaks (e.g., Hunaidi, Wang, Bracken, Gambino, & Fricke, 2004).

Large-scale commercialization of accelerometers has recently extended the scope of their use to the life sciences. For example, by examining patterns in output, biologists have used accelerometers to assess a wide range of animal activities like sleeping, gliding, diving for food, soaring, and grazing as well as the rate at which animals expend energy in the wild (e.g., Kato, Ropert-Coudert, Gremillet, & Cannell, 2006; Tanaka, Takagi, & Naito, 2001; Tsuda et al., 2006; Watanabe, Izawa, Kato, Ropert-Coudert, & Naito, 2005; Wilson, Shepard, & Liebsch, 2008; Yoda et al., 1999). In humans, studies of physical activity (for a meta-analysis see Bornstein, Beets, Byun, & McIver, 2011) and sleep (e.g., Teti, Shimizu, Crosby, & Kim, 2016; Yoon, Kripke, Youngstedt, & Elliott, 2003) are most common. To measure physical activity, accelerometers are attached close to the body's center of mass (e.g., hip, waist, lower back), while the device measures and records acceleration. Researchers then use this data to calculate kilocalories expended or to classify participants' levels of exertion (e.g., sedentary, light, moderate, vigorous, very vigorous). In sleep studies, participants typically wear an activity-monitoring, wristwatch-like device containing accelerometers to measure movements during sleep (Sadeh & Acebo, 2002). Innovative practitioners have also used accelerometers to identify depressive and manic episodes in bipolar patients (Gruenerbl et al., 2014), detect hand tremors (Ang, Khosla, & Riviere, 2003), examine movement and gait dynamics in stroke patients (Mizuike, Ohgi, & Morita, 2009), and observe hand flapping and body rocking in children with autism (Albinali, Goodwin, & Intille, 2009). Moreover, of late, researchers have begun to use accelerometer-generated data to identify specific activities including walking, jogging, sitting, standing, climbing up or down stairs, watching TV, eating, reading, vacuuming, and brushing teeth (e.g., Bao & Intille, 2004; Brezmes, Gorricho, & Cotrina, 2009; Choudhury et al., 2008; Kwapisz, Weiss, & Moore, 2010; Ravi, Dandekar, Mysore, & Littman, 2005).

While accelerometer research has a longer history in the physical and life sciences, social scientists have recently begun to utilize accelerometers for similar purposes. For example, anthropologists have used accelerometry technology to examine activity and sleep patterns in indigenous and cross-cultural populations (e.g., Madimenos, Snodgrass, Blackwell, Liebert, & Sugiyama, 2011; Samson, Crittenden, Mabulla, Mabulla, & Nunn, 2017; Snodgrass et al., 2016). And, sociologists have used findings from sleep disruption studies using accelerometers to argue that racial discrimination increases negative health outcomes for African Americans through the pathway of sleep disruption (Goosby, Straley, & Cheadle, 2017).

MEASURING AGGRESSION

Given their widespread applicability, it is surprising that the use of accelerometers to assess social behavior has largely been overlooked. To illustrate how sociologists, social psychologists, and group researchers might use accelerometers, we describe four studies that demonstrate the ability of accelerometers to measure aggression. There are a number of classifications and dimensions of aggression (Ramírez & Andreu, 2006). In this paper, we are interested in active, direct, physical aggression in which aggression is used as a means to achieve a goal. Aggression is an exemplary case, given the challenges associated with observing and measuring aggressive behavior.

To date, previous measures of aggression fall into one of two categories. Outside of the lab, researchers have relied on self-report measures of aggression (e.g., Buss & Perry, 1992; Orpinas & Frankowski, 2001; Perlman & Hirdes, 2008), which are limited for a number of reasons (Capaldi & Crosby, 1997; Hilton, Harris, & Rice, 1998; Hilton, Harris, & Rice, 2003; Krahe, Reimer, Scheinberger-Olwig, & Fritsche, 1999; Wolfe et al., 2001). For example, people have a tendency to inaccurately recall past behavior (Hilton et al., 1998; Offer, Kaiz, Howard, & Bennett, 2000; Schwarz, 1999; Skogan, 1986) and to present themselves more favorably (DeMaio, 1984; Schwarz, 1999). Because aggression is generally considered undesirable, aggression measures may be especially prone to these biases. Moreover, misrepresentation may depend on group membership (Deal & Wampler, 1986; Hilton et al., 2003; Morse, 1995; Schwarz, 1999). For example, gender norms discourage physical aggression in women, while encouraging physical aggression in (some) men (Archer, 2004; Eagly & Steffen, 1986). Such patterns may lead women to underreport and men to overreport aggressive behavior.

Inside the lab, researchers have relied on various proxies to measure aggression. To uncover underlying mechanisms, social psychologists and group processes' researchers often seek to observe human behavior in real-time under carefully controlled conditions. Yet, ethical reasons prevent placing participants in situations in which they could inflict or suffer harm. Consequently – although laboratory conditions need not perfectly correspond with real-world phenomena – aggression research has employed particularly artificial methods. For example, researchers have prompted participants to punch a punching pad (e.g., Bosson, Vandello, Burnaford, Weaver, & Wasti, 2009), write about their aggressive thoughts and feelings (e.g., Calvert & Tan, 1994), take money away from a fictitious participant (e.g., Cherek, Moeller, Schnapp, & Dougherty, 1997; Moeller et al., 1996; Pietras et al., 2005), verbally attack a confederate (e.g., Rohsenow & Bachorwoski, 1984; Wheeler & Caggiula, 1966), and inflict discomfort on another with noxious stimuli such as shocks or noise blasts (e.g., Anderson & Dill, 2000; Anderson & Murphy, 2003; Buss, 1961; Ferguson & Rueda, 2009). While useful, these measures have been criticized on a number of counts (see Ferguson, 2007; Ferguson & Rueda, 2009; Ritter & Eslea, 2005; Tedeschi & Quicgley, 1996). For example, their relationship to real-world aggression is unclear and, as measures of physical aggression, they suffer from low face validity. Some measures – like punching a pad or writing about aggressive thoughts and feelings – fail to incorporate interaction with a target (Baron & Richardson, 1994). Other measures, like withholding money and the use of verbal attacks, entail interaction but lack physicality. Consequently, these measures may not correlate with physical aggression. Accordingly, Ferguson and Rueda (2009) call for the development of measures that boast higher face validity and that allow for greater face-to-face contact between participants and the targets of their aggression. Below, we present the results of four studies that use accelerometers, in combination with readily available video game technology, to answer this call.

EQUIPMENT, METHOD, AND TERMINOLOGY

Across all studies, we made use of two tri-axial wireless accelerometers, two receivers, and a software development kit.[2] The accelerometers were sewn into straps that participants then wore on their wrists. The receivers were plugged into a nearby computer and the software was installed on the same computer. These devices allowed us to record motion, time, and x-, y- and z-axial acceleration for each participant between 500 and 700 times per second.

In addition to the accelerometers, we made use of the Nintendo Wii, although other gaming systems could be used to employ a similar approach. The Wii comes with a wireless primary controller (nicknamed the "Wiimote") and a smaller controller (called the "Nunchuk") that connect via a cord. These devices are used to play games, including the boxing game that comes standard with the system and was used in our studies. To play the game, the player holds the Wiimote in one hand and the Nunchuk in the other and boxes (i.e., punches with his or her hands). As the player moves, his or her avatar duplicates these movements on screen.[3]

An avatar is a digital representation of someone. Avatars vary in photographic and behavioral realism, meaning that they can look very similar to, or very different from, the person they represent and they can crudely or precisely mimic real-life behavior. Wii avatars have low photographic realism but high behavioral realism. High behavioral realism − even when combined with extremely low photographic realism − produces the experience of genuinely acting and reacting to others (Bailenson, Blascovich, Beall, & Loomis, 2001; Bailenson, Yee, Merget, & Schroeder, 2006; Garau et al., 2003; Heeter, 1992). Crucially, this sense of realism allows researchers to study behaviors that, to date, have been difficult or impossible to simulate in laboratory settings (e.g., violence, sexual behavior, assessing and responding to emergency situations) (Blascovich et al., 2002).

STUDY 1

The purpose of Study 1 was to introduce the measure and to establish its concurrent validity. Concurrent validity is established by associating a measure with a preexisting indicator, considered to be valid often by reason of its incontestable face validity. Intentional aggression − that is, asking people to play the boxing game aggressively − meets this criterion, perhaps more so than any other. For our aggression measure to be concurrently valid, it should be highly associated with intentionally aggressive game play. When people are asked to play the game more aggressively, they should score high on the aggression measure captured by the accelerometers; when people are asked to play the game less aggressively, they should score low on the aggression measure.

Methods and Procedure

We recruited 28 faculty, staff, and students (8 men; 20 women) at a university in the northeastern United States to participate. Each participant consented to take part in the study and was asked about his or her Wii experience. All participants had at least some Wii experience, making it unnecessary to provide any extra instruction. Participants put on the two wrist straps (one on each hand) into which the accelerometers were sewn and were instructed to play the boxing game twice: once in an "aggressive way" and once in a "normal way." The order in which participants were instructed to play was counter-balanced. Each participant used the same preselected, gender-neutral avatar to represent him or herself and played against the machine.[4] Afterward, each participant was paid US$2.00.

Data Collection and Analysis

We collected 30 seconds of accelerometer data for each participant on each hand in both the normal and aggressive conditions. Data collection began 5 seconds after the start of game play and was saved in Excel files. Then, using LabVIEW®, a graphical programming environment that allows users to write programs for data analysis, we condensed the data into two aggression measures: dominant- and nondominant-hand average peak acceleration. To compute average peak acceleration, we computed a resultant of the three acceleration vectors ($x^2 + y^2 + z^2$) for each sweep. We then graphed each participant's resultant acceleration and totaled the number of "peaks" (i.e., punches) in the resultant graphs.[5] We then averaged the maximum acceleration point across all peaks and converted the measure back into the original measurement unit by taking its square.

Results

Paired-samples t-tests were conducted to compare average peak acceleration across conditions. There was a significant difference in dominant-hand average peak acceleration between the normal ($M = 6.172$, SD $= 2.585$) and aggressive ($M = 9.229$, SD $= 2.345$) conditions, $t(27)=6.057$, $p < 0.001$. There was also a significant difference between conditions for data collected from participants' nondominant hands ($M = 6.313$, SD $= 2.499$; $M = 9.187$, SD $= 2.224$), $t(27)= 6.417$, $p < 0.001$. These differences equate to a 49.5% and a 45.5% increase in average peak acceleration, respectively, confirming that accelerometer data can be used to detect intentional differences in aggression.

STUDY 2

In Study 2, we again sought to establish the concurrent validity, as well as the stability and representative reliability, of our aggression measure. Stability reliability involves replication over time; representative reliability involves replication across subpopulations. Consequently, we repeated Study 1 using similar methods five years later at a large Midwestern university. Due to funding constraints, Study 2 examined the feasibility of our method with the use of a single accelerometer attached to participants' dominant hand. The replication was part of a larger group of studies about masculinity. Consequently, only undergraduate men were recruited ($N = 17$) to participate. This was apropos given the overrepresentation of women in Study 1. Participants received extra credit in a sociology course in exchange for participation.

Results

Again, a paired-samples *t*-test was conducted to compare dominant-hand average peak acceleration across conditions. Again, we found that average peak acceleration was significantly higher when participants were asked to play the game aggressively ($M = 8.233$, SD = 3.763) than when they were asked to play the game normally ($M = 5.930$, SD = 2.103), $t(16)=3.199$, $p < 0.01$. Independently, Studies 1 and 2 establish the measure's concurrent validity by demonstrating their ability to detect variation between more and less aggression within participants. Conjointly, the studies verify that the measure is both stably and representatively reliable. Study 2 also suggests that future researchers may save money by investing in only one accelerometer.

STUDY 3

In Study 3, to establish predictive validity, we compare our measure with an existing, commonly used measure of physical aggression. Buss and Perry's (1992) physical aggression subscale, a component of the Buss and Perry aggression questionnaire (BPAQ), consists of nine self-report items designed to assess trait aggression (e.g., "I have become so mad that I have broken things." "Once in a while, I can't control the urge to strike another person."). The BPAQ's four-factor structure has been validated in multiple populations and languages (e.g., Evren, Çinar, Güleç, Çelik, & Evren, 2011; Madran, 2013; Reyna, Ivacevich, Sanchez, & Brussino, 2011; Santisteban, Alvarado, & Recio, 2007). Additionally, the measure has been found to correlate with self-reported aggressive acts (Archer & Webb, 2006; Archer, Holloway, & McLoughlin, 1995; Burton, Hafetz, & Henninger, 2007; Diamond & Magaletta, 2006; Evren et al., 2011; Harris, 1997; Madran, 2013).

Relatively little research, however, has examined the relationship between the BPAQ and behavioral measures of aggression and these few studies have yielded mixed results. For example, although researchers have correlated the BPAQ with peer reports of men's aggression (Buss & Perry, 1992; O'Connor, Archer, & Wu, 2001) and used the measure to differentiate between incarcerated and nonincarcerated men (Garcia-Leon et al., 2002; Pechorro, Barroso, Poiares, Oliveira, & Torrealday, 2016), others find little correlation between the BPAQ and staff ratings of male offenders (Morren & Meesters, 2002) or the severity of criminal charges (Williams, Boyd, Cascardi, & Poythress, 1996).

In addition, this small body of work has largely excluded women. This is problematic because women are less likely than men to report engaging in physical aggression, presumably for social desirability reasons (Archer, 2004; Burton et al., 2007; Buss & Perry, 1992) and social desirability is negatively correlated with BPAQ scores (Harris, 1997). Thus, it remains unknown how self-reported physical aggression, as measured by the BPAQ, will correlate with a behavioral measure of women's physical aggression. Consequently, in this study, we explore whether our accelerometer measure correlates with the BPAQ physical aggression subscale and we explore this relationship separately for men and for women.

Methods

A total of 66 participants (33 men and 33 women) at a selective liberal arts college in the northeast ($N = 34$) and a research-intensive university in the northeast ($N = 32$) were recruited to participate. Both laboratories were set up in the following way. Two computer stations were created and separated by a large curtain. A large table was placed roughly six feet from the curtain in order to hold the Wii console and a 32-inch flat screen television. One participant was scheduled to participate at a time; however, participants were led to believe that their opponent was also a participant. In actuality, the participant's opponent was an undergraduate research assistant trained as a confederate. The confederate sat at one computer station; the participant sat on the other side of the curtain at the other computer station. The confederate arrived early to ensure that the participant did not see the confederate outside of the scripted procedure.

After consenting to participate, the experimenter told both "participants" (i.e., the participant and the confederate) that the purpose of the study was to investigate how various personality types play video games. The experimenter went on to explain that both participants would complete a personality survey, create an avatar, and play a game using the Nintendo Wii, but that they could not do these activities in the same order because only one avatar could be created at a time. The experimenter instructed the actual participant to create his or her avatar first. The experimenter then led the participant through a short tutorial on how to create an avatar in his or her likeness (called a "Mii") using the WiiMote. For example, participants were able to choose their head shape; hair color and style; eye color, shape, and placement; body size; and clothing. The experimenter gave the participant 8 min to create his or her avatar. Meanwhile, the confederate completed the online survey portion of the study.

After the participant finished creating his avatar, the participant and the confederate switched tasks: The participant completed the survey and the confederate completed the tutorial and created his avatar. (To ensure consistency across participants, the confederate created an identical, generic avatar each time.) The survey, labeled "Personality Survey," contained the nine physical aggression subscale items (Buss & Perry, 1992), as well as 91 randomly selected, randomly presented items ostensibly related to various personality traits. These 91 questions served to bolster the cover story and conceal the fact that the study was about aggression.

Next, the experimenter instructed both the participant and the confederate to attach the accelerometers to their dominant wrists and complete a short tutorial, explaining how to play the boxing game. They then played the game against one another using their Mii characters, while the experimenter collected the participant's accelerometer data between 5 seconds and 35 seconds of game play. To control for the confederate ability, the confederate repeated the same three moves to the tune of "Hot Cross Buns" for the duration of each round. Pretesting revealed that this did not arouse suspicion and that the confederate maintained consistent average peak acceleration across rounds.

After playing the game, the participant returned to the computer to answer several final questions about his desire to do well on the task, his feelings regarding his avatar, and his level of suspicion. All participants were debriefed and paid US$10 for their participation.

Results and Discussion

Correlation and multiple regression analyses were conducted to examine the relationship between Buss and Perry's physical aggression subscale and average peak acceleration. We found no significant correlation between the two measures in the full sample; however, for men, trait aggression was positively and significantly correlated with average peak acceleration ($R^2 = 0.405$, $p < 0.05$), indicating that men with higher self-reported physical trait aggression also had higher average peak acceleration scores. Among women, physical trait aggression was not significantly correlated with average peak acceleration ($R^2 = -0.058$). To further assess the robustness of our results, we estimated two additional models controlling for Wii experience ($\beta = 1.270$, $p < 0.05$) and for both Wii experience and participants' desire to do well on the task ($\beta = 1.339$, $p < 0.05$). Again, we found a significant, positive relationship between physical trait aggression and average peak acceleration among men.

There are several possible reasons for this pattern of results. On the one hand, our measure may be unreliable with respect to gender. However, we do not think this is the case given that, in Studies 1 and 2, the accelerometer data were able to discern between more and less aggressive game play in both men and women. On the other hand, the physical aggression component of the BPAQ may not be representatively reliable. For example, women may be less honest than men when answering questions about physical aggression; men may overstate, and women may understate, aggression; or men and women may interpret questions about aggression differently. Although a subpopulation analysis of the Buss and Perry questionnaire is beyond the scope of this study, previous research finds that being male is more robustly related to physical aggression (Gerevich, Bácskai, & Czobor, 2007), lending credence to this interpretation.

STUDY 4

The purpose of Study 4 was to determine whether, using our accelerometer measure, we could reproduce a well-established theoretical finding about aggression. Previous work finds that threatened masculinity is associated with a variety of aggressive responses. For example, threatened men have been found to compensate by expressing increased support for war (Willer, Rogalin, Conlon, & Wojnowicz, 2013), completing a word task with aggressive words rather than neutral words (Vandello, Bosson, Cohen, Burnaford, & Weaver, 2008), exhibiting greater tolerance for violence against women (Munsch & Willer, 2012), sexually harassing women over the computer (Maass, Cadinu, Guarnieri, & Grasselli, 2003), selecting a punching task over a puzzle-solving task (Bosson et al., 2009), and punching a pad more forcefully as measured by a pressure pad (Bosson et al., 2009). In this study, we also test the hypothesis that men who undergo a masculinity threat will display more aggression than men who do not undergo such a threat; however, we assess aggression with our accelerometer-generated measure, average peak acceleration.

Methods

We collected data from 94 undergraduate men at a large Midwestern university.[6] Participants were told that the purpose of the study was to investigate whether various personality types prefer different versions of the Wii Boxing game. As before, participants watched a tutorial and created Mii characters, while a confederate completed the survey portion of the study. The participant and confederate then switched tasks.

The survey, labeled "Gender Identity Test," contained the experimental manipulation and has been used successfully in past masculinity threat research (e.g., Maass et al., 2003; Munsch & Willer, 2012; Willer et al., 2013). In actuality, participants completed the Bem Sex Role Inventory (BSRI; Bcm, 1974). The BSRI consists of a list of 60 adjectives: 20 associated with masculinity (e.g., "dominant"), 20 associated with femininity (e.g., "compassionate"), and 20 associated with neither masculinity nor femininity (e.g., "truthful"). Respondents indicated the degree to which each adjective described them (1 = "never or almost never true," 7 = "always or almost always true"). After completing the inventory, participants were told that the experimenter would review their results and provide feedback. Two minutes later, the experimenter handed participants a sealed envelope containing their gender identity score. In truth, scores received by participants were randomly determined prior to the beginning of the study. Participants were either given a score of 32 or 11 as indicated on a number line. Scores of 32 were shown to be just inside the average range for women (threat condition); scores of 11 were shown to be squarely in the average range for men (no-threat condition).

After exposure to the manipulation, participants watched a brief tutorial about how to play the boxing game, and then competed against the confederate, while the experimenter collected participants' accelerometer data in the same manner described above. Finally, participants answered a series of basic demographic questions, were fully debriefed, and received either extra credit or US$10 for their participation.

Results

During debriefing, two participants indicated that they knew their test results were fallacious, one participant did not open his envelope and thus was not

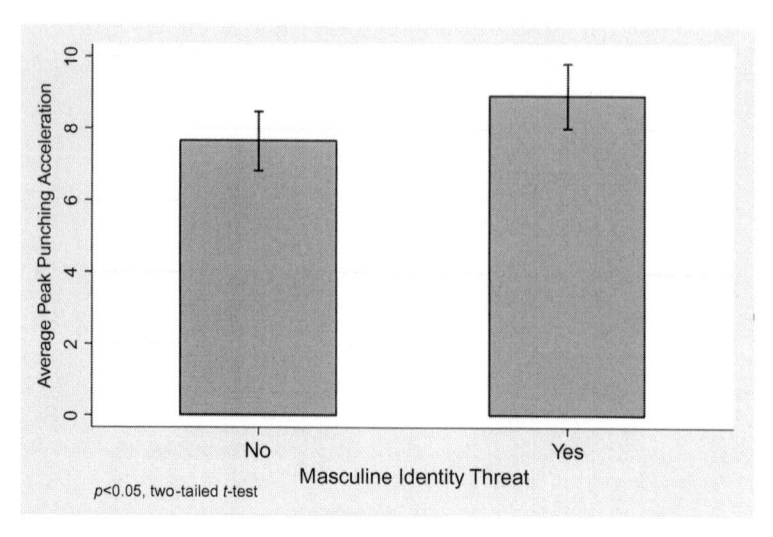

Fig. 1. Average Peak Punching Acceleration by Exposure to Masculine Identity Threat, $N = 90$.

exposed to the manipulation, and one participant was given incorrect test results (i.e., a number that was not 11 or 32). These four participants were excluded from the analyses, resulting in a sample of 90 participants.

Fig. 1 displays average peak acceleration by condition. Results of an independent sample t-test reveal that threatened men were significantly more aggressive than nonthreatened men, $t(88) = -2.090$, $p < 0.05$. Participants who did not experience a masculinity threat yielded a mean peak acceleration score of 7.64 (SD = 0.41). Participants who experienced a masculinity threat yielded a mean peak acceleration score approximately 17% higher ($M = 8.91$, SD = 0.45). Thus, our study replicates previous research that finds threatened masculinity is associated with increased aggression using accelerometer-generated data.

DISCUSSION AND CONCLUSIONS

Taken together, the results of our work demonstrate the utility of accelerometers for measuring aggression in laboratory settings. We found that nondominant- (Study 1) and dominant-hand (Studies 1 and 2) average peak acceleration allows for differentiation between intentionally more and less aggressive behavior in both men and women. We also found that, for men, dominant-hand average peak acceleration correlates with a previously validated, self-report measure of physical aggression (Study 3). We found no correlation between the accelerometer and self-report measures in women. This is not surprising, however, given the gendered ways in which men and women express – and are expected to express – aggression (Archer, 2004; Archer & Coyne, 2005; Eagly & Steffen, 1986), suggesting that behavioral measures captured in real-time may more reliably gauge aggression across subgroups. Future research should identify situations, in which women engage in physically aggressive behavior and determine whether accelerometers successfully correlate with aggression in these situations. We then demonstrated the utility of accelerometers for testing a well-documented theory of aggression in a sample of young men (Study 4).

In light of the replication crisis in science, we are encouraged by these results. The results of many scientific studies, particularly from examinations like ours that rely on relatively small sample sizes, are difficult or impossible to replicate. Yet, Study 2 repeated Study 1 using the same methods, different subjects, and different experimenters. Further, as Munafò and Smith (2018) argue, robust research requires multiple lines of evidence. Our studies made use of multiple approaches to address our research question and came to similar conclusions. Thus, our work contributes to an ongoing conversation concerning the development of a shared, reliable, valid, and ethical measure of aggression that can be employed in laboratory settings (e.g., Ferguson & Rueda, 2009; Giancola & Chermack, 1998; Giancola & Zeichner, 1995; Ritter & Eslea, 2005; Tedeschi & Quigley, 1996, 2000). Our larger intention, however, is to begin a conversation about the ways, in which social scientists, broadly, and group processes researchers, specifically, might incorporate accelerometer technology into existing research programs. Consequently, aggression is meant to serve as an example case.

In thinking about some of the principle theoretical constructs in group processes research, we see a number of possibilities for the use of accelerometers. For example, given that individuals who like each other tend to mimic one another (Chartrand & Bargh, 1999; Lakin, Jefferis, Cheng, & Chartrand, 2003), researchers interested in affinity or social cohesion could use accelerometers to measure mimicry (i.e., positive correlations between participants' accelerometer data) (Kalimeri, Lepri, Kim, Pianesi, & Pentland, 2011). To date, researchers have almost exclusively relied on self-report measures or third-party observers; however, accelerometers allow for the collection of reliable, objective, real-time data and boast a much more precise level of measurement. Moreover, because accelerometers continuously collect data for extended periods of time, researchers can assess changes in affiliation – for example, before, during, and after an experimental stimulus.

Accelerometer data might also be used to measure emotion. To date, experience sampling (e.g., asking participants how they feel), coding facial behavior (e.g., coding the emotion expressed and its intensity from video footage), and measuring autonomic physiology (e.g., taking participants' blood pressure) are the three most common ways to measure emotional responses empirically. But emotions are embodied experiences. Slumped posture is associated with disappointment and negative affect; upright, expansive posture is associated with success and positive affect (Bull, 1978; James, 1932; Mendels, 1970; Riskind & Gotay, 1982; Weisfeld & Beresford, 1982). Thus, researchers could use accelerometers to detect emotion by examining postures and gait patterns associated with mood. Alternatively, researchers might use accelerometers to control for participant engagement by detecting on and off task behaviors (e.g., leaning forward, sitting upright, slumping in the chair, fidgeting).

In addition, because some cultures are more expressive (e.g., gesture faster, take up more space) than others, accelerometer data have been used to infer cultural background (Rehm, Bee, & André, 2008). In a similar manner, group processes' researchers could use accelerometer data to detect changes in expressivity in response to a stimulus (e.g., threat, social exclusion, stigma); or, given that accelerometer data are positively correlated with walking speeds (Rowlands, Thomas, Eston, & Topping, 2004), to gauge flight responses. Because high-status actors tend to speak more, gesture more assertively, and take up more space (Hall & Friedman, 1999; Henley, 1977; Leffler, Gillespi, & Conaty, 1982; Mast, 2002), researchers could also use accelerometers to differentiate between high- and low-status members in a task group.

Accelerometers might aid in the collection of data outside of the lab as well. This is important because some behaviors of interest to social scientists — for example, the amount of time people spend watching TV or sleeping — are impractical to collect in a laboratory setting. Asking participants to wear an accelerometer outside of the lab — or, as the data become more accessible, using accelerometer data from participants' cell phones — would allow researchers to collect data for longer periods of time, aggregate data collected over hours or days, and eliminate social desirability and recall bias concerns known to affect the reporting of certain behaviors (e.g., sleep, cigarette use, frequency, and duration of exercise). Further, accelerometers have fairly low subject burden compared to more traditional approaches like time diaries. In addition, researchers could make use of accelerometers in combination with other equipment like cameras; microphones; and heart rate, skin conductance, and brain activity monitors to study an even wider array of activities. New research pairing accelerometer data with global positioning system (GPS) data imply that researchers can even detect the context of particular activities (Randell & Muller, 2000). For example, one could study differences in expressivity, engagement, or dominance behaviors at work and at home.

While accelerometers hold promise for being remarkably generative in terms of collecting a host of socio-behavioral measures, they are not without limitations. For one, accelerometers can be expensive. For example, the accelerometers, receivers, and software used in the above studies cost approximately US$3000. A second drawback is that extracting more complicated features from the raw data requires a number of processing steps, yet few social scientists have the coding skills necessary to do this themselves. A good programmer can write code to assess gestures and behaviors from accelerometer-generated data, but hiring a programmer is an added expense. Of course, as accelerometers gain traction, it is likely that researchers will share their code with one another. Third, like other forms of technology, on occasion the equipment may fail to function. Indeed, in Study 4, we lost approximately 7% of our data due to technical difficulties and other researchers have reported similar problems (e.g., Hooker & Masters, 2016; Van Coevering et al., 2005). Similarly, accelerometer placement can influence output. Accelerometers provide data whether or not they are securely attached to research participants (Gjoreski, Luštrek, & Gams, 2011; Olguõn & Pentland, 2006). When accelerometers are loosely attached, the device is more moveable, artificially increasing activity counts (Martin, Olsen, Duncan, & Duerr, 2016). Finally, like other studies that involve the collection of real-world data, compliance is a concern. For example, in one study, a full 32% of participants reported they did not wear their accelerometer at some point during a three-day study (Hooker & Masters, 2016). To ease this concern, however, researchers can call or text participants periodically to remind them to wear the equipment.

Despite these limitations, the price and size of accelerometers continues to decline and accelerometry technology is rapidly advancing. Over the past few years, researchers have begun to experiment with the use of accelerometers for detecting the kinds of social gestures and behaviors described above (e.g., Kalimeri et al., 2011; Kools, 2012; Olguín, Gloor, & Pentland, 2009; Vossen, 2012) and it is only a matter of time before they are widely adopted. We offer this paper with the hope that it will generate a dialog between group processes and accelerometry scholars and that it will motivate social scientists to integrate this technology into their research in innovative ways.

NOTES

1. Since the accelerometer itself can only measure acceleration in one direction, triaxial accelerometers actually contain three accelerometers, aligned perpendicular to one other, in order to measure acceleration in any direction.

2. We purchased ours from Microstrain®; however, a number of companies have comparable products.

3. The Wiimote and Nunchuk are also equipped with accelerometers. Accelerometer data are transmitted to the console and translated into the movements seen on screen. It was not feasible, however, to gather this data directly from the Wii.

4. The Nintendo Wii allows players to either play against a fictive component whose performance is preprogrammed (the machine) or to play against another player also equipped with a Wiimote and Nunchuk. In Studies 1 and 2, participants played against the machine. In Studies 3 and 4, they played against a confederate.

5. Accelerometer data collected from punching shows multiple peaks. The larger peaks reflect punches, while other, smaller peaks may simply reflect small hand movements. To separate the punches from extraneous movement, only peaks that reached at least 50% of the participants' maximum acceleration were counted as punches. This method was validated by counting punches in real time and comparing the result to the number of punches detected by our algorithm. While we used a cutoff of 50% in this study; other researchers may choose to use different thresholds, depending on their purposes.

6. Eight additional people participated in the study; inadvertently, however, their accelerometer data were not recorded.

ACKNOWLEDGMENTS

The authors would like to thank Steve Benard, Hannah Bolte, Shelley Correll, Susan Fisk, Beth Hirsh, Jelani Ince, Deb King, Ed Lawler, Peter Lista, Viktor Przebinda, Richard Serpe, Catherine Taylor, and Lindy Williams for their guidance on this project, as well as the many research assistants who helped our experiments run smoothly.

REFERENCES

Albinali, F., Goodwin, M. S., & Intille, S. S. (2009). Recognizing stereotypical motor movements in the laboratory and classroom: A case study with children on the autism spectrum. Paper presented at Proceedings of the 11th International Conference on Ubiquitous Computing. Orlando, FL.

Anderson, C. A., & Dill, K. E. (2000). Video games and aggressive thoughts, feelings, and behavior in the laboratory and in life. *Journal of Personality and Social Psychology, 78*(4), 772–790. doi:10.1037//0022-3514.78.4.772

Anderson, C. A., & Murphy, C. R. (2003). Violent video games and aggressive behavior in young women. *Aggressive Behavior, 29*(5), 423–429. doi:10.1002/ab.10042

Ang, W. T., Khosla, P. K., & Riviere, C. N. (2003). Design of all-accelerometer inertial measurement unit for tremor sensing in hand-held microsurgical instrument. Paper presented at IEEE International Conference on Robotics and Automation. Taipei, Taiwan.

Archer, J. (2004). Sex differences in aggression in real-world settings: A meta-analytic review. *Review of General Psychology, 8*(4), 291–322. doi:10.1037/1089-2680.8.4.291

Archer, J., & Coyne, S. M. (2005). An integrated review of indirect, relational, and social aggression. *Personality and Social Psychology Review, 9*(3), 212–230. doi:10.1207/s15327957pspr0903_2

Archer, J., Holloway, R., & McLoughlin, K. (1995). Self-reported physical aggression among young men. *Aggressive Behavior, 21*(5), 325–342. doi:10.1002/1098-2337(1995)21:5325::AID-AB24802105033.0.CO;2-R

Archer, J., & Webb, I. A. (2006). The relation between scores on the Buss-Perry Aggression Questionnaire and aggressive acts, impulsiveness, competitiveness, dominance, and sexual jealousy. *Aggressive Behavior, 32*(5), 464–473. doi:10.1002/ab.20146

Bailenson, J. N., Blascovich, J., Beall, A. C., & Loomis, J. M. (2001). Equilibrium theory revisited: Mutual gaze and personal space in virtual environments. *Presence-Teleoperators and Virtual Environments, 10*(6), 583–598. doi:10.1162/105474601753272844

Bailenson, J. N., Yee, N., Merget, D., & Schroeder, R. (2006). The effect of behavioral realism and form realism of real-time avatar faces on verbal disclosure, nonverbal disclosure, emotion recognition, and copresence in dyadic interaction. *Presence-Teleoperators and Virtual Environments, 15*(4), 359–372. doi:10.1162/pres.15.4.359

Bao, L., & Intille, S. S. (2004). Activity recognition from user-annotated acceleration data. In A. Ferscha & F. Mattern (Eds.), *Pervasive: International conference on pervasive computing* (pp. 1–17). Paper presented at Second International Pervasive Computing Conference, Vienna Austria, April, 21–23.

Baron, R. A., & Richardson, D. R. (1994). *Human aggression.* New York, NY: Plenum Press.

Bem, S. L. (1974). The measurement of psychological androgyny. *Journal of consulting and clinical psychology, 42*(2), 155.

Blascovich, J., Loomis, J., Beall, A. C., Swinth, K. R., Hoyt, C. L., & Bailenson, J. N. (2002). Immersive virtual environment technology as a methodological tool for social psychology. *Psychological Inquiry, 13*(2), 103–124. doi:10.1207/S15327965PLI1302_01

Bornstein, D. B., Beets, M. W., Byun, W., & McIver, K. (2011). Accelerometer-derived physical activity levels of preschoolers: A meta-analysis. *Journal of Science and Medicine in Sport, 14*(6), 504–511. doi:10.1016/j.jsams.2011.05.007

Bosson, J. K., Vandello, J. A., Burnaford, R. M., Weaver, J. R., & Wasti, S. A. (2009). Precarious manhood and displays of physical aggression. *Personality and Social Psychology Bulletin, 35*(5), 623–634. doi:10.1177/0146167208331161

Brezmes, T., Gorricho, J.-L., & Cotrina, J. (2009). Activity recognition from accelerometer data on a mobile phone. In S. Omatu, M. P. Rocha, J. Bravo, F. Fernandez, E. Corchado, A. Bustillo, & J. M. Corchado (Eds.), *Distributed computing, artificial intelligence, bioinformatics, soft computing, and ambient assisted living* (pp. 796–799). Paper presented at International Work Conference on Artificial Neural Networks, Salamanca, Spain, June, 10–12. Berlin: Springer.

Bull, P. (1978). The interpretation of posture through an alternative methodology to role play. *British Journal of Social and Clinical Psychology, 17*(1), 1–6. doi:10.1111/j.2044-8260.1978.tb00888.x

Burton, L. A., Hafetz, J., & Henninger, D. (2007). Gender differences in relational and physical aggression. *Social Behavior and Personality*, *35*(1), 41–50. doi:10.2224/sbp.2007.35.1.41

Buss, A. H. (1961). *The psychology of aggression*. Hoboken, NJ: John Wiley & Sons.

Buss, A. H., & Perry, M. (1992). The aggression questionnaire. *Journal of Personality and Social Psychology*, *63*(3), 452–459. doi:10.1037/0022-3514.63.3.452

Calvert, S. L., & S. L. Tan. (1994). Impact of virtual reality on young adults' physiological arousal and aggressive thoughts: Interaction versus observation. *Journal of Applied Developmental Psychology*, *15*(1), 125–139. doi:10.1016/0193-3973(94)90009-4

Capaldi, D. M., & Crosby, L. (1997). Observed and reported psychological and physical aggression in young, at-risk couples. *Social Development*, *6*(2), 184–206. doi:10.1111/1467-9507.00033

Chartrand, T. L., & Bargh, J. A. (1999). The Chameleon effect: The perception-behavior link and social interaction. *Journal of Personality and Social Psychology*, *76*(6), 893–910. doi:10.1037//0022-3514.76.6.893

Cherek, D. R., Moeller, F. G., Schnapp, W., & Dougherty, D. M. (1997). Studies of violent and nonviolent male parolees: Laboratory and psychometric measurements of aggression. *Biological psychiatry*, *41*(5), 514–522. doi:10.1016/S0006-3223(96)00059-5

Choudhury, T., Consolvo, S., Harrison, B., LaMarca, A., LeGrand, L., Rahimi, A., ... Hightower, J. (2008). The mobile sensing platform: An embedded activity recognition system. *IEEE Pervasive Computing*, *7*(2), 32–41. doi:10.1109/MPRV.2008.39

Deal, J., & Wampler, K. (1986). Dating violence: The primacy of previous experience. *Journal of Social and Personal Relationships*, *3*(4), 457–471. doi:10.1177/0265407586034004

DeMaio, T. J. (1984). Social desirability and survey measurement: A review. In C. F. Turner & E. Martin (Eds.), *Surveying subjective phenomena* (pp. 257–274). New York, NY: Russell Sage Foundation.

Diamond, P. M., & Magaletta, P. R. (2006). The short-form Buss-Perry aggression questionnaire (BPAQ-SF) – A validation study with federal offenders. *Assessment*, *13*(3), 227–240. doi:10.1177/1073191106287666

Eagly, A., & Steffen, V. (1986). Gender and aggressive behavior: A meta-analytic review of the social psychological literature. *Psychological Bulletin*, *100*(3), 309–330. doi:10.1037//0033-2909.100.3.309

Evren, C., Çinar, O., Güleç, H., Çelik, S., & Evren, B. (2011). The validity and reliability of the Turkish version of the Buss-Perry's Aggression Questionnaire in male substance dependent inpatients. *The Journal of Psychiatry and Neurological Sciences*, *24*(4), 283–295. doi:10.5350/DAJPN2011240404

Ferguson, C. J. (2007). Evidence for publication bias in video game violence effects literature: A meta-analytic review. *Aggression and Violent Behavior*, *12*(4), 470–482. doi:10.1016/j.avb.2007.01.001

Ferguson, C. J., & Rueda, S. M. (2009). Examining the validity of the modified Taylor competitive reaction time test of aggression. *Journal of Experimental Criminology*, *5*(2), 121–137. doi:10.1007/s11292-009-9069-5

Garau, M., Slater, M., Vinayagamoorthy, V., Brogni, A., Steed, A., & Sasse, M. A. (2003). The impact of avatar realism and eye gaze control on perceived quality of communication in a shared immersive virtual environment. In *Proceedings of the SIGCHI conference on human factors in computing systems*, Ft. Lauderdale, FL, April, 5–10 (pp. 529–536). New York, NY: ACM. https://doi.org/10.1145/642611.642703

Garcia-Leon, A., Reyes, G. A., Vila, J., Perez, N., Robles, H., & Ramos, M. M. (2002). The aggression questionnaire: A validation study in student samples. *Spanish Journal of Psychology*, *5*(1), 45–53. doi:10.1017/S1138741600005825

Gerevich, J., Bácskai, E., & Czobor, P. (2007). The generalizability of the Buss–Perry aggression questionnaire. *International Journal of Methods in Psychiatric Research*, *16*(3), 124–136. doi:10.1002/mpr.221

Giancola, P. R., & Chermack, S. T. (1998). Construct validity of laboratory aggression paradigms: A response to Tedeschi and Quigley (1996). *Aggression and Violent Behavior*, *3*(3), 237–253. doi:10.1016/S1359-1789(97)00004-9

Giancola, P., & Zeichner, A. (1995). Construct validity of a competitive reaction-time aggression paradigm. *Aggressive Behavior*, *21*(3), 199–204. doi:10.1002/1098-2337(1995)21:3199::AID-AB24802103033.0.CO;2-Q

Gjoreski, H., Luštrek, M., & Gams, M. (2011). Accelerometer placement for posture recognition and fall detection. In *Intelligent environments*. Paper presented at 7th International Conference on Intelligent Environments, Nottingham, UK, July 25–28 (pp. 47–54). https://doi.org/10.1109/IE.2011.11

Goosby, B. J., Straley, E., & Cheadle, J. E. (2017). Discrimination, sleep, and stress reactivity: Pathways to African American-White cardiometabolic risk inequities. *Population Research and Policy Review*, *36*(5), 699–716.

Gruenerbl, A., Osmani, V., Bahle, G., Carrasco, J. C., Oehler, S., Mayora, O., ... Lukowicz, P. (2014, March). Using smart phone mobility traces for the diagnosis of depressive and manic episodes in bipolar patients. In *Proceedings of the 5th augmented human international conference* (p. 38). ACM.

Hall, J. A., & Friedman, G. B. (1999). Status, gender, and nonverbal behavior: A study of structured interactions between employees of a company. *Personality and Social Psychology Bulletin*, *25*(9), 1082–1091. doi:10.1177/01461672992512002

Harris, J. A. (1997). A further evaluation of the aggression questionnaire: Issues of validity and reliability. *Behaviour Research and Therapy*, *35*(11), 1047–1053. doi:10.1016/S0005-7967(97)00064-8

Heeter, C. (1992). Being there: The subjective experience of presence. *Presence: Teleoperators and Virtual Environments*, *1*(2), 262–271.

Henley, N. (1977). *Body politics: Power, sex, and nonverbal communication*. Englewood Cliffs, NJ: Prentice Hall.

Hilton, N. Z., Harris, G. T., & Rice, M. E. (1998). On the validity of self-reported rates of interpersonal violence. *Journal of Interpersonal Violence*, *13*(1), 58–72. doi:10.1177/088626098013001004

Hilton, N. Z., Harris, G. T., & Rice, M. E. (2003). Correspondence between self-report measures of interpersonal aggression. *Journal of Interpersonal Violence*, *18*(3), 223–239. doi:10.1177/0886260502250065

Hooker, S. A., & Masters, K. S. (2016). Purpose in life is associated with physical activity measured by accelerometer. *Journal of Health Psychology*, *21*(6), 962–971. doi:10.1177/1359105314542822

Hunaidi, O., Wang, A., Bracken, M., Gambino, T., & Fricke, C. (2004, May). Acoustic methods for locating leaks in municipal water pipe networks. In *International conference on water demand management* (pp. 1–14). Jordan: Dead Sea. Retrieved from https://pdfs.semanticscholar.org/5f80/372cc31bad76d66f23e7cda896d65d0610db.pdf

James, W. T. (1932). A study of the expression of bodily posture. *Journal of General Psychology*, *7*(2), 405–436.

Kalimeri, K., Lepri, B., Kim, T., Pianesi, F., & Pentland, A. (2011). Automatic modeling of dominance effects using granger causality. In A.A. Salah & B. Lepri (Eds.), *Human behavior understanding*. Paper presented at the Second International Workshop on Human Behavior Understanding, Amsterdam, The Netherlands, November 16 (pp. 124–133). Berlin Heidelberg: Springer-Verlag.

Kato, A., Ropert-Coudert, Y., Gremillet, D., & Cannell, B. (2006). Locomotion and foraging strategy in foot-propelled and wing-propelled shallow-diving seabirds. *Marine Ecology Progress Series*, *308* 293–301. doi:10.3354/meps308293

Kools, J. A. N. (2012). *Recognizing non-verbal social behavior with accelerometers*. Unpublished master's thesis. Department of Artificial Intelligence, University of Amsterdam, Amsterdam, The Netherlands.

Krahe, B., Reimer, T., Scheinberger-Olwig, R., & Fritsche, I. (1999). Measuring sexual aggression – The reliability of the sexual experiences survey in a German sample. *Journal of Interpersonal Violence*, *14*(1), 91–100. doi:10.1177/088626099014001006

Kwapisz, J. R., G. M. Weiss, & S. Moore. (2010). Cell phone-based biometric identification. In *Fourth IEEE international conference on biometrics: Theory applications and systems*. Washington, DC, September, 27–29. https://doi.org/10.1109/BTAS.2010.5634532

Lakin, J. L., Jefferis, V. E., Cheng, C. M., & Chartrand, T. L. (2003). The chameleon effect as social glue: Evidence for the evolutionary significance of nonconscious mimicry. *Journal of Nonverbal Behavior*, 27(3), 145–162. doi:10.1023/A:1025389814290

Leffler, A., Gillespi, D., & Conaty, J. (1982). The effects of status differentiation on nonverbal behavior. *Social Psychology Quarterly*, 45(3), 153–161. doi:10.2307/3033648

Liu, X., Guo, J., Bai, C., Sun, X., & Mou, R. (2015). Drop test and crash simulation of a civil airplane fuselage section. *Chinese Journal of Aeronautics*, 28(2), 447–456. doi:10.1016/j.cja.2015.01.007

Lynch, J. P., Wang, Y., Loh, K. J., & Yi, J. H. (2006). Performance monitoring of the Geumdang Bridge using a dense network of high-resolution wireless sensors. *Smart Materials and Structures*, 15(6), 1561–1575. doi:10.1088/0964-1726/15/6/008

Maass, A., Cadinu, M., Guarnieri, G., & Grasselli, A. (2003). Sexual harassment under social identity threat: The computer harassment paradigm. *Journal of Personality and Social Psychology*, 85(5), 853–870. doi:10.1037/0022-3514.85.5.853

Madimenos, F. C., Snodgrass, J. J., Blackwell, A. D., Liebert, M. A., & Sugiyama, L. S. (2011). Physical activity in an indigenous Ecuadorian forager-horticulturalist population as measured using accelerometry. *American Journal of Human Biology*, 23(4), 488–497.

Madran, H. A. D. (2013). The reliability and validity of the Buss-Perry Aggression Questionnaire (BAQ): Turkish version. *Turkish Journal of Psychiatry*, 24(2), 124–129. Retrieved from http://www.turkpsikiyatri.com/Data/UnpublishedArticles/7pradb.pdf

Martin, K. W., Olsen, A. M., Duncan, C. G., & Duerr, F. M. (2016). The method of attachment influences accelerometer-based activity data in dogs. *BMC Veterinary Research*, 13(1), 48. doi:10.1186/s12917-017-0971-1

Mast, M. S. (2002). Dominance as expressed and inferred through speaking time: A meta-analysis. *Human Communication Research*, 28(3), 420–450. doi:10.1111/j.1468-2958.2002.tb00814.x

Mendels, J. (1970). *Concepts of depression*. New York, NY: John Wiley & Sons.

Mizuike, C., Ohgi, S., & Morita, S. (2009). Analysis of stroke patient walking dynamics using a triaxial accelerometer. *Gait & Posture*, 30(1), 60–64. doi:10.1016/j.gaitpost.2009.02.017

Moeller, F. G., Dougherty, D. M., Swann, A. C., Collins, D., Davis, C. M., & Cherek, D. R. (1996). Tryptophan depletion and aggressive responding in healthy males. *Psychopharmacology*, 126(2), 97–103.

Morren, M., & Meesters, C. (2002). Validation of the Dutch version of the aggression questionnaire in adolescent male offenders. *Aggressive Behavior*, 28(2), 87–96. doi:10.1002/ab.90010

Morse, J. (1995). Beyond the conflict tactics scale: Assessing gender differences in partner violence. *Violence and Victims*, 10(4), 251.

Munafò, M. R., & Smith, G. D. (2018). Repeating experiments is not enough. *Nature*, 553(7689), 399–401.

Munsch, C. L., & Willer, R. (2012). The role of gender identity threat in perceptions of date rape and sexual coercion. *Violence against Women*, 18(10), 1125–1146. doi:10.1177/1077801212465151

O'Connor, D. B., Archer, J., & Wu, F. W. C. (2001). Measuring aggression: Self-reports, partner reports, and responses to provoking scenarios. *Aggressive Behavior*, 27(2), 79–101. doi:10.1002/ab.2

Offer, D., Kaiz, M., Howard, K. I., & Bennett, E. S. (2000). The altering of reported experiences. *Journal of the American Academy of Child and Adolescent Psychiatry*, 39(6), 735–742. doi:10.1097/00004583-200006000-00012

Olguõn, D. O., & Pentland, A. S. (2006, October). Human activity recognition: Accuracy across common locations for wearable sensors. In *Proceedings of 2006 10th IEEE international symposium on wearable computers*, Montreux, Switzerland (pp. 11–14). Citeseer. Retrieved from http://vismod.media.mit.edu/pub/tech-reports/TR-603.pdf

Olguín, D., Gloor, P. A., & Pentland, A. (2009). Capturing individual and group behavior with wearable sensors. In *Proceedings of AAAI spring symposium on human behavior modeling, series papers from the AAAI spring symposium, no. SS-09-04*. Palo Alto, CA: AAAI Press.

Orpinas, P., & Frankowski, R. (2001). The aggression scale: A self-report measure of aggressive behavior for young adolescents. *The Journal of Early Adolescence, 21*(1), 50–67. doi:10.1177/0272431601021001003

Pechorro, P., Barroso, R., Poiares, C., Oliveira, J. P., & Torrealday, O. (2016). Validation of the Buss-Perry Aggression Questionnaire − Short form among Portuguese juvenile delinquents. *International Journal of Law and Psychiatry, 44*, 75–80. doi:10.1016/j.ijlp.2015.08.033

Perlman, C. M., & Hirdes, J. P. (2008). The Aggressive Behavior Scale: A new scale to measure aggression based on the minimum data set. *Journal of the American Geriatrics Society, 56*(12), 2298–2303. doi:10.1111/j.1532-5415.2008.02048.x

Pietras, C. J., Lieving, L. M., Cherek, D. R., Lane, S. D., Tcheremissine, O. V., & Nouvion, S. (2005). Acute effects of lorazepam on laboratory measures of aggressive and escape responses of adult male parolees. *Behavioural Pharmacology, 16*(4), 243–251. doi:10.1097/01.fbp.0000170910.53415.77

Ramírez, J. M., & J. M. Andreu. (2006). Aggression, and some related psychological constructs (anger, hostility, and impulsivity): Some comments from a research project. *Neuroscience & Biobehavioral Reviews, 30*(3), 276–291.

Randell, C., & Muller, H. (2000). Context awareness by analysing accelerometer data. In *The fourth international symposium on wearable computers*. Atlanta, GA. https://doi.org/10.1109/ISWC.2000.888488

Ravi, N., N. Dandekar, P. Mysore, & M. L. Littman. (2005). Activity recognition from accelerometer data. In *Proceedings of the 17th conference on innovative applications of artificial intelligence*. Paper presented at American Association for Artificial Intelligence, Pittsburgh, PA, July, 9–13 (pp. 1541–1546). Retrieved from http://www.aaai.org/Papers/IAAI/2005/IAAI05-013

Rehm, M., Bee, N., & André, E. (2008). Wave like an Egyptian: Accelerometer based gesture recognition for culture specific interactions. In *Proceedings of the 22nd British HCI group annual conference on people and computers: Culture, creativity, interaction*, September, 1–5 (pp. 13–22). Liverpool: British Computer Society.

Reyna, C., Ivacevich, M. G. L., Sanchez, A., & Brussino, S. (2011). The Buss-Perry Aggression Questionnaire: Construct validity and gender invariance among Argentinean adolescents. *International Journal of Psychological Research, 4*(2), 30–37. doi:10.21500/20112084.775

Riskind, J. H., & Gotay, C. C. (1982). Physical posture: Could it have regulatory or feedback effects on motivation and emotion? *Motivation and Emotion, 6*(3), 273–298. Retrieved from https://www.researchgate.net/profile/Carolyn_Gotay/publication/227054597_Physical_Posture_Could_It_Have_Regulatory_or_Feedback_Effects_on_Motivation_and_Emotion/links/00b49536668a0c5939000000.pdf

Ritter, D., & Eslea, M. (2005). Hot sauce, toy guns, and graffiti: A critical account of current laboratory aggression paradigms. *Aggressive Behavior, 31*(5), 407–419. doi:10.1002/ab.20066

Rohsenow, D., & Bachorwoski, J. (1984). Effects of alcohol and expectancies on verbal aggression in men and women. *Journal of Abnormal Psychology, 93*(4), 418–432. doi:10.1037/0021-843X.93.4.418

Rowlands, A. V., Thomas, P. W. M., Eston, R. G., & Topping, R. (2004). Validation of the RT3 tri-axial accelerometer for the assessment of physical activity. *Medicine and Science in Sports and Exercise, 36*(3), 518–524. doi:10.1249/01.MSS.0000117158.14542.E7

Sadeh, A., & Acebo, C. (2002). The role of actigraphy in sleep medicine. *Sleep Medicine Reviews, 6*(2), 113–124.

Samson, D. R., Crittenden, A. N., Mabulla, I. A., Mabulla, A. Z., & Nunn, C. L. (2017). Hadza sleep biology: Evidence for flexible sleep-wake patterns in hunter-gatherers. *American Journal of Physical Anthropology, 162*(3), 573–582.

Santisteban, C., Alvarado, J. M., & Recio, P. (2007). Evaluation of a Spanish version of the Buss and Perry aggression questionnaire: Some personal and situational factors related to the aggression scores of young subjects. *Personality and Individual Differences, 42*(8), 1453–1465. doi:10.1016/j.paid.2006.10.019

Schwarz, N. (1999). Self-reports: How the questions shape the answers. *American Psychologist, 54*(2), 93–105. doi:10.1037/0003-066X.54.2.93

Skogan, W. G. (1986). Methodological issues in the study of victimization. In E. A. Fattah (Ed.), *From crime policy to victim policy* (pp. 80–116). London: Palgrave Macmillan.
Snodgrass, J. J., Liebert, M. A., Cepon-Robins, T. J., Barrett, T. M., Mathur, A., Chatterji, S., & Kowal, P. (2016). Accelerometer-measured physical activity among older adults in urban India: Results of a study on global ageing and adult health substudy. *American Journal of Human Biology*, 28(3), 412–420.
Tanaka, H., Takagi, Y., & Naito, Y. (2001). Swimming speeds and buoyancy compensation of migrating adult chum salmon Oncorhynchus keta revealed by speed/depth/acceleration data logger. *Journal of Experimental Biology*, 204(22), 3895–3904. Retrieved from http://jeb.biologists.org/content/jexbio/204/22/3895.full.pdf
Tedeschi, J. T., & Quigley, B. M. (1996). Limitations of laboratory paradigms for studying aggression. *Aggression and Violent Behavior*, 1(2), 163–177. doi:10.1016/1359-1789(95)00014-3
Tedeschi, J. T., & Quigley, B. M. (2000). A further comment on the construct validity of laboratory aggression paradigms: A response to Giancola and Chermack. *Aggression and Violent Behavior*, 5(2), 127–136. doi:10.1016/S1359-1789(98)00028-7
Teti, D. M., Shimizu, M., Crosby, B., & Kim, B. R. (2016). Sleep arrangements, parent–infant sleep during the first year, and family functioning. *Developmental Psychology*, 52(8), 1169.
Tsuda, Y., Kawabe, R., Tanaka, H., Mitsunaga, Y., Hiraishi, T., Yamamoto, K., & Nashimoto, K. (2006). Monitoring the spawning behaviour of chum salmon with an acceleration data logger. *Ecology of Freshwater Fish*, 15(3), 264–274. doi:10.1111/j.1600-0633.2006.00147.x
Van Coevering, P., Harnack, L., Schmitz, K., Fulton, J. E., Galuska, D. A., & Gao, S. J. (2005). Feasibility of using accelerometers to measure physical activity in young adolescents. *Medicine and Science in Sports and Exercise*, 37(5), 867–871. doi:10.1249/01.MSS.0000162694.66799.FE
Vandello, J. A., Bosson, J. K., Cohen, D., Burnaford, R. M., & Weaver, J. R. (2008). Precarious manhood. *Journal of Personality and Social Psychology*, 95(6), 1325–1339. doi:10.1037/a0012453
Vossen, D. L. (2012). *Detecting speaker status in a social setting with a single triaxial accelerometer.* Unpublished master's thesis. Department of Artificial Intelligence, University of Amsterdam, Amsterdam, The Netherlands.
Walter, P. L. (1999). Review: Fifty years plus of accelerometer history for shock and vibration (1940–1996). *Shock and Vibration*, 6(4), 197–207. Retrieved from http://downloads.hindawi.com/journals/sv/1999/281718.pdf
Watanabe, S., Izawa, M., Kato, A., Ropert-Coudert, Y., & Naito, Y. (2005). A new technique for monitoring the detailed behaviour of terrestrial animals: A case study with the domestic cat. *Applied Animal Behaviour Science*, 94(1–2), 117–131. doi:10.1016/j.applanim.2005.01.010
Weisfeld, G. E., & Beresford, J. M. (1982). Erectness of posture as an indicator of dominance or success in humans. *Motivation and Emotion*, 6(2), 113–131. doi:10.1007/BF00992459
Wheeler, L., & Caggiula, A. R. (1966). The contagion of aggression. *Journal of Experimental Social Psychology*, 2(1), 1–10. doi:10.1016/0022-1031(66)90002-3
Whelan, M. J., Gangone, M. V., Janoyan, K. D., & Jha, R. (2009). Highway bridge assessment using an adaptive real-time wireless sensor network. *IEEE Sensors Journal*, 9(11), 1405–1413. doi:10.1109/JSEN.2009.2026546
Willer, R., Rogalin, C. L., Conlon, B., & Wojnowicz, M. T. (2013). Overdoing gender: A test of the masculine overcompensation thesis. *American Journal of Sociology*, 118(4), 980–1022. doi:10.1086/668417
Williams, T. Y., Boyd, J. C., Cascardi, M. A., & Poythress, N. (1996). Factor structure and convergent validity of the aggression questionnaire in an offender population. *Psychological Assessment*, 8(4), 398–403. doi:10.1037/1040-3590.8.4.398
Wilson, R. P., Shepard, E. L. C., & Liebsch, N. (2008). Prying into the intimate details of animal lives: use of a daily diary on animals. *Endangered Species Research*, 4(1–2), 123–137. doi:10.3354/esr00064
Wolfe, D. A., Scott, K., Reitzel-Jaffe, D., Wekerle, C., Grasley, C., & Straatman, A. L. (2001). Development and validation of the conflict in adolescent dating relationships inventory. *Psychological Assessment*, 13(2), 277–293. doi:10.1037//1040-3590.13.2.277

Yoda, K., Sato, K., Niizuma, Y., Kurita, M., Bost, C. A., Le Maho, Y., & Naito, Y. (1999). Precise monitoring of porpoising behaviour of Adelie penguins determined using acceleration data loggers. *Journal of Experimental Biology, 202*(22), 3121–3126. Retrieved from http://jeb.biologists.org/content/jexbio/202/22/3121.full.pdf

Yoon, I. Y., Kripke, D. F., Youngstedt, S. D., & Elliott, J. A. (2003). Actigraphy suggests age-related differences in napping and nocturnal sleep. *Journal of Sleep Research, 12*(2), 87–93.

MODELING SMALL GROUP STATUS AND POWER DYNAMICS USING VOCAL ACCOMMODATION

Joseph Dippong and Will Kalkhoff

ABSTRACT

Purpose — *We review literature linking patterns of vocal accommodation in the paraverbal range of the voice to small group structures of status and dominance. We provide a thorough overview of the current state of vocal accommodation research, tracing the development of the model from its early focus on patterns of mutual vocal adaptation, to the current focus on structural factors producing patterns of unequal accommodation between group members. We also highlight gaps in existing knowledge and opportunities to contribute to the development of vocal accommodation as an unobtrusive, nonconscious measure of small group hierarchies.*

Approach — *We trace the empirical development of vocal accommodation as a measure of status and power, and discuss connections between vocal accommodation and two prominent theoretical frameworks: communication accommodation theory (CAT) and expectation states theory. We also provide readers with a guide for collecting and analyzing vocal data and for calculating two related measures of vocal accommodation.*

Findings — *Across multiple studies, vocal accommodation significantly predicts observers' perceptions regarding interactants engaged in debates and interviews. Studies have specifically linked vocal accommodation to perceptions of relative power or dominance, but have not shown a relationship between accommodation and perceptions of prestige.*

Research Implications — *Vocal accommodation measures have clear applications for measuring and modeling group dynamics. More work is needed to understand how accommodation functions in clearly-defined status situations, how the magnitude of status differences affects the degree of accommodation inequality, and how vocal accommodation is related to other correlates of social status, including openness to influence and contributions to group tasks.*

Keywords: Status; prestige; dominance; vocal accommodation; biosociology; interactional synchrony

Scholars who study group processes employ a variety of methodological tools for measuring and modeling group-level status and power structures. The most common approaches to assessing the behavioral consequences of interaction within status-heterogeneous groups include experimental tasks to measure influence between actors (cf. Moore, 1968), questionnaires designed to assess expectations, beliefs, and perceptions (Cheng, Tracy, Foulsham, Kingstone, & Henrich, 2013; Rashotte & Webster, 2005; Zeller & Warnecke, 1983), and observational measures of verbal and nonverbal task cues (McLeer, Frederick, Markovsky, & Barnum, 2011; Ridgeway, Berger, & Smith, 1985). Taken together, these methods are useful for addressing a wide range of research questions, and the strengths and weaknesses of each approach are generally well known. At the same time, each of the previously mentioned methods assesses behaviors that are largely under research participants' conscious control (i.e., deciding whether to change one's opinion based on the contradictory feedback from a task partner, or selecting a particular response on a questionnaire). Given the well-documented performative aspects of interaction (e.g., Goffman, 1959), it is worth considering if and how researchers might observe interactions unobtrusively and model status and power structures in a way that bridges the gap between what people *say* they believe vs what they *actually* believe.

Research on vocal accommodation (Gregory, 1994; Gregory, Green, Carrothers, Dagan, & Webster, 2001; Kalkhoff, Thye, & Gregory, 2017) suggests that certain frequencies within the human voice may hold the key to differentiating between what group members are able to tell us about their status- and power-based perceptions, and the true – perhaps consciously inaccessible – content of those perceptions. Communications scholars have long posited that our voices transmit much more information than the manifest verbal content of any particular message (Ekman, 1965; Ekman & Friesen, 1969). Paraverbal factors, such as vocal pitch, speech rate, and fluency, are often more crucial than the manifest content of speech in determining how others perceive us (Gregory, Webster, & Huang, 1993; Mehrabian, 1971). Vocal accommodation research builds on well-established theoretical paradigms within communications and social psychology to examine and explain a unique and seemingly invisible communication channel that reveals our perceptions of specific interaction partners and shapes how they perceive us in return.

Of particular importance to group processes scholars, evidence suggests that group members convey information about their perceptions of each other's relative status and power through patterns of nonconscious adaptation within the lower, paraverbal frequency band of the voice below 500 Hz (Gregory &

Webster, 1996; Kalkhoff et al., 2017). Because manipulation of the paraverbal frequencies occurs outside of an individual's conscious awareness (Gregory, Kalkhoff, Harkness, & Paull, 2009), measures of vocal accommodation offer researchers the potential to unobtrusively assess and model microsocial status and power hierarchies in a way that largely bypasses group members' conscious self-presentation motives. A growing body of research indicates that quantitative indicators of vocal accommodation reveal a clear picture of the group status and power structure as it emerges and stabilizes or shifts throughout interaction.

In this paper, we review theory and research linking patterns of vocal accommodation to individuals' locations within small group status and power structures. We begin with an overview of the central concepts and processes involved in behavioral convergence and vocal accommodation. Second, we discuss theoretical and empirical work connecting vocal accommodation to actors' relative position within interactional hierarchies of power and prestige. Third, we outline a number of future directions for research in this area, highlighting currently unanswered questions about the relationship between structural location and vocal accommodation as well as the need for further testing of existing arguments. Finally, for readers interested in researching vocal accommodation, we describe the most common procedures for collecting and analyzing vocal spectral data. Our goal is to encourage group processes' scholars to take up vocal accommodation measures as they seek to address current research questions and open new lines of social psychological inquiry.

TEMPORAL SYMMETRY AND THE RHYTHM OF INTERACTION

The process of vocal accommodation is rooted in a seemingly universal component of communication – interactional synchrony (Condon & Sander, 1974). Across a variety of contexts, social interaction frequently possesses a powerful rhythmic component (Condon & Sander, 1974; Kalkhoff, Dippong, & Gregory, 2011). Whether we consider friends sitting in a coffee shop who seem to spontaneously take a drink at the same time, or a group of unacquainted runners who intuitively find a common stride as they race together, even casual observation reveals that interaction can generate a rhythm that coordinates the behaviors of all those involved (Gregory, 1990). This apparently nonconscious synchronization of speech and behavior over time is temporal symmetry (Zerubavel, 1981). As we will argue, underlying differences in how individuals contribute to producing symmetry plays a vital role in revealing interactants' status and power perceptions.

Highlighting the rhythmic nature of interaction, previous scholars have employed music as a metaphor to describe the processes of mutual adaptation and temporal symmetry (Schutz, 1976). In essence, the musical metaphor casts social interactants as improvising performers; they follow a common score, while at the same time adjusting to each other's idiosyncrasies to avoid disrupting the collective harmony and rhythm (Gregory, 1983). Hall's (1981) analysis of children's playground behaviors provides a compelling illustration of the rhythm and musicality of interaction. Not only did Hall (1981) observe children in multiple subgroups moving with each other to the beat of a single overarching rhythm, but he also found that the beat was steady and consistent enough that video recordings of the children playing could be overlaid with unrelated musical recordings, such that the playground action appeared to move according to the same rhythm as the song. On this point, Kalkhoff and colleagues (2011, p. 937) note that "individual actors [...] align their interactional patterns with others within the immediate social environment, becoming 'swept up' in the movements of a larger collective." The rhythmic nature of group interaction is so well documented that it may represent a fundamental component of human social behavior (Condon, 1986).

As suggested above, interaction takes on a rhythmic or musical nature when individuals occupying the same social space synchronize their behaviors in some way in response to their own and each other's speech and movements. The convergence of individual actions toward a common, collective pattern of behavior serves to minimize social differences between actors and promote smooth interaction (Giles & Coupland, 1991). Importantly, group synchrony produces convergence not only in interactants' outward, observable behaviors, but also in inward, biological processes that occur outside of conscious awareness and control (Condon & Ogston, 1967; Kalkhoff et al., 2011).

Outward Interactional Synchrony

In one of the most influential early analyses of temporal symmetry, Condon and Ogston (1967) meticulously analyzed audiovisual recordings of mothers and fathers interacting with their children to examine patterns of behavioral synchronization. Viewing films frame-by-frame, Condon and Ogston (1967) observed two distinct forms of outward synchrony that occur during interaction: self-synchrony and interactional synchrony. Regarding *self-synchrony*, Condon and Ogston (1967) observed that individuals synchronize their bodily gestures with their *own* speech patterns. Self-synchrony occurs when, for example, a speaker's eyes widen as he or she reveals a particularly intriguing fact (Condon & Ogston, 1967). This type of synchrony typically occurs outside of actors' conscious awareness, and as such cannot easily be intentionally manipulated.

With *interactional* synchrony, individuals outwardly coordinate their speech and movement with the speech and movement of *other actors* within the social environment. To this end, Condon and Ogston (1967) observed that parents and children shared patterns of movement, including both the direction and the velocity of movement. Furthermore, the family groups shared patterns of vocal pitch and vocal stress. The synchronous behaviors revealed such a high level of coordination that Condon and Ogston (1967, p. 229) note, "Metaphorically, the three interactants looked like puppets moved by the same set of strings." Interestingly, unique forms of behavioral synchronization occurred simultaneously between the child and the two different parents, such that when one parent was speaking, the behaviors of the two nonspeaking family members would synchronize both with each other and with the speaker. The overall synchrony of the interaction was composed of smaller segments of rhythm converging into a single overarching pattern. Interactional synchrony, then, organizes the behaviors of groups as a whole as well as the behaviors of subgroups within the larger social setting.

The act of synchronizing behaviors with an interaction partner does not appear to reflect a learned or conscious process, but rather may be a natural human inclination. Illustrating this point most clearly, Condon and Sander's (1974) analysis of early interactions between neonates and parents reveals that infants synchronize their behaviors with caretaker voices as early as the first day of life. The one- and two-day-old children in Condon and Sander's (1974) study coordinated their movements with adult voices, independent of any eye contact, and regardless of whether the child heard her or his biological parents' voices or recordings of other parents. Importantly, the newborns did not synchronize their actions with recordings that did not contain a human voice. Condon and Sanders' (1974) research suggests that behavioral synchrony can occur (1) prior to any intensive socialization effects and (2) regardless of whether the hearer comprehends the manifest content of the speech. These two features of interactional synchrony point to the possibility that humans innately attune to rhythmic cues within interaction partners' voices.

Inward Interactional Synchrony

Just as interaction partners synchronize their observable outward behaviors, interaction also creates a sort of inward temporal symmetry, whereby individuals synchronize biological processes that occur below the level of conscious control. Condon and Ogston (1967) demonstrated inward synchrony in the form of shared patterns of the bioelectric activity in the brain. Connecting pairs of interaction partners to a 12-channel EEG, Condon and Ogston (1967) observed that the EEG pens associated with the scalp electrodes on both participants appeared to change synchronously. Such interbrain synchronization "occurs when brain wave activity across multiple individuals becomes 'phase locked' [...] [whereby EEG signals] for electrode pairs across two individuals begin to 'dance' in harmony as if being driven by a single person" (Thye & Kalkhoff, 2015, p. 39). The bioelectric activity of the speaker and listener coordinate in much the same way as speech patterns and hand gestures synchronize. More recently, researchers have begun to identify specific brain regions and EEG frequency bands that are involved in interbrain synchronization during various types of interactive tasks (Kalkhoff et al., 2015).

Gregory (1983) identified a second form of inward synchrony, observing that during interaction, individuals nonconsciously modulate certain frequencies of the vocal spectrum in a manner that causes the actors' voices to converge toward a common point. By quantitatively analyzing sequential segments of conversation, Gregory (1983; Gregory & Hoyt, 1982) found that over the course of interaction, frequencies of group members' voices come together to generate a sort of collective "vocal fingerprint" that is unique to the interacting dyad. The degree of convergence between two actors' voices is substantial to the point that, using a straightforward statistical routine, it is possible to accurately separate the vocal frequencies of an interacting pair from those of other actors within a larger pool of speakers (Gregory & Hoyt, 1982; Gregory, 1983; Gregory, 1986). As such, patterns of vocal convergence represent distinguishing emergent properties of specific interactions.

VOCAL DYNAMICS, SPEECH CONVERGENCE, AND COMMUNICATION ACCOMMODATION

Like other auditory stimuli, human speech reflects a combination of hundreds of individual acoustic frequencies that we interpret as a unitary sound. The audio signals of the human voice are produced when the lungs pass air across vocal folds (i.e., the vocal chords) within the larynx, causing the folds to vibrate. As the acoustic signal passes from the larynx into the laryngopharynx and sinuses, the tones are modified, resulting in an overall frequency range from 1 Hz to over 3,900 Hz (Gregory, 1983). Fig. 1 shows an example of an acoustic waveform for the full range of vocal frequencies in a segment of speech occurring between two actors. Waveforms like this depict changes in vocal intensity (measured in decibels). The complex speech waveform depicted in Fig. 1 models changes in the amplitude within the time domain (Gregory & Kalkhoff, 2007). To analyze convergence and accommodation, these complex waveforms must be "deconstructed" into their constituent frequencies.

Researchers typically employ fast Fourier transform (FFT) algorithms to separate the complex speech waveform, which is necessary to calculate measures of frequency change. Gregory (1986) likens acoustic FFT analysis to passing light through a prism; just as a prism separates visible light into its component

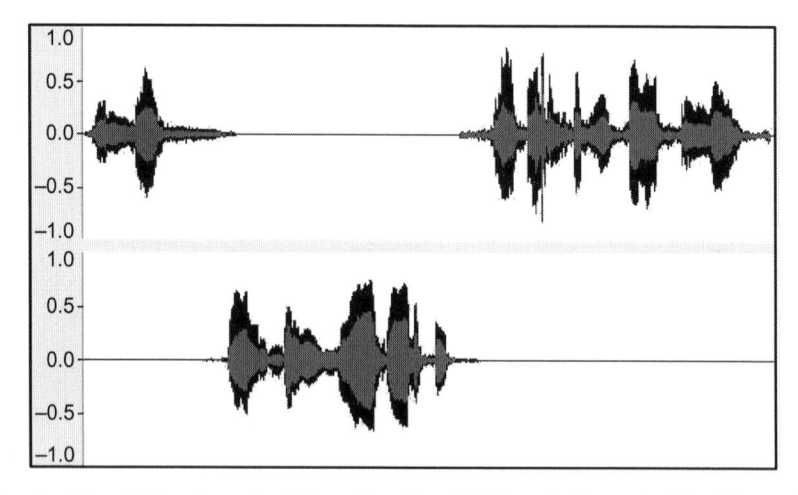

Fig. 1. Vocal Waveform for Interacting Dyad. Values Indicate the Vocal Intensity in Decibels (db). *Note*: Used with permission from Audacity ® Dominic Mazzoni, https://www.audacityteam.org.

frequencies, performing FFT on an acoustic signal separates the audible signal into its component frequencies. Given a segment of speech, the FFT transformation produces the average amplitude at each frequency across the entire segment.

Quantitatively, FFT summarizes the audio signal for a segment of speech by plotting acoustic frequencies for a given utterance or sound on the x-axis against the average amplitude at that frequency on the y-axis. Separating the acoustic waveform into its constituent frequencies converts the time domain to the frequency domain (see Gregory & Kalkhoff, 2007 for an in-depth discussion of FFT calculations). Fig. 2 presents a sample FFT plot for a 60-s utterance, with each bar representing the vocal amplitude at a specific frequency. As can be seen in Fig. 2, FFT transformation produces hundreds of distinct vocal amplitude values. This allows researchers to isolate specific frequency ranges that may be of theoretical or empirical interest. By comparing the shape of FFT plots for two or more actors across multiple temporal points groups, we can assess similarities and differences that emerge over the course of interaction; groups with a high degree of vocal symmetry produce very similar FFT plots (Gregory & Hoyt, 1982).

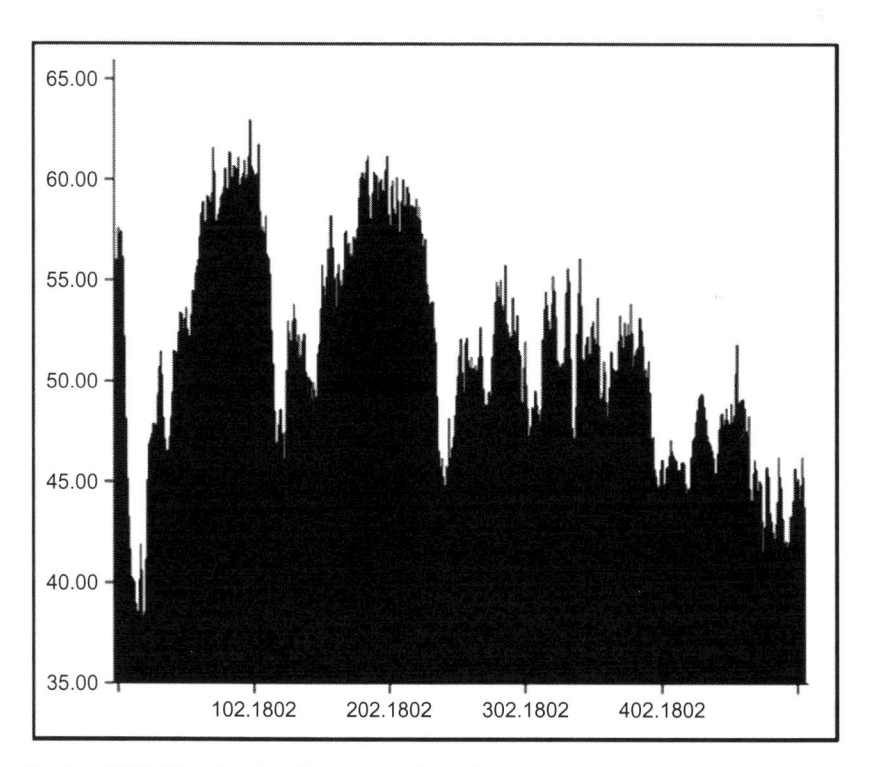

Fig. 2. FFT Plot for 60-s Segment of Speech. *Note*: Values on the x-axis indicate the vocal frequency, ranging from 1 to 500 Hz. Values on the y-axis indicate the amplitude at each frequency, Averaged across the entire speech segment.

For analytical purposes, the full vocal range described above can be conceptually divided into subsets of frequency bands. The verbal range of the voice includes frequencies greater than 500 Hz, and contains the acoustic signals that we would consider recognizable speech (Gregory, 1990). Frequencies in the verbal range are produced and manipulated under the speaker's conscious control, and carry the manifest informational content of a vocal utterance. Conversely, frequencies in the paraverbal range (at or below 500 Hz) are less easily consciously manipulated (Bachorowski, 1999). Although frequency convergence occurs across the full vocal range, substantial literature links dynamics in the paraverbal band to such important group outcomes as solidarity (Kalkhoff et al., 2011), communication quality (Gregory, Dagan, & Webster, 1997), cohesiveness (Gregory et al., 2009); task success (Kalkhoff, Gregory, & Melamed, 2009); social status perceptions (Gregory & Webster, 1996), and dominance perceptions (Gregory & Gallagher, 2002; Kalkhoff et al., 2017). As such, analyses of temporal symmetry in speech focus primarily on frequencies within the paraverbal band.

Vocal Synchrony and Paraverbal Frequencies

The earliest research on vocal symmetry focused on synchrony as a cooperative outcome produced through mutual behavioral adaptation between interaction partners. Following this assumption, Gregory (1983) analyzed recordings of conversations between an interviewer and members of the United States Air Force, examining how interactants' vocal patterns overlapped as conversation progressed. Using bivariate correlations, Gregory (1983) compared the interviewer's vocal patterns across eight frequency bands (ranging from 10 Hz to 3,988 Hz) to those of the Airman with whom he was interacting, revealing a significant relationship between interactants' voices across three time segments. Bolstering evidence of temporal vocal symmetry, Gregory also compared vocal patterns between the interviewer and all possible "virtual" partners, demonstrating a much closer match between actual conversation partners and virtual partners.[1] Furthermore, the relationship between actors' voices shifted across different phases of interaction, with each temporal segment producing a unique form of adaptation (Gregory, 1983).

Subsequent research reinforced Gregory's (1983; Gregory & Hoyt, 1982) initial findings regarding vocal symmetry in interaction. Over a series of studies, Gregory and colleagues replicated his early results and demonstrated vocal convergence in interviewer–interviewee dyads (Gregory, 1986, 1990) as well as between members of experimental task groups (Gregory et al., 1997). Recent advances in data collection technology and analysis procedures have led to the development of a growing body of the literature supporting and extending Gregory's early claims. Vocal convergence within the paraverbal frequency band, then, is a well-documented phenomenon.

Whereas initial research indicated symmetry in several separate frequency bands, later work identified frequencies in the lower vocal spectrum as the critical locus of vocal convergence. Gregory (1990) compared FFT values for interaction partners using three separate frequency thresholds – below 2,000 Hz, below 500 Hz, and below 200 Hz – and observed the strongest evidence for convergence within the frequencies below 500 Hz. Importantly, the frequency band below 500 Hz contains the fundamental frequency of the voice, which listeners perceive largely as tone or pitch (Fry, 1979; Gregory et al., 1997). Gregory's (1990) results echo findings from the previous research noting fundamental frequency symmetry (cf. Lieberman, 1967) and establish the paraverbal band as the region of greatest theoretical importance for understanding vocal convergence.

From Convergence to Accommodation

While refining his model of cooperative vocal convergence, Gregory (1994) observed something unexpected: Analyses of interview data revealed that statistical procedures could not only differentiate true interactions from virtual interactions, but could also differentiate vocal characteristics between group members based on their roles. To this end, Gregory (1994) observed that interactants contribute unequally to the act of convergence – one group member's voice often demonstrates greater temporal variability across the paraverbal band, while the other member's vocal characteristics remain relatively stable throughout the interaction. Stated differently, when one member of an interacting dyad fails to contribute adequately to the process of producing vocal convergence, the other member "puts in more work," so to speak, to reach a point of vocal symmetry. Frequency variability provides a starting point for unobtrusively differentiating between actors' perceptions of each other, based solely on the roles they play in producing convergence.

Employing the framework of communication accommodation theory (CAT; Giles & Coupland, 1991; Giles, Mulac, Bradac, & Johnson, 1987; Giles & Smith, 1979), Gregory (1994) lays the foundations for a theoretical model explaining role-based differences in contributions to vocal convergence. Building on CAT's notion that speakers and listeners employ speech convergence to optimize conditions for accurate conveyance and interpretation of communication content, Gregory (1994) posits that convergence processes are not limited to easily observed paraverbal characteristics like vocal pitch, speech tempo, and cadence, but rather that they occur across the full range of vocal content, including paraverbal frequency variability. Later, Gregory and Webster (1996) elaborated on the relationship between the communication accommodation and fundamental frequency convergence to explain how between-actor differences in social status and dominance contribute to differences in the amount of effort that group members put toward achieving vocal convergence.

The elaboration of status and dominance as factors affecting temporal symmetry led to a noteworthy shift in the theory and research on vocal dynamics. Rather than examining symmetry as a process of mutual vocal *convergence*, research began to reflect the language of vocal *accommodation*. Regarding the differences between convergence and accommodation, Gregory and Webster (1996, p. 1232) state that "convergence involves studying how partners merge voice elements to one another, with no specific attention devoted to their roles in producing the adaptation [...] [and] accommodation emphasizes studying how partners perform a service" to interaction partners. Through the lens of CAT, we see the effects of social structure on the process of convergence, as social roles influence which group members provide interactional services, and which members receive them (e.g., who defers to whom). Because CAT is central to understanding the relationship between the social structure and vocal accommodation, we provide an overview of the central arguments of the theory before discussing its bearing on vocal convergence processes.

Communication Accommodation Theory

As a theory of communication, CAT posits that during interaction, individuals adjust their behaviors relative to their partners to maximize the likelihood of successful message transmission and interpretation (Gallois, Ogay, & Giles, 2005; Giles & Coupland, 1991). While CAT accounts for two forms of behavioral adjustment – convergence to emphasize similarity between actors, and divergence to emphasize the distinctiveness of individuals – we focus our discussion entirely on the process of convergence. Although vocal dynamics likely reflect both convergence and divergence processes, our interests are primarily in understanding how status differences affect group members' contributions toward convergence. This is not to say that vocal divergence is irrelevant to group process scholars, but rather that vocal accommodation research has yet to empirically address the causes and consequences of divergence processes.

CAT sets forth three propositions related to the production, magnitude, and reception of converging behaviors (Street & Giles, 1982; Thakerar, Giles, & Cheshire, 1982). Regarding production, CAT posits that "People are more likely to converge toward the speech patterns of their recipients when they desire recipients' approval and when the perceived costs of doings so are proportionally lower than the anticipated rewards" (Gallois et al., 2005, p. 125). Concerning the magnitude of convergence, CAT argues that increased need for social approval is related to greater convergence, and that situational factors can increase or decrease motivations for approval. Lastly, in terms of reception, recipients of accommodation evaluate such attempts positively when it results in "optimal sociolinguistic distance" (Gallois et al., 2005, p. 125), depending on the perceived motives of the speaker. Overall, accommodation behaviors originate from and are shaped by an actor's need for social approval, self-presentation motives, situational constraints (including roles and identities), communication needs, and rational considerations of the costs of accommodation (Giles et al., 1987).

Communication accommodation serves both cognitive and affective functions (Gallois et al., 2005; Giles, Scherer, & Taylor, 1979). The cognitive function of accommodation is fairly straightforward: speakers converge to the behaviors of their recipients in order to improve message comprehension (Gallois et al., 2005; Giles et al., 1987). Affectively, speech accommodation functions to increase similarity between actors and reduce social distance, which also serves to increase accurate communication (Gallois et al., 2005; Giles & Coupland, 1991). Based on these functions, Giles and Coupland (1991) argue that status and power differences produce inequality in terms of how group members contribute to the overall goal of reduced social distance. Specifically, lower-status actors typically adjust their behaviors to match those of higher-status actors. While both actors contribute to the process of convergence, lower-status actors "provide a convenience" to higher-status actors (Gregory & Webster, 1996, p. 1232) by putting in the lion's share of the accommodation effort (Giles & Coupland, 1991). That lower-status actors accommodate higher-status partners makes sense in light of the CAT's emphasis on social approval seeking, in that status characteristics shape a group's distribution of positive evaluations and social approval (Berger, Fisek, Norman, & Zelditch, 1977).

Evidence for a Relationship between Status, Dominance, and Vocal Accommodation

CAT's central premises map neatly onto Gregory's (1994; Gregory & Webster, 1996) observations regarding vocal frequency convergence. Assuming that vocal frequency convergence abides by the same rules that govern other forms of speech convergence, Gregory's vocal status model predicts that in achieving vocal synchrony, lower-status group members modulate their voices to accommodate higher-status members. Whereas higher-status actors' paraverbal frequencies remain relatively stable across the interaction, lower-status actors' frequencies tend to move more dramatically toward those of their higher-status counterparts. Accordingly, researchers can ascertain the underlying status and power structure of a group simply by observing patterns of paraverbal frequency accommodation. And because this form of inward synchrony reflects a process of nonconscious behavioral adaptation, the magnitude of an actor's vocal accommodation serves as an unobtrusive indicator of her or his perceptions of relative status and power vis-à-vis an interaction partner.

Gregory and Webster (1996) provided the first test of the vocal status model, analyzing a series of televised interviews between talk show host Larry King and a variety of celebrity guests, including sitting presidents and vice presidents, other politicians and major candidates, and celebrity athletes and entertainers. Using FFT and principle components factor analysis (a procedure we describe later in this paper), Gregory and Webster (1996, Study 2) derived measures of vocal accommodation between Larry King and each interview partner, and found that Mr King tended to accommodate higher-status partners, while lower-status partners tended to accommodate the interviewer. This finding was confirmed by additional analyses by Gregory and Webster (1996, Study 3), in which they compared the derived vocal accommodation results to ratings of interviewer and interviewee status obtained from a sample of almost 600 raters. As expected, observers' ratings of status corresponded closely to the patterns of vocal accommodation observed in the interview data.

In a further test of central arguments of the vocal status model, Gregory and colleagues (2001) analyzed recordings of interactions between experimental participants engaged in a collective problem-solving task. Because communication occurs across both audio and visual channels, Gregory et al. (2001) sought to validate their theoretical model by isolating the effects of the vocal channel on perceptions of status and dominance. By comparing results from group members who could see their interaction partners to group members who could not, and by restricting group members' ability to hear vocal frequencies in either the verbal or paraverbal range, Gregory and colleagues demonstrated the primacy of the vocal channel in communication accommodation.[2] That is, vocal accommodation predicts group members' perceptions of each other independent of any visual cues.

Gallagher, Gregory, Bianchi, Hartung, and Harkness (2005) further developed the vocal status model by incorporating elements of expectation states theory into their analyses of interview data.[3] Examining interactions between medical students and simulated patients, Gallagher and colleagues (2005) found that asymmetry in vocal convergence between interviewer and interviewee emerged when the interaction involved tasks related to the interviewers' area of expertise (biomedical assessment), but was absent when the group task did not activate differential performance expectations between actors. This finding is consistent with the expectation states theory, which posits that behavioral inequalities of attention, favor, and influence emerge when individuals in task groups develop differential competency expectations for each other based on the group's distribution of status and ability (Berger et al., 1977).

Moore's (2008) research on vocal dynamics within multiactor, status-differentiated groups further articulates the theoretical connection between the vocal accommodation and expectation states theory. Laying out a theoretical model of fundamental frequency accommodation as an expressive task cue, Moore (2008, p. 58) develops the concept of "expressive legitimacy cues," and argues that vocal accommodation functions as an expression of lower-status, less powerful group members' endorsement of the group structure. In other words, Moore (2008) posits that status differences produce differences in vocal accommodation, and accommodation lends legitimacy to structural inequality.

A related line of research, focusing on presidential debates and election outcomes, provides further indirect evidence of a relationship between social status and vocal accommodation. Analyzing vocal accommodation in presidential debates across eight election cycles, Gregory and Gallagher (2002) found that measures of accommodation predicted viewers' perceptions of the debate "winner" in six of the eight election cycles and predicted the final outcome of the popular vote for all eight elections. Likewise, Kalkhoff and Gregory (2008) examined how vocal accommodation patterns affected postdebate poll results from three presidential debates during the 2008 election. In this study, vocal accommodation did not predict the perceived debate winner, but Kalkhoff and Gregory (2008) uncovered evidence that vocal accommodation tracked temporal shifts in the dominance hierarchy as it emerged between Barack Obama and John McCain in each debate. Measures of accommodation, then, are useful not just for summarizing the outcome of an entire interaction, but also for modeling group dynamics in settings where actors contest the status order and compete for influence. Although the debate studies do not directly measure status, dominance, and prestige, they underscore the core principles guiding vocal accommodation research: We attune to interactional dynamics in the paraverbal range, and those dynamics shape how we perceive and respond to others.

A preponderance of the research described above assumes that vocal accommodation functions as a paraverbal signal of dominance by a higher-status actor and deference by a lower-status actor. In other words, the existing research largely employs the concepts of power/dominance and status/prestige interchangeably, thereby creating theoretical and conceptual confusion. The following question has arisen: Does vocal accommodation reflect a status process or a power process? Given that the expectation states literature asserts that perceptions of competence and prestige are potentially the most important correlates of social status (Ridgeway & Walker, 1995), a critical task for vocal accommodation scholars is to develop a clear understanding of the distinct roles of dominance and prestige in shaping patterns of accommodation.

To examine the relationship between vocal accommodation and perceptions of dominance and prestige, Kalkhoff and colleagues (2017) analyze vocal data from three televised debates from the *Piers Morgan Live* television program that aired in 2014. Specifically, Kalkhoff et al. (2017) measured accommodation patterns between Mr Morgan and his guests and collected data from panels of observers who rated each actor using established measures of dominance and prestige (please see Cheng et al., 2013). Regression analyses showed that vocal accommodation significantly predicted observers' perceptions of group members' relative dominance, but not perceptions of their prestige. That is, less accommodating actors were rated as more dominant, but not more prestigious. Importantly, Kalkhoff et al. found that observers rated less accommodating actors as more dominant even when viewing modified versions of the interviews with the paraverbal signals filtered out. These results challenge earlier work (i.e., Gregory et al., 2001) that suggests that vocal accommodation conveys status information independent of other social signals.

Unanswered Questions and Opportunities for Theoretical Development

Over the past several decades, the vocal status model has received substantial empirical support. Nonetheless, a number of questions about the relationship between group structure and vocal accommodation remain unanswered. In this section, we discuss what we consider the four most pressing current areas for the theoretical development.

First, the relationship between accommodation and prestige requires clarification. While Kalkhoff and colleagues' (2017) recent research (described above) provides an important step in assessing the different structural bases of vocal accommodation (i.e., status/prestige vs power/dominance), their analyses focused on televised interviews between actors who were largely behaving in competitive and antagonistic ways toward each other. The competitive nature of the situation, coupled with the weakly defined status structure of the group likely did not invoke assessments of competence, ability, and prestige. Because group members in collective and cooperative task settings (as opposed to competitive task settings like debates) tend to assess status in terms of perceived ability and prestige (Berger et al., 1977), it is possible that vocal accommodation reflects such perceptions under specific structural conditions. Stated differently, while vocal accommodation reflects status differences in general, it may reflect perceptions of dominance and prestige differently, depending on which of the two dimensions serves as the foundation for the group hierarchy. As Kalkhoff et al. (2017) have argued, future work can address this gap in knowledge by assessing perceptions within collective task groups.

On a related point, existing vocal accommodation research falls somewhat short of definitively testing the status-accommodation link. The reliance on observers' ratings has necessarily created a research model in which more often than not, researchers begin with observed accommodation differences and infer backward to status or dominance differences. While this approach has produced impressive results, further work is needed to establish the correct temporal ordering of effects, which would require researchers to asses or manipulate status differences prior to measuring accommodation. Furthermore, prior studies have largely examined accommodation in weakly defined status situations, such as debates and interviews, where it is unclear whether group members themselves even perceive a status difference. By experimentally inducing status differences between group members prior to interaction, researchers can clarify the direction of causality between vocal accommodation and status perceptions.

Second, most of the research on the relationship between the group structure and vocal accommodation has focused on the perceptions of observers who are external to the group interaction; we have virtually no information on how vocal accommodation affects the perceptions that group members themselves form for each other. Given social psychological research on actor–observer differences in perception (Jones & Nisbett, 1971), it is potentially problematic to develop a measure of group structure that fails to account for actors' own perceptions. A crucial next step in developing the vocal status model is to collect data on group members' perceptions *and* observers' perceptions. This information will provide a clearer understanding of how vocal accommodation reflects the internal status structure of a group and allow us to identify similarities and differences between actors and observers' perceptions.

Third, researchers have established that vocal accommodation predicts certain types of perceptions, but have not directly assessed its relationship to other status-related behaviors. To this end, Berger et al. (1977, p. 38, emphasis in original) list four behavioral outcomes associated with interaction in mixed-status groups:

> [These four behaviors] form what we think of as the observable *power and prestige order* of the group. This order includes: (1) *action opportunities*, which are requests by one individual for activity from another [...] (2) *performance outputs*, which are attempts to make some contribution to accomplishing the task [...] (3) *reward actions*, which are communicated evaluations made of performance outputs or persons [...] and (4) *influence*, which is a change of evaluation or opinion as a consequence of a disagreement by another.

Understanding group members' status-based perceptions is certainly important for quantitatively modeling group structures, but we do not know the extent to which perceptions translate into outward behaviors (again, largely due to reliance on perceptions of external raters). For example, we do not yet know if vocal accommodation predicts group members' openness to influence or contributions to group tasks. If so, the question remains as to whether these effects are independent of the effects of status-based performance expectations. It is quite possible that vocal accommodation mediates the relationship between expectations and behaviors, but this can only be established by collecting behavioral data.

And four, while we know that status perceptions are positively related to vocal accommodation, research has yet to examine how closely the two variables track each other. That is, does the magnitude of status difference affect the magnitude of accommodation difference? By comparing magnitudes of accommodation inequality in groups with relatively large status differences to those with smaller status differences, we can assess whether accommodation differences increase proportionally with status differences or if vocal accommodation reflects status as a binary higher-versus-lower comparison.

Although substantial questions about the relationship between vocal accommodation and status remain, we do not see these questions, either individually or collectively, as flaws or shortcomings that undermine the core components of the vocal status model. As it stands, vocal accommodation has clear applications for modeling group status structures. We encourage readers to see the questions we raise as opportunities to contribute to a burgeoning area of social scientific inquiry. Each of the questions raised here represents a path toward theoretical refinement and an invitation to engage with the vocal accommodation paradigm. For scholars who are interested in tackling these important questions but are uncertain about how to collect and analyze vocal data, in the next section we provide a brief overview of the most common methods and statistical procedures involved in collecting vocal data and assessing convergence and accommodation.

PROCEDURES FOR MEASURING VOCAL ACCOMMODATION

Aside from providing readers with a review of the empirical and theoretical literature linking vocal accommodation to group structure, we hope to encourage interested scholars to contribute to the ongoing development of knowledge about vocal accommodation by employing measures of accommodation in their own research. In what follows, we describe methods for collecting and preparing audio files for analysis, and for conducting statistical analyses of convergence and accommodation. We discuss approaches to analyzing existing recordings and for collecting audio recordings specifically for FFT analysis. Additionally, a detailed procedural manual for calculating vocal accommodation measures, including software settings, is available online (see Kalkhoff et al., 2017, online appendix).

Unlike many other approaches to vocal analysis, the approach we describe does not focus exclusively on variation in the fundamental frequency. Research on fundamental frequency variability has largely failed to establish a clear relationship between vocal dynamics and social rank. For example, in an experiment conducted by Ko, Sadler, and Galinsky (2015), bystanders did not draw inferences about social rank based on interactants' "pitch variability," which was measured in terms of variability in the fundamental frequency. Differences in findings between our approach and the fundamental frequency approach are likely due to the fact that the fundamental frequency approach relies on much less information. That is, the fundamental frequency is, by definition, only one frequency. Focusing on fundamental frequency dynamics alone excludes information on other sources of variability across the lower vocal spectrum. The approach we describe includes information on all frequencies below 500 Hz, and as such, captures the full range of sources of paraverbal vocal variability.

Researchers can collect audio recordings specifically for conducting acoustic analyses like those we discuss here, or they can analyze vocal data acquired from other sources. In fact, most of the audio recordings employed in vocal accommodation research were collected for reasons other than FFT analysis, so they typically contain voices from multiple actors, as well as ambient sounds, within a single audio track. On the upside, using the procedures we describe, it is possible to analyze interactions derived from virtually any audio or video recording. On the downside, analyzing recordings that contain multiple different voices, such as recorded interviews (i.e., Gregory, 1983) or televised debates (i.e., Gregory & Gallagher, 2002; Kalkhoff & Gregory, 2008), is substantially more labor intensive than analyzing clean recordings.

Preparing Existing Recordings

Many researchers make recordings of discussion groups or interviews during the course of data collection. Recordings like these, as well as other "secondary" recordings (e.g., televised interviews or radio broadcasts), provide an excellent data source for scholars interested in acoustic analysis. Such data sources are often easily obtained, but require an extra level of editing and file preparation prior to analysis. For digital video recordings, the data preparation process begins with creating an audio-only recording of the interaction, which can be accomplished using any number of free audio or video editing programs.[4] Once the researcher has an audio-only file, it is necessary to edit the recordings to remove ambient noises and instances of cross-talk (two or more actors speaking simultaneously), as these factors can produce unreliable FFT results. Aside from removing nuisance events from the recording, the editing process also involves isolating the speech of interactants on separate audio tracks, such that each track contains the voice of only one person. In separating group members into multiple files, video can provide visual reference for determining which actor is speaking at any point in time.

Collecting Original Audio Data for FFT Analysis

A controlled laboratory environment provides an ideal setting for eliminating sources of ambient noise and for creating clean, high-quality recordings that require minimal editing. Optimal conditions for recording audio data would mimic the qualities of a professional recording studio: separate microphones for each actor, group members isolated in separate, soundproof rooms, professional quality microphones, and professional data acquisition hardware and analysis software. While such a setup might seem cost prohibitive, researchers can currently acquire the equipment and software listed above for under US$2,500 (based on the cost of equipment for collecting data in dyadic groups). For researchers who do not have access to an ideal setup, it is possible to approximate optimal conditions within virtually any space or budget constraints.

The most important piece of equipment involved in collecting vocal data is the microphone, and there are several different factors that affect the quality of audio data. First, because vocal accommodation occurs in the frequencies below 500 Hz, it is important to select microphones with a frequency response range that extends as low as possible. Microphones with a frequency response range that extends to 40 Hz or lower are best suited for collecting vocal data. Furthermore, condenser microphones tend to have flatter frequency response curves (less dramatic response drop-off), so they are preferable to most of the dynamic microphones. Lastly, researchers should select a microphone with low impedance (less than 600 ohms). Medium impedance microphones (600–10,000 ohms) should be used with the shortest possible microphone cable, as response drops off substantially with long cables. High-impedance microphones (>10,000 ohms), while typically quite inexpensive, are not suitable for collecting the type of audio data necessary to conduct FFT analysis.

For the best audio quality, group members should be stationed in separate rooms, each with his or her own microphone. Unidirectional condenser lavalier microphones are well suited for vocal data collection. By utilizing individual lavalier microphones for data collection, along with separate microphone headsets for participant communication, researchers can record participants' voices on separate audio channels using the lavalier mics, thus eliminating the need to remove cross-talk and manually separate actors' speech. In the absence of individual microphones, it is also possible to use a single omnidirectional microphone to record the voices of multiple people, as long as interactants are seated within five feet of the microphone to ensure a strong signal. Recordings that employ a single microphone must be cleaned and edited to isolate group members' speech on separate audio tracks. For researchers who do not have access to a laboratory with participant isolation rooms, using individual participant microphones is still the best option.

Aside from microphones, data collection also requires computer audio interface hardware and a computer with data-acquisition software. Audio interface hardware, such as the Roland QuadCapture, serve as mixing boards with microphone jacks and preamplifiers, and they connect to a computer via standard USB port. Audio interfaces allow users to record speech from multiple microphones to separate audio channels, eliminating the need to manually separate group members' speech. When data collection requires more than two microphones, it may be more practical to use an external mixing board with a greater number of audio inputs; a variety of audio equipment suppliers offer inexpensive USB mixing boards with four to 16 channels.

Data Preparation and Analysis

When done properly, collecting original data or acquiring and separating secondary audio data produces one audio file for each member of an interacting group, which contains only one group member's voice. Examining vocal symmetry over time necessitates that each group member's recording be further divided into multiple temporal segments, depending on the researcher's needs.[5] Most often, it is suitable to separate each file into three equal segments, signifying the beginning, middle, and end of discussion. Dividing files intro three equal segments, a dyadic group will produce a total of six audio files (beginning, middle, and end for Actor A, and beginning, middle, and end for Actor B). This provides researchers with the temporal sequence necessary to track vocal convergence over the entire interaction. To produce a reliable FFT result, each segment must contain at least 10 s of speech.

Once cleaned and separated, the recorded speech is transformed via FFT. A variety of acoustic analysis programs are available to perform this transformation, though we recommend SpectraPlus software. Performing FFT analysis on a temporal segment of conversation produces a long-term average spectra (LTAS). LTAS are simply an FFT result, indicating a group member's average amplitude for each component frequency across the temporal segment. LTAS represent the more or less-stable features of the voice for a given utterance, averaging out inconsequential momentary irregularities in speech (Pittam, 1987). FFT values for each LTAS segment should be copied into a spreadsheet for data analysis.

Fig. 3 depicts the LTAS output for a dyadic group in a spreadsheet form. Though the output in Fig. 3 is truncated, for the LTAS depicted here, frequencies range from approximately 2–500 Hz. Frequency values are listed in the first column, and function primarily as a reference point. Frequency labels are not employed in data analyses, except for the purpose of selecting the appropriate frequency range. Each subsequent column then represents the average amplitude at each frequency for each temporal segment. These FFT values provide the basis for metrics of convergence and accommodation.

Modeling Vocal Accommodation

The acoustic analysis result (AAR) statistic summarizes a group status and dominance structure based on the patterns of paraverbal accommodation. Data analysis begins by importing FFT data into a data analysis program such as SPSS. Calculating AAR involves including LTAS for all group members as variables in a principle components factor analysis. For example, returning to

Frequency (Hz)	A_Beginning	A_Middle	A_End	B_Beginning	B_Middle	B_End
2.1802	−57.843781	−59.438206	−60.220383	−57.629814	−57.786057	−63.081699
3.2703	−56.584244	−59.574181	−59.67667	−56.995831	−58.058464	−62.148331
4.3605	−57.06839	−59.951721	−60.278667	−56.952	−57.829865	−61.793972
5.4506	−59.515881	−58.565498	−60.352943	−56.605614	−57.244801	−61.676556
6.5407	−60.418888	−57.704369	−58.727268	−56.280617	−57.646332	−61.771759
7.6308	−56.492062	−57.599354	−56.089958	−56.184689	−58.173172	−61.957153
8.7209	−52.781109	−56.915276	−54.287292	−56.452145	−58.764648	−61.086349
9.811	−50.635818	−56.681057	−52.797577	−55.417713	−59.219036	−60.811501
10.9012	−50.151669	−56.985783	−52.344479	−55.350002	−59.578342	−60.137291
11.9913	−50.222389	−56.699772	−52.689423	−55.656448	−60.041424	−58.40221
13.0814	−48.078156	−57.076679	−53.304703	−53.885654	−60.434486	−58.072643
14.1715	−46.652905	−56.641064	−53.103939	−54.136917	−60.991875	−58.021042
15.2616	−47.14262	−56.750549	−52.925262	−52.814796	−61.347702	−57.272629
16.3517	−48.108597	−55.893005	−52.6133	−51.946724	−60.19886	−57.373909
17.4419	−48.475262	−55.049458	−49.157379	−53.493065	−59.951878	−58.10?
18.532	−49.036629	−54.434563		−52.004	−59.772743	
19.6221	−50.927933					
20.7122						
21.8?						

Fig. 3. A Truncated Piece of FFT Output for LTAS in a Two-actor Group.
Note: Frequencies range from 2.1802 to 499.2733 Hz.

Fig. 3, calculating AAR for the interaction depicted would require including the six LTAS variables in a single factor analysis model (again, the frequency label variable is not included in the analysis). Performing the factor analysis with varimax rotation typically produces a two-factor solution, with factor one representing vocal stability and factor two representing variability. Alternatively, factor one can be seen as representing dominance, with factor two representing deference (Gallagher et al., 2005; Gregory & Webster, 1996). Under certain circumstances, such as when accommodation differences are small, analysis will extract only one factor. However, given the extensive existing information on the factor structure of paraverbal stability, it is appropriate to constrain the analysis to produce a two-factor solution (Gregory & Webster, 1996).

Computing AAR simply involves calculating the arithmetical mean of each group member's factor one loading from the rotated factor matrix. Higher-status actors are associated with greater paraverbal vocal stability, and thus higher AAR scores. Conversely, lower-status actors are associated with greater paraverbal frequency variability, and thus produce lower AAR scores. To assess the status structure of a group, then, one need only compare the rank ordering of AAR values across group members. Factor two loadings are, in most cases, mirror images of factor one loadings, and as such, are inversely related to status.

Researchers can directly employ AAR values as independent and dependent variables in a variety of statistical models. Additionally, it is possible to convert AAR scores into a metric of status known as acoustic expectation standing (AES, see Fisek, Berger, & Norman, 1991 for an overview of the concept of expectation standing). Calculating AES involves converting AAR values into proportions: Divide each group member's AAR score by the sum of all group members' AAR score. In many analyses, particularly involving groups larger than two, AES may be preferable to AAR in that AES possesses a considerably more straightforward interpretation. That is, AES values provide a clear picture of the group status structure by assigning to each member a proportional share of the available status, based on the patterns of vocal accommodation. Again, for detailed, step-by-step instructions on how to compute vocal accommodation measures, see the online appendix in Kalkhoff et al. (2017).

It is worth noting that AAR and AES reflect the relative stability/variability of actors' paraverbal vocal frequencies, and not convergence or accommodation per se. It is possible that under certain conditions, higher-status actors will demonstrate greater vocal variability than their lower-status counterparts. For example, when a higher-status group member nonconsciously *diverges* from a lower-status partner, this might manifest as a low AAR value. Researchers who employ AAR or AES may find it useful to assess the overall degree of convergence between actors alongside measures of the vocal stability. Assessing convergence and divergence requires employing Gregory's (1983) bivariate correlational approach to analyzing vocal data. Vocal convergence is discernable between actors when their LTAS curves are significantly and positively related across time points, while inverse relationships indicate vocal divergence (Gregory & Webster, 1996). Utilizing a combination of convergence and stability measures can increase confidence that AAR or AES is in fact measuring accommodation.

CONCLUSION

Because many of the cognitive processes underlying status and power dynamics in small groups occur outside of group members' conscious awareness, relying on conscious indicators of status beliefs can be problematic for modeling group structures. To this end, Wagner (2007, p. 131) notes, "actors' accounts of their [...] behavior are colored by other processes like self-presentation and consistency; even if they can recall their experience accurately, their representation of it (to themselves and especially to others) is likely to be distorted." In this paper, we have reviewed literature linking patterns of nonconscious vocal accommodation to status and dominance hierarchies in small groups. The significance of vocal accommodation for research on groups is that it holds the potential to bypass cognitive biases and recall effects to model status and power dynamics, using one nonconscious process to measure another.

Taken as a whole, the vocal status model rests on solid empirical and theoretical footing. Evidence from multiple studies provides strong support for the contention that vocal accommodation both reflects and conveys information relevant to group members' relative standing within small group hierarchies of status and power. Starting with an observed difference in vocal accommodative behaviors, we can infer status and dominance differences between actors (Gregory & Webster, 1996; Kalkhoff et al., 2017). It is also possible that, starting with knowledge of a group's status structure, we can predict the vocal accommodation structure that will emerge, though there is considerably less evidence for this (Gallagher et al., 2005; Moore, 2008). Furthermore, the theoretical underpinnings of this model — CAT and expectation states theory — are very well-established and well-supported explanations for behaviors that emerge in status-differentiated groups.

Vocal accommodation, then, shows great promise as an unobtrusive indicator of status and dominance perceptions and of group structures more generally. That being said, there is considerable theoretical and empirical work left to do to clarify how vocal accommodation functions and how it reflects different bases of social differentiation (status/prestige vs power/dominance). To encourage readers to contribute to refining our knowledge of vocal accommodation and status, we have provided a methodological overview that explains procedures for analyzing existing recordings and for collecting original vocal data. The two metrics of accommodation we discuss (AAR and AES) are versatile and easy to calculate. That is, researchers can employ vocal accommodation measures to ascertain the underlying status and dominance structure of groups of any size, in limited or open interaction, within any particular set of scope conditions, and in naturalistic or laboratory settings.

NOTES

1. Virtual interactions involved comparing the interviewer's vocal patterns from each conversation to the vocal patterns of every possible interaction partner in the dataset. Analyses of virtual interactions demonstrated a much weaker relationship between the interviewer and virtual partners than with the interviewer and actual partners. This procedure rules out the possibility that vocal patterns correlate generally, and not with specific interaction partners.

2. It is worth noting that participants in Gregory et al. (2001) completed the experimental task in status-equal dyads. As such, the study does not provide evidence for accommodation as a status-based process, but it does provide support for the model of paraverbal frequency accommodation generally.

3. For an overview of expectation states theory, see Correll and Ridgeway (2003).

4. For older audio and video recordings that exist on actual physical tape (i.e., VHS or 1/8″ cassette), it is necessary to create digital copies of the media for analysis. Many audiovisual editing services produce digital copies inexpensively.

5. Moore (2008) employs a different approach in which he analyzes convergence iteratively across several speaking turns, and limits his analyses verbal exchanges that occur within the first 3 min of interaction (see Moore, 2008 and Moore & Tucker, 2011 for more details).

ACKNOWLEDGMENTS

The research reported here was funded under award W911NF-17-1-0008 from the US Army Research Office/Army Research Laboratory. The views expressed are those of the authors and should not be attributed to the Army Research Office/Army Research Laboratory.

REFERENCES

Bachorowski, J. A. (1999). Vocal expression and perception of emotion. *Current directions in psychological science, 8*(2), 53–57.

Berger, J., Fisek, M. H., Norman, R. Z., & Zelditch, M. (1977). *Status characteristics and social interaction: An expectation-states approach.* New York, NY: Elsevier.

Cheng, J. T., Tracy, J. L., Foulsham, T., Kingstone, A., & Henrich, J. (2013). Two way to the top: Evidence the power and prestige are distinct yet viable avenues to social rankand influence. *Journal of Personality ad Social Psychology, 104*(1), 103–125.

Condon, W. S. (1986). Communication, rhythm, and structure. In J. Evans & M. Clynes (Eds.), *Rhythm in psychological, linguistic, and musical processes* (pp. 55–77). Springfield, IL: Thomas.

Condon, W. S., & Ogston, W. D. (1967). A segmentation of behavior. *Journal of Psychiatric Research, 5*(3), 221–235.

Condon, W. S., & Sander, L. W. (1974). Neonate movement is synchronized with adult speech: Interactional participation and language acquisition. *Science, 183*(4120), 99–101.

Correll, S. J., & Ridgeway, C. L. (2003). Expectation states theory. In J. Delamater (Ed.), *Handbook of Social Psychology* (pp. 29–51). New York, NY: Kluwer.

Ekman, P. (1965). Differential communication of affect by head and body cues. *Journal of Personality and Social Psychology, 2*(5), 726–735.

Ekman, P., & Friesen, W. V. (1969). Non-verbal leakage and clues to deception. *Psychiatry, 32*(1), 88–106.

Fisek, M. H., Berger, J., & Norman, R. Z. (1991). Participation in heterogeneous and homogenous groups: A theoretical integration. *American Journal of Sociology, 97*(1), 114–142.

Fry, D. B. (1979). *The physics of speech.* Cambridge: Cambridge University Press.

Gallagher, T. J., Gregory Jr, S. W., Bianchi, A. J., Hartung, P. J., & Harkness, S. K. (2005). Examining medical interview asymmetry using the expectation states approach. *Social Psychology Quarterly, 68*(3), 187–203.

Gallois, C., Ogay, T. T., & Giles, H. (2005). Communication accommodation theory: A look back and a look ahead. In W. B. Gundykunst (Ed.), *Theorizing About Intercultural Communication* (pp. 121–148). Thousand Oaks, CA: Sage.

Giles, H., & Coupland, N. (1991). *Language, contexts, and consequences.* Pacific Grove, CA: Brooks.

Giles, H., Mulac, A., Bradac, J. J., & Johnson, P. (1987). *Annals of the International Communication Association, 10*(1), 13–48.

Giles, H., Scherer, K. R., & Taylor, D. M. (1979). Speech markers in social interaction. In K. R. Scherer & H. Giles (Eds.), *Social markers in speech* (pp. 343–381). Cambridge: Cambridge University Press.

Giles, H., & Smith, P. (1979). Accommodation theory: Optimal levels of convergence. In H. Giles & R. N. St Clair (Eds.), *Language and social psychology* (pp. 45–65). Baltimore, MD: University Park Press.

Goffman, E. (1959). *The presentation of self in everyday life.* Garden City, NY: Doubleday.

Gregory Jr, S. W. (1983). A quantitative analysis of temporal symmetry in microsocial relations. *American Sociological Review, 48,* 129–135.

Gregory Jr, S. W. (1986). Social psychological implications of voice frequency correlations: Analyzing conversation partner adaptation by computer. *Social Psychology Quarterly, 49*(3), 237–246.

Gregory Jr, S. W. (1990). Analysis of fundamental frequency reveals covariation in interview partners' speech. *Journal of Nonverbal Behavior, 14*(4), 237–251.

Gregory Jr, S. W. (1994). Sounds of power and deference: Acoustic analysis of macro social constraints on micro interaction. *Sociological Perspectives, 37*(4), 497–526.

Gregory Jr, S. W., Dagan, K. A., & Webster, S. W. (1997). Evaluating the relation of vocal accommodation in conversation partners' fundamental frequencies to perceptions of communication quality. *Journal of Nonverbal Behavior, 21*(1), 23–43.

Gregory Jr, S. W., & Gallagher, T. J. (2002). Spectral analysis of candidates' nonverbal vocal communication: Predicting U.S. presidential election outcomes. *Social Psychology Quarterly*, 65(3):298–308.
Gregory Jr, S. W., Green, B. E., Carrothers, R. M., Dagan, K. A., & Webster, S. W. (2001). Verifying the primacy of voice fundamental frequency in social status accommodation. *Language and Communication*, 21, 37–60.
Gregory Jr, S. W., & Hoyt, B. R. (1982). Conversation partner mutual adaptation as demonstrated by Fourier series analysis. *Journal of Psycholinguistic Research*, 11(1), 35–46.
Gregory Jr, S. W., & Kalkhoff, W. (2007). Analyzing sequences of interactive voice data using fast Fourier transform analysis. *The Mathematical Sociologist*, 11(1), 7–11.
Gregory Jr, S. W., Kalkhoff, W., Harkness, S. K., & Paull, J. L. (2009). Targeted high and low speech frequency bands to right and left ears respectively improve task performance and perceived sociability in dyadic conversations. *Laterality*, 14(4), 423–440.
Gregory Jr, S. W., & Webster, S. W. (1996). A nonverbal signal in voices of interview partners effectively predicts communication accommodation and social status perceptions. *Journal of Personality and Social Psychology*, 70(6), 1231–1240.
Gregory Jr, S. W., Webster, S. W., & Huang, G. (1993). Voice pitch and amplitude convergence as a metric of quality in dyadic interviews. *Language & Communication*, 13(3), 195–217.
Hall, E. T. (1981). *Beyond culture*. New York, NY: Doubleday.
Jones, E. E., & Nisbett, R. E. (1971). *The actor and the observer: Divergent perceptions of the causes of behavior*. New York, NY: General Learning Press.
Kalkhoff, W., Dippong, J., & Gregory Jr, S. W. (2011). The biosociology of solidarity. *Sociology Compass*, 5(10), 936–948.
Kalkhoff, W., & Gregory Jr, S. W. (2008). Beyond the issues: Nonverbal vocal communication, power rituals, and "rope-a-dopes" in the 2008 presidential debates. *Current Research in Social Psychology*, 14(3), 39–51.
Kalkhoff, W., Gregory Jr, S. W., & Melamed, D. (2009). The effects of dichotically enhanced electronic communication on crash risk and performance during simulated driving. *Perceptual and Motor Skills*, 108, 449–464.
Kalkhoff, W. Thye, S. R., & Gregory Jr, S. W. (2017). Nonverbal adaptation and audience perceptions of dominance and prestige. *Social Psychology Quarterly*, 80(4), 342–354.
Kalkhoff, W., Thye, S. R., Lawler, E. J., Pollock, J. Miller, B., Pfeiffer, M., & Girard, D. (2015). Affect, behavior, and brain coordination in social exchange. Paper presented at the Annual Meeting of the American Sociological Association, August 21, Chicago, IL.
Ko, S. J., Sadler, M. S., & Galinsky, A. D. (2015). The sound of power: Conveying and detecting hierarchical rank through voice. *Psychological Science*, 26(1), 3–14.
Lieberman, P. (1967). *Intonation, perception, and language*. Cambridge, MA: The MIT Press.
McLeer, J., Frederick, J., Markovsky, B., & Barnum, C. (2011). Standardizing open interaction coding for status processes. In *Advances in group processes* (pp. 33–58). Bingley: Emerald Publishing.
Mehrabian, A. (1971). *Silent messages* (Vol. 8). Belmont, CA: Wadsworth.
Moore, C. D. (2008). *Legitimacy, status, and the acoustic signature of deferential speech*. Unpublished doctoral dissertation. University of Georgia.
Moore, C. D., & Tucker, T. N. (2011). *VFF Training Manual: A Brief Tutorial for Calculating Vocal Fundamental Frequency (VFF) Using PRAAT*. Unpublished manuscript.
Moore, J. C. (1968). Status and influence in small group interactions. *Sociometry*, 31(1), 47–63.
Pittam, J. (1987). The long-term spectral measurement of voice quality as a social and personality marker: A review. *Language and Speech*, 30(1), 1–12.
Rashotte, L. S., & Webster Jr, M. (2005). Gender status beliefs. *Social Science Research*, 34(3), 618–633.
Ridgeway, C. L., Berger, J., & Smith, L. (1985). Nonverbal cues and status: An expectation states approach. *American Journal of Sociology*, 90(5), 955–978.
Ridgeway, C. L., & Walker, H. A. (1995). Status structures. In K. Cook, G. Fine, & J. House (Eds.), *Sociological perspectives on social psychology* (pp. 281–310). Boston, MA: Allyn and Bacon.
Schutz, A. (1976). *Collected papers II: Studies in social theory*. New York, NY: Springer.

Street, R. L., & Giles, H. (1982). Speech accommodation theory: A social cognitive approach to language and speech behavior. In M. E. Roloff & C. R. Berger (Eds.), *Social cognition and communication* (pp. 193–226). Beverly Hills, CA: Sage.

Thakerar, J. N., Giles, H., & Cheshire, J. (1982). Psychological and linguistic parameters of speech accommodation theory. In C. Frasier & K. R. Scherer (Eds.), *Advances in the social psychology of language* (pp. 205–255). Cambridge: Cambridge University Press.

Thye, S. R., & Kalkhoff, W. (2015). Theoretical perspectives on power and resource inequality. In J. D. McCleod, E. J. Lawler, & M. Schwalbe (Eds.), *Handbook of the social psychology of inequality* (pp. 27–47). New York, NY: Springer.

Wagner, D. G. (2007). Symbolic interaction and expectation states theory: Similarities and differences. *Sociological Focus*, *4*(2), 121–137.

Zeller, R. A., & Warnecke, R. B. (1983). The utility of intervening constructs in experiments. *Sociological Methods and Research*, *2*(1), 85–110.

Zerubavel, E. (1981). *Hidden rhythms: Schedules and calendars in social life*. Chicago, IL: University of Chicago Press.

IDENTITY THEORY PARADIGM INTEGRATION: ASSESSING THE ROLE OF PROMINENCE AND SALIENCE IN THE VERIFICATION AND SELF-ESTEEM RELATIONSHIP

Kelly L. Markowski and Richard T. Serpe

ABSTRACT

Purpose — *The purpose of this paper was to empirically integrate the structural and perceptual control programs in the identity theory. This integration involved examining how the structural concepts of prominence and salience moderate the impact that the perceptual control process of nonverification has role-specific self-esteem.*

Methodology/approach — *We use survey data from normative and counter-normative conditions in the parent and spouse identities to test a series of structural equation models. In each model, we test the direct impacts of prominence, salience, and nonverification on worth, efficacy, and authenticity. We also test interaction effects between prominence and nonverification as well as salience and nonverification on the three self-esteem outcomes.*

Findings — *Out of the 24 possible interaction effects, only three were significant. By contrast, the expected positive effects of prominence on worth were supported among all identities, while the expected positive effects of salience on self-esteem were supported only among normative identities. Also as expected, the negative effects of nonverification on self-esteem were supported, though most strongly among counter-normative identities.*

Practical Implications — *Our findings indicate that the structural and perceptual control concepts have independent effects on self-esteem. Thus, future research should incorporate both programs when examining identity processes on self-esteem. However, depending on the normativity or counter-normativity of the identities of interest, research may find it useful to focus on concepts from one program over the other.*

Originality/value of Paper — *This paper is a test of integration of the two research paradigms in the identity theory, which addresses the micro−macro problem in a unique way.*

Keywords: Research paper; identity theory; self-esteem; prominence; salience; verification

As a key subfield of sociology, much research within sociological social psychology concerns itself with the relationship between individuals and the larger society in which they participate. Commonly referred to as the micro−macro problem (Coleman, 1986; Wiley, 1988), social psychologists often take one of two approaches to this issue. The first concerns how social structure and patterns of interaction shape individuals, including their thoughts, feelings, and actions (i.e., macro to micro). The second concerns how individuals and their interactions shape social structures within society (i.e., micro to macro). While those within the symbolic interactionist tradition (Blumer, 1980; Mead, 1934) tend to organize their work from the latter approach, those who employ the structural symbolic interactionist tradition (Stryker, 1980) are unique since the perspective incorporates both approaches. Within this framework, interaction serves as the bridge between the micro- and macrolevels, allowing reciprocal interplay between the two. In this way, a structural symbolic interactionist framework specifies that it is through interaction that the macrolevel organizes the micro- and that the microlevel can impact the macrolevel.

Evolving from this framework, the identity theory (Burke, 1991; Burke & Stets, 2009; McCall & Simmons, 1978; Stryker, 1968, 1980) is useful because it clearly translates the macro- and microlevels into measureable concepts, allowing for empirical tests of the general relationships. In one articulation of the identity theory, the structural program calls attention to the ways in which social structures impact the structure of the self in terms of identities, and subsequently, how identities impact individuals' behaviors across situations. In another articulation of the identity theory, the perceptual control program[1] calls attention to the ways in which perceptions of identity meanings as well as actual identity meanings in the self-structure impact behavior. Put simply, the structural program focuses on identity processes external to the individual, while the perceptual control program focuses on identity processes internal to the individual (Burke & Stryker, 2016). That said, it is clear that both articulations meet at the concept of behavior (Stryker & Burke, 2000), and it is from behavior in interaction that both acknowledge how identity processes can impact social structures over time.

Though each articulation of identity theory takes a unique perspective on the micro−macro problem, the foregoing suggests that the two articulations of identity theory overlap. Indeed, several assessments of the state of identity theory research made over the last two decades note the complementary nature of the two programs and call for research that theoretically and empirically integrates the two as a "unified" identity theory (Burke & Stets, 2009; Burke & Stryker, 2016; Serpe & Stryker, 2011; Stets & Serpe, 2013; Stryker & Burke, 2000). While research has begun to pursue integration, this integration has followed only two of three possible paths. Specifically, some research has examined the impact of structural categories on perceptual control processes (i.e., incorporating macro concepts into microlevel processes), while other research has examined the impact of perceptual control concepts within structural processes (i.e., incorporating additional microlevel concepts into the macro-to-micro process). The third path is possible, however, and has been unexplored to date: Structural and perceptual control concepts might interact such that structural concepts condition the impact that perceptual control processes have on mutual outcomes, such as behavior or other self-outcomes. This third path has been theorized in the past research (Burke, 1991), but the authors know of no research that has empirically assessed the extent to which these predictions capture individuals' identity-related experiences.

It is this third path that we pursue in this paper. In order to do so, we draw upon theoretical speculations made regarding the moderating role of salience and prominence in the verification process. We also build upon work that has examined the simultaneous (but not interactive) effects of prominence as well as nonverification on mutual outcomes (Stets, Brenner, Burke, & Serpe, 2017). We are interested in how salience and prominence (i.e., structural concepts) strengthen or weaken the impact that verification (i.e., a key perceptual control concept) has on self-esteem. In conducting what we believe to be the first test of this kind, we explore the extent to which the two programs are contingent upon one another in their impact on a central aspect of the self-concept.

This work is important for several reasons. Specifically, our work directly contributes to the refinement of identity theory as a unified theory while also adding to the integration of two closely related literatures: identity and self-esteem. However, our work is also important in the larger scheme of sociological social psychology because it serves as a unique way to explore the micro−macro problem. In pursuing a new integration of programs within the identity theory, we are able to address the question: To what extent do stable, macroaspects of society, as reflected in the self, condition how micro, internal processes lead to self-esteem?

IDENTITY THEORY

Sociological social psychology is replete with theories and perspectives that elaborate the link between individuals, including their thoughts, feelings, and actions, and the structural features of the societies in which they participate. The theory of interest in this paper derives from a structural symbolic interactionist perspective (Stryker, 1980): identity theory (Burke, 1991; Burke & Stets, 2009; McCall & Simmons, 1978; Stryker, 1968, 1980). In this context, identities refer to the meanings associated with who individuals are in social situations. These meanings can derive from internalized roles based on social positions that individuals occupy (i.e., role identities), from relationships individuals have to others as a member of a group (i.e., group identities), or from the meanings associated with qualities that individuals use to regard themselves as unique from others (i.e., person identities) (Burke & Stets, 2009; Stets & Serpe, 2013). With the exceptions we note below, identity theory research has largely progressed in two empirically isolated yet parallel streams of research. We elaborate the focus of each of the two programs[2] below. We then highlight not only the differences between the two, but also the key similarities that have led to the previous empirical integrations upon which we build in this study.

Structural Program

Deriving directly from his exposition on structural symbolic interactionism, Stryker (1968, 1980) posited what is now referred to as the structural program of identity theory. In this program, scholars examine the process by which features of social structural arrangements impact the organization of the self as it impacts likely behavior. In its original formulation, social structure was operationalized as the number and affective intensity of the ties that link individuals based on an identity. These concepts are referred to as interactional and affective commitment, respectively. The idea is that the more committed the individuals are to others in their interactional networks based on holding an identity, the greater the likelihood that individuals will invoke the identity across situations. This latter concept is referred to as *identity salience*. Implied by the salience concept is the idea that identities are cognitively organized into a hierarchy according to likely enactment. In this way, relationship structures are reflected in the structure of the self in terms of identity salience. Importantly, not only has the commitment-identity salience link been supported by research, but identity salience has also been shown to predict the frequency of identity-related behaviors that individuals enact (Callero, 1985; Markowski, 2016; Serpe, 1987; Serpe & Stryker, 1987; Stryker & Serpe, 1982).

Recent refinements of the structural program have clarified this basic macro-to-micro process in two ways. First, scholars have further clarified the concept of social structure beyond interactional and affective commitment. Identity theorists now demarcate among large social structure, or the most macroaspects along which social life is stratified (e.g., race/ethnicity, gender), intermediate social structure, or more localized contexts (e.g., neighborhoods), and proximate social structure, or the social relationships closest to individuals (e.g., kinship, clubs) (Merolla, Serpe, Stryker, & Schultz, 2012; Stryker, Serpe, & Hunt, 2005; Yarrison, 2016). In this case, the most macrostructures impact the most microstructures, which further impact the commitment-identity salience-behavior link. Second, scholars have incorporated another concept as part of the operationalization of the self. In addition to identity salience, *identity prominence* refers to individuals' subjective assessments of how important an identity is to how individuals see themselves as people (McCall & Simmons, 1978). Similar to salience, the prominence concept also implies cognitive hierarchical arrangement reflective of relationship structures. Identity prominence impacts identity salience (Brenner, Serpe, & Stryker, 2014), and commitment impacts both operationalizations of the self as the microlevel (Yarrison, 2013).

Perceptual Control Program

Burke (1991) posited what is now referred to as the perceptual control program of identity theory. In this program, scholars commonly examine the mechanism by which behavior results from the comparison between meanings an individual holds for herself in an identity vs the meanings she perceives others hold for her in the identity. The meanings that a person associates with her identities are referred to as the identity standard or self-view, and the meanings that the person thinks others hold for her identity are referred to as reflected appraisals. Driven by the desire for consistency between these two kinds of meanings, the idea is that individuals compare the meanings between the self-view and reflected appraisals. Mismatches are called discrepancies or identity *nonverification*, and matches are called identity *verification*. In its original formulation, Burke (1991) specified that nonverification would lead to negative outcomes, like distress, while verification would lead to positive outcomes. The negative outcomes from nonverification serve to motivate the individual to behave in ways that would bring about a perceived change in the mind of others (or a change in one's self-view) such that meanings once again match and positive outcomes result.

Research has confirmed these basic microlevel relationships, while making an important theoretical refinement. Scholars have noted that mismatches in meanings, or nonverification, can occur in two ways: in a negative or positive fashion. In negative nonverification, an individual imagines that others hold a more negative self-view for her than she holds for herself. In positive nonverification, an individual imagines others hold a more positive self-view for her than she holds for herself. According to Burke (1991), any kind of nonverification (positive or negative) should lead to negative outcomes. The negative impact of both kinds of nonverification is the most consistent and robust finding in the context of emotions[3] (Stets & Burke, 2014a; Stets & Tsushima, 2001; Stets, 2005) as well as self-esteem outcomes (Burke & Harrod, 2005; Cast & Burke, 2002; Stets & Burke, 2014b).

Differences and Similarities between Programs

It should be clear from the foregoing that there are notable differences between the two programs of identity theory, especially as it regards the scope of the processes seen as central to each. The perceptual control program grants attention to the microlevel as assessed through individuals' perceptions of identity meanings. By contrast, the structural program grants attention to the macro- and microlevels by assessing the impact of social structures and patterns of interactions on the self-structure. Put plainly, the structural program assesses the macro-to-micro link by focusing on identity-related processes that are external to the individual, while the perceptual control program assesses the microlevel by focusing on identity-related processes that are internal to the individual. At the most base level, even operationalizations of the self are different, as one emphasizes likelihood of identity enactment as well as identity importance, while the other emphasizes identities' contents in terms of meaning.

In the larger literature, the emphasis on differences between the two programs has overshadowed the substantial overlap and compatibility of the two. Both programs derive from a structural symbolic interactionist perspective, where the ultimate goal is to understand and explain how social structures impact the self, which impacts behavior that reconstitutes social structure (Stryker & Burke, 2000). Despite differing emphases, both operate upon the assumption that society is comprised of complex webs of patterned interactions from which identities derive and in which identities are enacted. Both agree that identities refer to meanings associated with roles, group memberships, and characteristics unique to individuals, and that identities carry with them expectations for behavior. In addition to this shared foundation, each more or less assumes the process implied by the other, making the two complementary when taken in tandem. This position has been well laid out by a variety of scholars (Burke & Stets, 2009; Burke & Stryker, 2016; Serpe & Stryker, 2011; Stets & Serpe, 2013; Stryker & Burke, 2000).

IDENTITY THEORY PROGRAM INTEGRATION

In addition to scholars noting the complementary nature of the two programs of identity theory, these same scholars have articulated the theoretical and empirical need to integrate both programs into a unified identity theory. Possible integrations are threefold. The first involves incorporating macrolevel, structural identity model concepts into the microlevel, verification process central to the perceptual control program. The second involves the inverse: incorporating additional microlevel concepts central to the perceptual control program into the macro-to-micro articulation of the structural program. In addition to these two, we identify a third integration. The third integration involves examining how structural concepts and perceptual control concepts simultaneously operate to impact outcomes common to both programs. Within this third integration, the additional possibility exists that structural concepts condition the impact that the perceptual control process has on mutual outcomes.

Several studies serve as important steps toward unifying the theory. Pursuing the first type of integration, scholars have examined how the large social structure variables of gender, race/ethnicity, and education impact the identity verification process (Cast, Stets, & Burke, 1999; Stets & Cast, 2007; Stets & Harrod, 2004). In general, this research finds that individuals holding a more privileged position are more likely to have their identities verified. Pursuing the second type of integration, scholars have examined how the perceptual control concept of reflected appraisals relates to the structural concepts of identity prominence and identity salience (Merolla, 2016; Yarrison, 2016). This research finds that reflected appraisals impact identity salience and identity prominence.

Only one published study has assessed the third type of integration. Stets et al. (2017) examined the simultaneous impacts of prominence and nonverification on the likelihood to enter a science occupation. The authors know of no research to date that has empirically assessed the further possibility, in which structural concepts condition the impact that the identity verification process has on mutual outcomes. That said, key theoretical speculations have been made regarding the role of prominence and salience in the verification process.

In his original statement on the perceptual control model, Burke (1991) proposes a series of hypotheses outlining conditions under which nonverification leads to greater distress. He states the following: "Interruptions of the identity process causes [sic] greater distress when the interrupted identity is *highly salient* than when it is less important, i.e., higher levels of distress are associated with the interruption of identities that are most important to the person" (p. 841, emphasis in original). Though he uses *importance*, or identity prominence, interchangeably with the term *salience*, there is reason to believe that the statement should hold in both cases. First, subsequent work by Burke and Stets (2009) has clarified Burke's (1991) original proposition in the context of emotions, where they state: "Nonverified identities will be more likely to produce negative emotions when the identity is salient compared to when it is not salient" (p. 214). Second, and also in the context of emotions, McCall and Simmons (1978) hypothesize that threats in an identity that is high in prominence will lead to more negative emotions. Ellestad and Stets (1998) provide initial support for this speculation, where prominence was measured using one's anticipated emotional valence to being called a "good" or "bad" mother. Implied by these statements and initial support is the idea that prominence and salience moderate the ways which nonverification impacts outcomes. The theorized relationship is that positive and negative nonverification lead to more negative emotions when identities are prominent as well as when identities are salient compared to those that are not prominent or not salient.

SELF-ESTEEM

Though the theoretical speculations have been clarified in the context of emotions, we do not test emotions in this paper. Instead, we test self-esteem. We do this for two reasons. First, past research shows complementary findings in the verification process for negative emotions as well as self-esteem components. Nonverification leads to greater negative emotions in addition to lower self-esteem (Stets & Burke, 2014a, 2014b). Thus, the original statement, "Nonverified identities will be more likely to produce *negative emotions* when the identity is salient compared to when it is not salient" (Burke & Stets, 2009, p. 214, italics ours), becomes "Nonverified identities will be more likely to produce *lower self-esteem* when the identity is salient compared to when it is not salient." Second, past research has separately assessed the structural model and self-esteem as well as the perceptual model and self-esteem. Thus, past research regarding self-esteem is in a favorable position for the incremental step that our study takes regarding the integration between identity theory programs as well as the identity and self-esteem literatures (Ervin & Stryker, 2001).

Self-esteem refers to the sense of positive or negative appraisal or regard for one's self. This appraisal can refer to an overall global sense of self or to a specific domain (i.e., specific to a role) (Rosenberg, Schooler, Schoenbach, & Rosenberg, 1995). Furthermore, scholars have recognized that both global and role-specific self-esteem can each be broken down into three components: worth, efficacy, and authenticity (Stets & Burke, 2014b). Below, we describe each component of self-esteem in the context of identity research, which leads to our hypotheses regarding main effects before we propose our hypotheses for expected moderation effects.

Worth

The worth component of self-esteem involves a sense of belongingness or feeling accepted (Stets & Burke, 2014b). Until relatively recently, much research used the term self-esteem to mean self-worth (see e.g., Owens & Serpe, 2003). However, since the way in which "self-esteem" has been measured is nearly identical to the way in which "self-worth" is currently measured, we refer to the studies below using the "worth" terminology.

Within the structural program, Owens and Serpe (2003) examined worth as it impacted commitment and identity salience. However, as discussed further below, since a recent study found that prominence and salience impacted another component of self-esteem (Brenner, Serpe, & Stryker, 2017), we predict the following:

H1a. Prominence will positively impact role-specific worth.

H2a. Salience will positively impact role-specific worth.

Within the perceptual control program, most of the empirical tests have examined the impact that verification has on self-esteem. Since nonverification has been found to negatively impact worth (Burke & Harrod, 2005; Stets & Burke, 2014b), we predict the following:

H3a. Nonverification will negatively impact role-specific worth.

Efficacy

The efficacy component of self-esteem involves a sense of control or feeling that one has the ability to have an effect on the environment (Stets & Burke, 2014b). Within the structural program, Brenner et al. (2017) found that prominence and salience impacted efficacy. Thus, we predict the following:

H1b. Prominence will positively impact role-specific efficacy.

H2b. Salience will positively impact role-specific efficacy.

Within the perceptual control program, nonverification has been found to negatively impact efficacy (Burke & Harrod, 2005; Stets & Burke, 2014b). Thus, we predict the following:

H3b. Nonverification will negatively impact role-specific efficacy.

Authenticity

The authenticity component of self-esteem involves a sense of feeling true to one's self (Stets & Burke, 2014b). Though authenticity has been relatively neglected in research within the structural program, we expect similar relationships and thus make similar predictions for authenticity as worth and efficacy. We predict the following:

H1c. Prominence will positively impact role-specific authenticity.

H2c. Salience will positively impact role-specific authenticity.

Within the perceptual control program, nonverification has been found to negatively impact authenticity (Stets & Burke, 2014b). Thus, we predict the following:

H3b. Nonverification will negatively impact role-specific authenticity.

Moderation Effects on Worth, Efficacy, and Authenticity

Though the above hypotheses regard expected main effects of prominence, salience, and nonverification on worth, efficacy, and authenticity, we take our predictions a step further in order to test the third kind of integration. Guided by the theorized moderation effects of prominence and salience on the impact that nonverification has on self-esteem (Burke, 1991; McCall & Simmons, 1978), we also predict the following:

H4a. Nonverification will lead to lower role-specific worth for identities that are highly prominent.

H4b. Nonverification will lead to lower role-specific efficacy for identities that are highly prominent.

H4c. Nonverification will lead to lower role-specific authenticity for identities that are highly prominent.

H5a. Nonverification will lead to lower role-specific worth for identities that are highly salient.

H5b. Nonverification will lead to lower role-specific efficacy for identities that are highly salient.

H5c. Nonverification will lead to lower role-specific authenticity for identities that are highly salient.

Normative vs Counter-normativity

Finally, in addition to examining how the structural and perceptual control processes interact to impact self-esteem, we take into account the normativity as well as counter-normativity of identities. Normative identities refer to those identities that are societally accepted such that individuals are expected to possess or acquire them; counter-normative identities refer to those identities that contradict societal expectations (Long, 2016; Stets & Serpe, 2013). For instance, it is widely accepted and expected that individuals will have children and become parents in adulthood. Thus, using the normative/counter-normative distinction, the parent identity is a normative identity, while those who do not have children (i.e., the childless[4]) fall within the counter-normative condition of the parent identity.

We suspect that this distinction is important because the failure to accept or attain normative identities violates societal meanings and expectations. As a result, holding a counter-normative identity is apt to impact the likelihood that these identities are verified, subjectively evaluated highly by the person, and likely to be enacted across social situations. However, since little research has theorized or examined these differences, we include this facet of our analysis as an exploratory component with general expectations as opposed to formal hypotheses. Thus, we expect similar general relationships as hypothesized above to hold for individuals with counter-normative identities, with some slight differences. Since normative identities are socially accepted, we expect that the positive effects of prominence and salience on worth, efficacy, and authenticity will be stronger among those with normative compared to counter-normative identities. Additionally, since counter-normative identities often lead to disapproval and/or ridicule (see e.g., Gillespie, 2003), we expect that the negative effect of nonverification on worth, efficacy, and authenticity will be stronger among those with counter-normative compared to normative identities.

METHOD

Data

The data for this study come from the multiple identities dataset, a cross-sectional survey administered online using nonfull probability sampling. In a nonfull probability sample, individuals elect to join the potential respondent pool by registering with a sampling vendor/company. As part of the registration process, individuals provide demographic information about themselves and agree to participate in surveys that apply to them in exchange for compensation through the sampling vendor (e.g., airline miles). Recent research on these non-probability-based web strategies has found that samples obtained are equivalent to traditional random digit dialing techniques (Braunsberger, Wybenga, &

Gates, 2007; Simmons & Bobo, 2015; Yeager et al., 2011). Based on the specified criteria for the survey, random samples of individuals from the total pool of qualified individuals are contacted electronically to participate in the survey. The original criteria for the survey included individuals who simultaneously held particular combinations of identities. Identities included in the survey included the parent identity, the spouse identity, and the religious identity. Each identity was broken down into two conditions, including the normative condition and the counter-normative condition (Long, 2016; Stets & Serpe, 2013). A total of just over 3,000 individuals participated in the survey. Half of the sample were parents, half were spouses, and half were religious.

Though specific identity combinations were pertinent to data collection, they are not central to this analysis. For this reason, each identity condition is examined separately, including the normative and counter-normative conditions of two identities: the parent and the spouse identities. For this analysis, the normative parent identity sample was refined to include parents who had children under the age of 18 living in the home (about 75% of parents), and both counter-normative condition samples were refined to include those individuals who held their counter-normative identity by choice (51% of childless and 40% of single individuals). The total sample thus included 1,126 parents, 789 childless, 1,016 spouses, and 478 single individuals.

The demographic breakdown of each sample is presented in Table 1. About half of the sample is female (coded as 1) in the childless and single conditions, while just over half of the parents and spouses are female. Mean ages across the sample is early 40s, ranging from 18 to 65. Majority of each sample has attended some college (1 = did not finish high school to 5 = obtained a graduate degree). Similarly, majority of each sample is white (coded as 1).

Variables and Measures

Prominence

Identity prominence was assessed through the inclusion of four items that asked participants to indicate how strongly they agreed with a series of statements related to how important the identity in question was to how they see themselves. All items were worded to reflect either the normative or the counter-normative identity condition that the participant indicated they held. The four

Table 1. Demographic Information by Identity and Condition.

	Parent Identity		Spouse Identity	
	Parent	Childless	Spouse	Single
n	1126	789	1016	478
% Female	67.20	53.93	61.48	50.11
Mean age	39.77	43.17	41.94	42.12
% Some college+	83.73	86.42	86.61	82.81
% White	77.52	84.25	83.25	79.28

items included the following: "Being a [identity] is an important part of my self-image," "Being a [identity] is an important reflection of who I am," "I have come to think of myself as a [identity]," and "I have a strong sense of belonging to the community of [identity]." Responses were anchored from 1 (*strongly disagree*) to 4 (*strongly agree*), and responses were averaged into an identity prominence score. Alpha reliability scores were high for both normative and counter-normative conditions, with parents at 0.832, childless at 0.843, spouses at 0.845, and the single at 0.812. See Table 2 for mean scores across identities and conditions as well as for the other measures discussed below.

Salience
Identity salience was assessed through the inclusion of four items that asked participants to imagine meeting for the first time a person of the same sex, a friend of a close friend, a friend of a family member, and a stranger. All items were worded to reflect either the normative or the counter-normative identity condition that the participant indicated they held. Items solicited the degree to which respondents would be likely to tell the new person about the identity in question. Responses were anchored from 1 (*almost certainly would not*) to 4 (*almost certainly would*), and responses were averaged into a salience score. Alpha reliability scores were high for both normative and counter-normative conditions, with parents at 0.859, childless at 0.968, spouses at 0.918, and the single at 0.942.

Nonverification
Nonverification was assessed through the inclusion of two separate items. The first assessed how positively the participants thought others in general viewed them as someone who held the identity in question. This is referred to as the reflected appraisal. The second assessed how positively the participants viewed themselves as someone who held the identity in question. This is referred to as the self-view or identity standard. Responses for both items were anchored from 0 (*not at all positively*) to 10 (*very positively*). To construct the nonverification item, scores from the self-view were subtracted from the reflected appraisal. Possible scores range from −10 to 10. A score of zero indicates identity verification where individuals perceive that others view them the same way that they view themselves. Positive scores indicate a condition of positive nonverification where individuals perceive that others view them more positively than they view themselves. Negative scores indicate a condition of negative nonverification where individuals perceive that others view them less positively than they view themselves. Research has confirmed that both kinds of nonverification lead to negative outcomes (Burke & Harrod, 2005; Stets & Burke, 2014a), leading to the decision to square the nonverification item prior to analyses. However, for reasons discussed below (e.g., ease of interpretation), we do not square the nonverification item and instead use the linear term in all analyses (Stets et al., 2017). Scores on this nonverification item can be interpreted with reference to positive nonverification, or the state in which individuals imagine others hold more positive views for the individual than the individual holds for herself.

Table 2. Descriptive Statistics by Identity and Condition.

	Prom.* Mean (SD) Reliability	Salience* Mean (SD) Reliability	Worth Mean (SD) Reliability	Efficacy Mean (SD) Reliability	Auth. Mean (SD) Reliability	Nonverif.* Mean (SD) Reliability
Parent identity						
Parent	3.49 (0.532)	3.50 (0.572)	3.37 (0.569)	2.85 (0.704)	3.03 (0.570)	−0.284 (1.25)
$n = 1{,}126$	(0.832)	(0.859)	(0.930)	(0.892)	(0.793)	–
Childless	2.47 (0.830)	2.60 (0.996)	3.50 (0.572)	3.39 (0.655)	3.26 (0.546)	−1.22 (2.27)
$n = 789$	(0.843)	(0.968)	(0.944)	(0.934)	(0.792)	–
Spouse identity						
Spouse	3.31 (0.605)	3.37 (0.686)	3.39 (0.568)	3.04 (0.772)	3.11 (0.590)	−0.308 (1.37)
$n = 1{,}126$	(0.845)	(0.918)	(0.939)	(0.936)	(0.782)	–
Single	2.95 (0.690)	2.88 (0.863)	3.42 (0.598)	3.16 (0.775)	3.12 (0.608)	−0.657 (1.97)
$n = 478$	(0.812)	(0.942)	(0.946)	(0.941)	(0.821)	–

Note: * = Scales were standardized prior to subsequent analyses.

Worth
Role-specific worth was assessed through the inclusion of seven items that asked participants to indicate the degree to which they agreed with each statement. These items as well as all items for efficacy and authenticity detailed below were adapted from Stets and Burke (2014b). The seven worth items included the following: (1) As someone who is a [identity], I feel that I am a person of worth, at least on an equal basis with others; (2) As someone who is a [identity], I feel that I have a number of good qualities; (3) As someone who is a [identity], I take a positive attitude toward myself; (4) As someone who is a [identity], on the whole, I am satisfied with myself; (5) As someone who is a [identity], I usually feel good about myself; (6) As someone who is a [identity], I feel I have much to offer as a person; and (7) As someone who is a [identity], I have a lot of confidence in the actions I undertake in my life. Responses were anchored from 1 (*strongly disagree*) to 4 (*strongly agree*), and responses were averaged into a worth score such that higher scores reflected greater levels of worth. Alpha reliability scores were high for both normative and counter-normative conditions, with parents at 0.930, childless at 0.944, spouses at 0.939, and the single at 0.946.

Efficacy
Role-specific efficacy was assessed through the inclusion of seven items that asked participants to indicate the degree to which they agreed with each statement. The seven items included the following: (1) As someone who is a [identity], there is no way that I can solve some of the problems I have; (2) As someone who is a [identity], I have little control over the things that happen to me; (3) As someone who is a [identity], there is little I can do to change many of the important things in my life; (4) As someone who is a [identity], I feel as if what happens is mostly determined by other people; (5) As someone who is a [identity], I certainly feel helpless at times; (6) As someone who is a [identity], sometimes I feel that I am not able to accomplish what I want; and (7) As someone who is a [identity], I often feel unable to deal with the problems of life. Responses were anchored from 1 (*strongly disagree*) to 4 (*strongly agree*). All items were reversed-coded such that higher scores reflected greater levels of efficacy. Responses were averaged into an efficacy score. Alpha reliability scores were high for both normative and counter-normative conditions, with parents at 0.892, childless at 0.934, spouses at 0.936, and the single at 0.941.

Authenticity
Role-specific authenticity was assessed through the inclusion of seven items that asked participants to indicate the degree to which they agreed with each statement. The seven items included the following: (1) As someone who is a [identity], I feel that most people don't know the "real" me; (2) As someone who is a [identity], I find I can almost always be myself;[5] (3) As someone who is a [identity], I feel people expect me to be different than I really am; (4) As someone who is a [identity], I think most people accept who I really am; (5) As someone

who is a [identity], I just wish I were more able to be myself; (6) As someone who is a [identity], I feel the way in which I generally act reflects the "real" me; and (7) As someone who is a [identity], I often do not feel that I am myself. Responses were anchored from 1 (*strongly disagree*) to 4 (*strongly agree*). Certain items were reversed-coded such that higher scores reflected greater levels of authenticity. Responses were averaged into an authenticity score. Alpha reliability scores were high for both normative and counter-normative conditions, with parents at 0.793, childless at 0.792, spouses at 0.782, and the single at 0.821.

RESULTS

Zero-order Correlations

The zero-order correlation coefficients among all variables of interest are presented in Table 3. Consistent with the previous research that shows correlations between prominence and salience (Stryker & Serpe, 1994), prominence and salience are significantly correlated across all identity conditions, ranging from 0.258 and 0.270 in the single and the parent identities to 0.298 and 0.370 in the spouse and childless identities. Prominence is related to all aspects of self-esteem in the normative identities (0.477, 0.166, and 0.285, respectively for parents; 0.436, 0.139, and 0.235, respectively for spouses) but is only correlated with worth in the counter-normative conditions (0.153 for the childless and 0.386 for the single). Correlations with salience are a bit more variable, showing significant coefficients with all aspects of self-esteem among parents (0.185 for worth, 0.075 for efficacy, and 0.161 for authenticity) but only showing significant coefficients with worth and efficacy among spouses (0.243 and 0.110, respectively) as well as only with worth for the single (0.156).

Consistent with prior research (Stets et al., 2017), prominence is negatively associated with positive nonverification, but only in the counter-normative conditions (−0.245 for the childless and −0.138 for the single). This means that identity importance is associated with higher levels of positive nonverification where individuals think others view them more positively than they view themselves. Salience is not associated with nonverification in any condition. Efficacy is negatively associated with nonverification again only in the counter-normative conditions (−0.130 among the childless and −0.176 among the single). Worth is negatively associated with nonverification in both counter-normative conditions (−0.156 for the childless and −0.170 for the single) as well as among parents (−0.113), while authenticity shows no correlations to nonverification in any condition. As one would expect, worth, efficacy, and authenticity show high correlations to one another across all identities (see Table 3). These preliminary results are important because they show the basic relationship structure among the constructs of interest. The correlation coefficients confirm the basic expectations for the positive association of prominence and salience as well as the negative association of nonverification on worth and efficacy (but not authenticity).

Table 3. Correlations among Normative and Counter-normative Identities.

	Prominence	Salience	Worth	Efficacy	Authenticity
Parent Identity					
Parent					
Salience	0.270***				
Worth	0.477***	0.185***			
Efficacy	0.166***	0.075*	0.345***		
Authenticity	0.285***	0.161***	0.528***	0.559***	
Nonverif.	−0.028	−0.012	−0.113***	−0.057	−0.059
Childless					
Salience	0.298***				
Worth	0.153***	0.074			
Efficacy	−0.017	0.015	0.530***		
Authenticity	0.006	0.012	0.627***	0.559***	
Nonverif.	−0.245***	−0.007	−0.156***	−0.130**	−0.069
Spouse Identity					
Spouse					
Salience	0.370***				
Worth	0.436***	0.243***			
Efficacy	0.139**	0.110**	0.420***		
Authenticity	0.235***	0.059	0.508***	0.645***	
Nonverif.	−0.061	0.037	−0.025	−0.045	−0.070
Single					
Salience	0.258***				
Worth	0.386***	0.156**			
Efficacy	0.029	−0.045	0.387***		
Authenticity	0.054	0.068	0.572***	0.628***	
Nonverif.	−0.138*	0.087	−0.170**	−0.176**	−0.109

Note: *$p < 0.05$; **$p < 0.01$; ***$p < 0.001$.

Structural Equation Modeling

To test our hypotheses, we use structural equation modeling techniques with full information maximum likelihood to preserve sample sizes. We conduct one structural equation model for each identity condition for a total of four structural equation models. We run separate models for each identity because direct, between group comparisons are not pertinent to our research questions. Structural equation modeling is appropriate to test our hypotheses because it allows us to account for multiple self-esteem outcomes simultaneously. It also allows us to account for the correlated error covariance structure between self-esteem components as well as the causal relationship between prominence and salience that has been demonstrated in prior literature (Brenner et al., 2014).

Fig. 1. Theoretical Model.

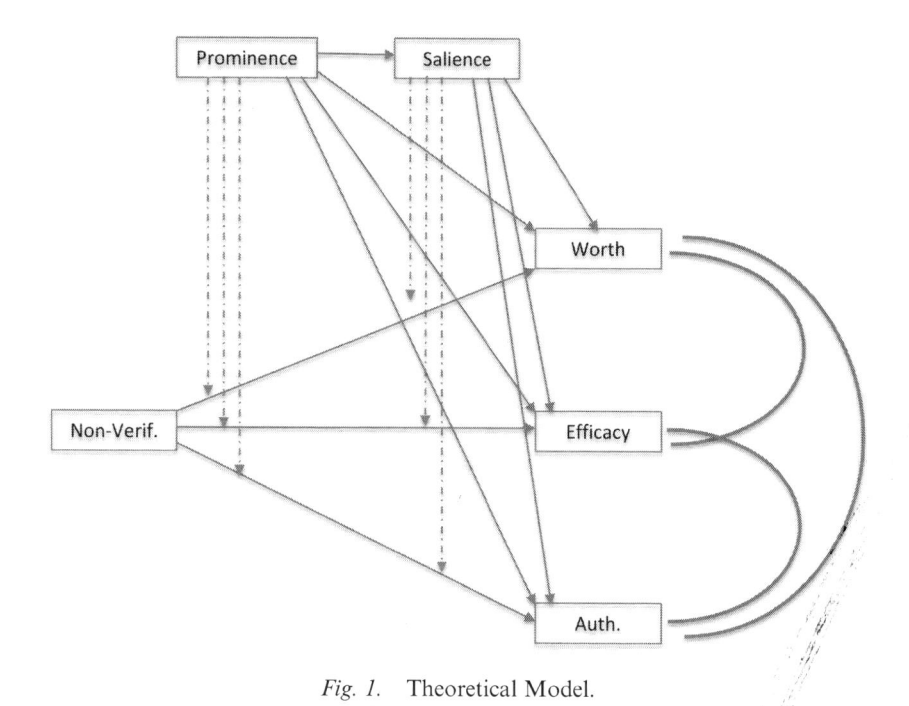

Fig. 1 shows the heuristic model tested for each identity condition. As shown in the model, the impact of prominence, salience, and nonverification are estimated separately and simultaneously on each of the three self-esteem outcomes. Additionally, interactions between prominence and nonverification as well as salience and nonverification are estimated on all self-esteem outcomes. Importantly, prominence, salience, and nonverification are included as observed variables using the calculation procedures for average scores discussed above. Similar to Marcussen and Gallagher (2017), we do this to preserve degrees of freedom. Additionally, we see it appropriate to forgo the use of latent constructs in our analyses for two additional reasons: First, using observed variables allows us to test interactions between nonverification and prominence as well as between nonverification and salience; and second, the items used in this study show high reliability scores, similar to other research (see e.g., Stets & Burke, 2014b).

Consistent with Marcussen and Gallagher (2017), we standardized the prominence, salience, and nonverification scores prior to constructing the interaction terms, such that the means of each variable equal zero and the standard deviations equal one. The interaction terms were included in the model by taking the cross-product of the standardized nonverification scores and the standardized prominence or salience scores. Finally, consistent with prior research (Stets et al., 2017), we only include the linear, as opposed to squared, nonverification terms in the model. This is for ease of interpretation of the interactions in the model. Structural equation model interaction coefficients can be interpreted with reference to situations of positive nonverification where one imagines others think more highly of the individual than they think of themselves in the identity.

Goodness of Fit Statistics

As a whole, the structural equation models provide a good fit for the data: $X^2(7) = 44.15$, $p < 0.001$ for parents; $X^2(7) = 8.06$, $p =$ ns for the childless; $X^2(7) = 14.03$, $p =$ ns for spouses; and $X^2(7) = 12.99$, $p =$ ns for the single. The RMSEA for the model fit among parents is higher than the 0.05 threshold (RMSEA $= 0.065$); however, the pclose statistic for this value is greater than 0.05, meaning that the model is not significantly different from a "close-fitting" model. The remaining three models show RMSEA statistics that are lower than the 0.05 threshold (RMSEA $= 0.014$ for childless; RMSEA $= 0.031$ for spouses; RMSEA $= 0.042$ for the single), and each of the associated pclose values is not significant. These statistics indicate that the model reasonably depicts relationships seen in the data among the four identity conditions of interest.

Worth

In the first part of our first three hypotheses (i.e., *H1a, H2a,* and *H3a*), we predict a positive effect of prominence on worth, a positive effect of salience on worth, and a negative effect of nonverification on worth. These hypotheses would be supported if the models showed the respective two positive and one negative coefficients for direct effects but not the interaction terms. In the first part of our fourth and fifth hypotheses (*H4a* and *H5a*), we predict a moderation effect of prominence and nonverification on worth as well as a moderation effect of salience and nonverification on worth. In this case, we expect a greater negative impact on self-esteem from nonverification when prominence and salience are high compared to low. The last two hypotheses would be supported if the models show significant and negative interaction terms, in which case, the direct effects would not be directly interpreted.

Table 4 presents the standardized structural equation model results for each of the four identity conditions. The top portion of Table 4 shows the results for worth across the four models. Prominence shows a significant and positive effect on worth in all identity conditions (0.442 for parents, 0.096 for the childless, 0.396 for spouses, and 0.321 for the single), supporting *H1a*. Salience shows a significant and positive effect on worth, but only in the normative conditions (0.060 for parents and 0.099 for spouses), supporting *H2a* for normative identities only. Nonverification shows a significant and negative effect on worth in three of the four conditions (-0.094 for parents, -0.140 for childless, and -0.120 for the single), supporting *H3a* in these three conditions.

Out of the eight possible interaction effects directly involving worth, only two of these effects are significant: one for nonverification and prominence (0.062) among parents, and one for nonverification and salience (0.075) among spouses. Interestingly, these effects are only found among normative identity conditions, and both are positive. These effects can be interpreted as

Table 4. Standardized Structural Equation Model Results for Role-specific Worth, Efficacy, and Authenticity by Identity and Condition.

	Parent Identity			Spouse Identity		
	Parent	Childless		Spouse	Single	

	Parent	Childless	Spouse	Single
Worth ←				
Prominence	0.442*** (0.026)	0.096* (0.045)	0.396*** (0.031)	0.321*** (0.050)
Salience	0.060* (0.030)	0.034 (0.045)	0.099** (0.034)	0.096 (0.053)
Nonverif.	−0.094*** (0.028)	−0.140** (0.047)	0.012 (0.033)	−0.120* (0.053)
Nonverif*prom	0.062* (0.030)	0.020 (0.051)	0.032 (0.035)	0.011 (0.067)
Nonverif*sal	0.039 (0.031)	−0.045 (0.048)	0.075* (0.035)	−0.019 (0.061)
Age	0.037 (0.027)	0.074* (0.037)	0.100*** (0.029)	0.144*** (0.045)
Female	−0.008 (0.028)	0.094** (0.038)	0.038 (0.030)	0.125** (0.046)
Education	−0.004 (0.028)	−0.039 (0.037)	−0.031 (0.031)	−0.024 (0.045)
White	−0.057* (0.027)	0.022 (0.037)	0.024 (0.029)	0.071 (0.045)
Efficacy ←				
Prominence	0.152*** (0.032)	−0.059 (0.046)	0.111** (0.036)	−0.042 (0.055)
Salience	0.040 (0.034)	0.041 (0.045)	0.084* (0.037)	0.007 (0.055)
Nonverif.	−0.052 (0.032)	−0.140** (0.047)	−0.027 (0.034)	−0.173** (0.055)
Nonverif*prom	0.051 (0.034)	−0.033 (0.052)	−0.004 (0.037)	−0.097 (0.068)
Nonverif*sal	0.002 (0.034)	0.009 (0.048)	0.056 (0.037)	0.083 (0.062)
Age	0.108*** (0.030)	0.088** (0.038)	0.135*** (0.032)	0.180*** (0.048)
Female	−0.001 (0.032)	0.047 (0.039)	0.087** (0.033)	−0.015 (0.049)
Education	−0.011 (0.032)	0.018 (0.038)	0.013 (0.038)	0.084 (0.048)
White	−0.014 (0.030)	0.023 (0.039)	−0.027 (0.032)	0.068 (0.047)

Table 4. (Continued)

	Parent Identity		Spouse Identity	
	Parent	Childless	Spouse	Single
Authenticity ←				
Prominence	0.237*** (0.030)	−0.051 (0.048)	0.240*** (0.035)	0.014 (0.057)
Salience	0.070* (0.033)	0.026 (0.047)	−0.006 (0.037)	0.083 (0.057)
Nonverif.	−0.065* (0.032)	−0.098* (0.050)	−0.027 (0.035)	−0.148** (0.058)
Nonverif*prom	0.028 (0.034)	0.052 (0.055)	0.021 (0.037)	0.043 (0.071)
Nonverif*sal	0.059 (0.034)	−0.025 (0.051)	0.080* (0.037)	0.059 (0.067)
Age	0.148*** (0.029)	0.081* (.039)	0.194*** (0.031)	0.213*** (0.049)
Female	0.102*** (0.031)	0.094** (0.040)	0.184*** (0.032)	0.091 (0.050)
Education	−0.060** (0.031)	−0.052 (0.039)	−0.012 (0.033)	0.037 (0.049)
White	0.006 (0.030)	0.068 (0.039)	0.022 (0.031)	0.140** (0.048)
Salience ←				
Prominence	0.263*** (0.030)	0.301*** (0.041)	0.382*** (0.030)	0.273*** (0.054)
Error cov.				
Worth*efficacy	0.290*** (0.029)	0.535*** (0.028)	0.376*** (0.029)	0.405*** (0.042)
Worth*auth.	0.458*** (0.026)	0.640*** (0.024)	0.453*** (0.027)	0.577*** (0.035)
Efficacy*auth.	0.531*** (0.024)	0.570*** (0.028)	0.634*** (0.021)	0.607*** (0.032)
LR-Chi^2	(7)=44.15***	(7)=8.06	(7)=14.03	(7)=12.99
RMSEA	0.065	0.014	0.031	0.042
CFI	0.965	0.998	0.994	0.989

Note: *$p < 0.05$; **$p < 0.01$; ***$p < 0.001$.

follows: Nonverification has on greater positive impact on worth for parents with highly prominent identities, and nonverification has a greater positive impact on worth for spouses with highly salient identities. This means that though these interaction effects are significant, the relationships directly contradict the expected nature of the effect. Thus, *H4a* and *H5a* find no support.

Last, though our analyses do not permit us to statistically compare the coefficients between normative and counter-normative identities, it is worth noting that the results appear to support our speculations. Specifically, salience only has a positive impact on worth among normative identities. Though prominence has an impact for both normative and counter-normative identities, the coefficients are stronger among normative identities. Finally, the negative nonverification coefficients are stronger among counter-normative identities.

Efficacy

In the second part of our first three hypotheses (i.e., *H1b, H2b,* and *H3b*), we predict identical effects as above regarding worth in the context of efficacy. Similarly, the second part of our fourth and fifth hypotheses (*H4b* and *H5b*) predict identical moderation effects as above regarding worth in the context of efficacy. The middle portion of Table 4 shows the results for efficacy across the four models. Prominence shows a direct and positive effect on efficacy among the normative conditions (0.153 for parents and 0.111 for spouses), supporting *H1b* in the normative conditions. Salience show a direct and positive effect on efficacy only in the spouse identity (0.084), supporting *H2b* only in the spouse condition. As expected, nonverification shows a direct and negative effect on efficacy, though only in the counter-normative conditions (−0.140 for the childless and −0.173 for the single). This means that hypothesis *H3b* is supported only in the counter-normative conditions. Interestingly, out of the eight possible interaction effects directly involving efficacy, none of these effects are significant. This means that *H4b* and *H5b* find no support from these results. However, again, it is worth noting that our results appear to support our speculations regarding differences between normative and counter-normative identities. Prominence and salience only have positive impacts on efficacy among normative identities, while nonverification only has a negative impact on efficacy among counter-normative identities.

Authenticity

In the third part of our first three hypotheses (i.e., *H1c, H2c,* and *H3c*), as well as the third part of our fourth and fifth hypotheses (*H4c* and *H5c*), we make identical predictions as above in the context of authenticity. The bottom portion of Table 4 shows the results for authenticity across the four models. Similar to results regarding efficacy, prominence also shows a direct and positive effect on authenticity among the normative conditions (0.277 for parents and 0.240 for spouses), supporting *H1c* in the normative conditions. Salience shows a direct and positive effect on authenticity only in the parent identity (0.070), supporting *H2c* only in the parent condition. Nonverification shows a direct and negative effect on authenticity in the counter-normative conditions (−0.098 for the childless and −0.148 for the single). This means that *H3c* is supported only in the counter-normative conditions.

Out of the eight possible interaction effects directly involving authenticity, only one of these effects are significant: one for nonverification and salience (0.080) among spouses. Again, this effect is only found among a normative identity conditions, and the coefficient is positive. This means that nonverification has on greater positive impact on atheneite among parents. Again, since the relationship directly contradicts the expected nature of the effect, we find no support for *H4c* or *H5c*. However, again, our speculations regarding differences between normative and counter-normative identities again appears to be supported. Like efficacy, prominence and salience only have positive impacts on authenticity among normative identities, while nonverification only has a stronger negative impact on efficacy among counter-normative identities.

Summary
Out of the 24 total possible interaction effects between prominence and nonverification as well as salience and nonverification, we only find significant coefficients three times across the models. Additionally, in all cases, the direction of the coefficients contradicts expectations. Thus, the lack of a robust pattern leads us to conclude that there is not significant support for the theorized moderation effects between prominence and nonverification or salience and nonverification. That said, the findings yield some interesting results regarding direct effects. Prominence consistently and positively impacts worth among all identities, while impacting efficacy and authenticity only among normative conditions. Although less consistently, salience also positively impacts worth, efficacy, and authenticity, but only among normative conditions. Last, nonverification negatively impacts worth, efficacy, and authenticity to varying degrees among both conditions, though coefficients appear to be stronger for counter-normative identities.

DISCUSSION

The purpose of this paper was to provide an empirical test of the integration between the structural and perceptual control models. Specifically, this integration involved assessing the moderating effect of structural concepts on the impact that the verification process has on shared outcomes. In this case, we relied on the previous theorizing (Burke, 1991; Burke & Stets, 2009; McCall & Simmons, 1978) to hypothesize the interaction effects of prominence and salience in the relationship between nonverification and the three components of self-esteem: worth, efficacy, and authenticity (Stets & Burke, 2014b). We also followed the previous research (see e.g., Stets et al., 2017) by assessing the simultaneous direct effects of prominence, salience, and nonverification on self-esteem. Using data from individuals who hold the parent, childless, spouse, and single identities, our results are important to the development and advancement of identity theory and broader sociological social psychological research in at least three ways.

First, this paper examines the direct effects of prominence, salience, and nonverification simultaneously in the context of role-specific self-esteem. While the previous research has examined prominence and salience as well as nonverification separately on self-esteem outcomes, the authors know of no work that has included concepts from both the structural and perceptual control paradigms within the identity theory as they interact to predict self-esteem. In general, our findings are consistent with the literature finding isolated effects, but our work advances prior research by illustrating that concepts from both threads within the identity theory operate as expected *at the same time*. This underscores the need for future identity research to incorporate concepts from both the structural and the perceptual control paradigms, because both exert independent effects on self-esteem outcomes.

Furthermore, and as suggested by our findings, prominence and salience may play a particularly important role among normative identities for all self-esteem components, while nonverification in the context of all self-esteem components may play a particularly important role among counter-normative identities. Though little research has theorized explicit differences between normative and counter-normative identity processes in the context of prominence, salience, or nonverification, we suspect that our results indicate that counter-normative individuals are more sensitive to verification processes due to the greater general disapproval and/or ridicule (see e.g., Gillespie, 2003) typically received for contradicting societal expectations. By contrast, it is perhaps this absence of general societal disapproval and/or ridicule as well as the acceptance of normative standards that explains why structural aspects as reflected in the self-structure are more important for normative individuals. In both cases, our results indicate that, depending on the identity context, self-esteem component of interest, and especially the normative or counter-normative status of the identity, one paradigm's concepts may serve as more important predictors of self-esteem than the concepts from the other paradigm.

Second, it is worth reiterating that many identity scholars have noted the complementary nature of the two identity theory programs, calling for integration of the two into a "unified" theory (Burke & Stets, 2009; Burke & Stryker, 2016; Serpe & Stryker, 2011; Stets & Serpe, 2013; Stryker & Burke, 2000). It is notable that research has pursued two types of integration: one where structural concepts are incorporated into analyses regarding the perceptual control model (Cast et al., 1999; Stets & Cast, 2007; Stets & Harrod, 2004), and one where perceptual control concepts are incorporated into analyses regarding the structural model (Merolla, 2016; Yarrison, 2016). However, despite previously theorized and hypothesized interaction effects between the structural program and the perceptual control program on mutually shared self-outcomes (Burke, 1991; Burke & Stets, 2009; McCall & Simmons, 1978), research has been slow to empirically assess this third kind of integration. We believe this study to be the first empirical test of this integration where structural concepts moderate the extent to which nonverification produces negative self-esteem outcomes. Importantly, our results suggest that the predicted relationships *do not* operate as expected. Out of the 24 tests, we find only three significant interaction effects — a pattern we conclude as lacking in robustness. Thus, at least in the context of self-esteem, structural and perceptual control processes are largely operating in parallel and simultaneous manners with little moderation between the two.

Last, though the expected moderation effects were not supported in the context of this research, we believe that such a test was important for its contribution to the larger body of sociological social psychological research regarding the micro—macro problem (Coleman, 1986; Wiley, 1988). Specifically, where a central task of sociological social psychology is specifying the relationship between macroaspects of society, such as social structures and institutions, as well as microaspects of society, such as individuals and their thoughts, feelings, and actions, the structural symbolic interactionist approach taken here brings something new to bear on this question. Identity prominence and identity salience typify macroaspects of society as reflected in the self and as the verification process illustrates a microlevel process that impacts behavior. As such, we were able to test the extent to which aspects of the macrolevel condition microlevel processes. Other research may find benefit in applying a similar approach to this guiding inquiry of sociological social psychology.

LIMITATIONS AND FUTURE RESEARCH

Though a key aspect of the structural symbolic interactionist approach is that it appreciates the reciprocal interplay between the micro- and macrolevels, our research admittedly falls short of examining the ways in which microlevel can impact the macrolevel. Specifically, though the structural and perceptual control models meet at the shared outcome of behavior (Stryker & Burke, 2000), our outcome of interest was self-esteem. Thus, to approximate the full potential offered by the structural symbolic interactionist frame, future research should endeavor to collect information regarding behavior that follows from the structural and perceptual control processes. Especially if such data were collected using a longitudinal design, research could empirically demonstrate the extent to which microlevel identity processes can impact back upon macrolevel social structures.

Despite this key limitation, our results provide a starting point for future research to examine the impact of nonverification and prominence or salience in other identity contexts as well as on other outcomes. Most directly, McCall and Simmons (1978) and Burke and Stets (2009) make their predictions for the moderating effect in the context of emotions. Though in this paper we examine role-specific self-esteem, the logical next step for future research is to test for moderation effects in the context of emotions. Research may also consider extending to other bodies of the literature to incorporate additional outcomes. For instance, Marcussen, Ritter, and Safron (2004), and more recently, Marcussen and Gallagher (2017), examine the moderating impact of commitment and salience on distress outcomes. Though this research draws upon identity discrepancy theory's (Large & Marcussen, 2000) attention to nonverification in the context of aspiration and obligation meanings within identity standards, such research serves as an important bridge to outcomes outside the context of self-esteem or emotions. Moving forward, then, future research should seek to replicate our analysis in other identities with other outcomes of interest, especially as these outcomes impact behavior and individuals' exertion of agency in altering their social relationships and network contexts.

NOTES

1. It should be noted that scholars originally referred to this program as "identity control theory" (see e.g., Burke, 2004), and prior to this, simply as "identity theory" (see e.g., Burke & Reitzes, 1991). However, given Stryker's (1968, 1980) work as well as the realization that it is *perceptions* that are controlled in Burke's (1991) model as opposed to *identities* per se, this program is now commonly referred to as the perceptual control model in more contemporary work (see e.g., Burke & Stets, 2009). Consistent with this recent change, we employ the "perceptual control program" terminology here to refer to the multitiude of theoretical and empirical work related to the perceptual control model.

2. In addition to the two programs discussed here, we acknowledge that the third program of identity theory exists: the interactional paradigm theorized by McCall and Simmons (1978). However, since the interactional paradigm has seen the least amount of theoretical and empirical development within the past four decades, our treatment of identity theory is restricted to the two elaborations that have garnered the most theoretical and empirical attention: the structural and perceptual control programs.

3. It is worth mentioning, however, that a recent study found that negative nonverification sometimes leads to more negative emotions than positive nonverification (Kalkhoff, Marcussen, & Serpe, 2016). The authors term this a "mixed-motivations" model. This was the case especially in the context of the spouse identity.

4. The previous literature regarding individuals without children tends to use both the "childless" and "childfree" designations in tandem to refer to those who accept as well reject negative perceptions implied by the linguistic choice of child*less* (see e.g., Gillespie, 2003). We acknowledge the implications of such linguistic choices; however, for parsimony, we use the term "childless" to refer to those individuals who have specifically chosen to not have children.

5. Among spouses, this item was negatively correlated with all other authenticity items. Thus, for the purposes of this analysis, this item was dropped from authenticity average scores only among spouses. Unfortunately, the data did not allow a comparison across responses for this item by levels of desiring change or levels of satisfaction. This should be examined in further research.

ACKNOWLEDGMENTS

This research was partially funded by a grant from the University Research Council at Kent State University. The authors would like to thank Kent State as well as Brooke L. Long and Fritz W. Yarrison for their foundational efforts and contributions, which culminated in the collection of the data used in this study. The authors would also like to thank the anonymous reviewer for their helpful comments and suggestions on an earlier draft of this paper.

REFERENCES

Blumer, H. (1980). Mead and Blumer: The convergent methodological perspectives of social behaviorism and symbolic interactionism. *American Sociological Review*, 45(3), 409–419.

Braunsberger, K., Wybenga, H., & Gates, R. (2007). A comparison of reliability between telephone and web-based surveys. *Journal of Business Research*, 60, 758–764.

Brenner, P. S., Serpe, R. T., & Stryker, S. (2014). The causal ordering of prominence and salience in identity theory: An empirical examination. *Social Psychology Quarterly*, 77(3), 231–252.

Brenner, P. S., Serpe, R. T., & Stryker, S. (2017). Role-specific self-efficacy as a precedent and product of the identity model. *Sociological Perspectives*, 61(1), 57–80.

Burke, P. J. (1991). Identity processes and social stress. *American Sociological Review*, 56(6), 836–849.

Burke, P. J. (2004). Identities and social structure: The 2003 Cooley-Mead award address. *Social Psychology Quarterly*, 67(1), 5–15.

Burke, P. J., & Harrod, M. J. (2005). Too much of a good thing? *Social Psychology Quarterly*, 68(4), 359–374.

Burke, P. J., & Reitzes, D. C. (1991). An identity theory approach to commitment. *Social Psychology Quarterly*, 54(3), 239–251.

Burke, P. J., & Stets, J. E. (2009). *Identity theory*. New York, NY: Oxford University Press.

Burke, P. J., & Stryker, S. (2016). Identity theory: Progress in relating the two strands. In J. E. Stets & R. T. Serpe (Eds.), *New directions in identity theory and research* (pp. 657–681). New York, NY: Oxford University Press.

Callero, P. L. (1985). Role-identity salience. *Social Psychology Quarterly*, 48(3), 203–215.

Cast, A. D., & Burke, P. J. (2002). A theory of self-esteem. *Social Forces*, 80(3), 1041–1068.

Cast, A. D., Stets, J. E., & Burke, P. J. (1999). Does the self conform to the view of others? *Social Psychology Quarterly*, 62(1), 68–82.

Coleman, J. S. (1986). Social theory, social research, and a theory of action. *American Journal of Sociology*, 91(6), 1309–1335.

Ellestad, J., & Stets, J. E. (1998). Jealousy and parenting: Predicting emotions from identity theory. *Sociological Perspectives*, 41(3), 639–668.

Ervin, L. H., & Stryker, S. (2001). Theorizing the relationship between self-esteem and identity. In T. J. Owens, S. Stryker, & N. Goodman (Eds.), *Extending self-esteem theory and research: Sociological and psychological currents* (pp. 29–55). New York, NY: Cambridge University Press.

Gillespie, R. (2003). Childfree and feminine: Understanding the gender identity of voluntary childless women. *Gender & Society*, 17(1), 122–136.

Kalkhoff, W., Marcussen, K., & Serpe, R. T. (2016). To thine own self be true? Clarifying the effects of identity discrepancies on psychological distress and emotions. *Social Science Research*, 58, 14–33.

Large, M. D., & Marcussen, K. (2000). Extending identity theory to predict differential forms and degrees of psychological distress. *Social Psychology Quarterly*, 63(1), 49–59.

Long, B. L. (2016). Stigmatized identities: Choice, accessibility, and authenticity. In J. E. Stets & R. T. Serpe (Eds.), *New directions in identity theory and research* (pp. 539–568). New York, NY: Oxford University Press.

Marcussen, K., & Gallagher, M. (2017). The role of aspirations and obligations in explaining the relationship between identity discrepancies and psychological distress. *Sociological Perspectives*, 60(6), 1019–1038.

Marcussen, K., Ritter, C., & Safron, D. J. (2004). The role of identity salience and commitment in the stress process. *Sociological Perspectives*, 47(3), 289–312.

Markowski, K. L. (2016). *Including the counter-normative in identity theory: The case of vegans and group participation on identity maintenance*. Unpublished master's thesis. Kent State University, Kent, OH.

McCall, G. J., & Simmons, J. L. (1978). *Identities and interactions*. New York, NY: Free Press.

Mead, G. H. (1934). *Mind, self, and society*. Chicago, IL: University of Chicago Press.

Merolla, D. M. (2016). Reflected appraisals and stereotype threat: The relationship between role and social identity feedback. In J. E. Stets & R. T. Serpe (Eds.), *New directions in identity theory and research* (pp. 412–442). New York, NY: Oxford University Press.

Merolla, D. M., Serpe, R. T., Stryker, S., & Schultz, W. (2012). Structural precursors to identity processes: The role of proximal social structures. *Social Psychology Quarterly, 75*, 149–172.

Owens, T. J., & Serpe, R. T. (2003). The role of self-esteem in family identity salience and commitment among blacks, latinos, and whites. In P. J. Burke, T. J. Owens, R. T. Serpe, & P. A. Thoits (Eds.), *Advances in identity theory research* (pp. 85–102). New York, NY: Kluwer Academic Publishers.

Rosenberg, M., Schooler, C., Schoenbach, C., & Rosenberg, F. (1995). Global self-esteem and specific self-esteem: Different concepts, different outcomes. *American Sociological Review, 60*, 141–156.

Serpe, R. T. (1987). Stability and change in the self: A structural symbolic interactionist explanation. *Social Psychology Quarterly, 50*(1), 44–55.

Serpe, R. T., & Stryker, S. (1987). The construction of self and reconstruction of social relationships. In E. Laweler & B. Markovsky (Eds.), *Advances in group processes* (pp. 41–66). Greenwich, CT: JAI Press.

Serpe, R. T., & Stryker, S. (2011). Interactionist perspective and identity theory. In J. Schwartz. K. Luyckx, & V. L. Vignoles (Eds.), *Handbook of identity theory and research* (pp. 225–248). New York, NY: Springer.

Simmons, A. D., & Bobo, L. D. (2015). Can non-full-probability internet surveys yield useful data? A comparison with full-probability face-to-face surveys in the domain of race and social inequality attitudes. *Sociological Methodology, 45*(1), 357–387.

Stets, J. E. (2005). Examining emotions in identity theory. *Social Psychology Quarterly, 68*(1), 39–56.

Stets, J. E., Brenner, P. S., Burke, P. J., & Serpe, R. T. (2017). The science identity and entering a science occupation. *Social Science Research, 64*, 1–14.

Stets, J. E., & Burke, P. J. (2014a). Emotions and identity nonverification. *Social Psychology Quarterly, 77*, 387–410.

Stets, J. E., & Burke, P. J. (2014b). Self-esteem and identities. *Sociological Perspectives, 57*(4), 409–433.

Stets, J. E., & Cast, A. D. (2007). Resources and identity verification from an identity theory perspective. *Sociological Perspectives, 50*(4), 517–543.

Stets, J. E., & Harrod, M. M. (2004). Verification across multiple identities. *Social Psychology Quarterly, 67*(2), 155–171.

Stets, J. E., & Serpe, R. T. (2013). Identity theory. In J. Delamater & A. Ward (Eds.), *Handbook of social psychology* (pp. 31–60). New York, NY: Springer.

Stets, J. E., & Tsushima, T. M. (2001). Negative emotion and coping responses within identity control theory. *Social Psychology Quarterly, 64*(3), 283–295.

Stryker, S. (1968). Identity salience and role performance: The relevance of symbolic interaction theory for family research. *Journal of Marriage and the Family, 30*(4), 558–564.

Stryker, S. (1980). *Symbolic interactionism: A social structural version.* Menlo Park, CA: Benjamin Cummings.

Stryker, S., & Burke, P. J. (2000). The past, present, and future of an identity theory. *Social Psychology Quarterly, 63*(4), 284–297.

Stryker, S., & Serpe, R. T. (1982). Commitment, identity salience, and role behavior: A theory and research example. In W. Ickes & E. S. Knowles (Eds.), *Personality, roles, and social behavior* (pp. 199–218). New York, NY: Springer.

Stryker, S., & Serpe, R. T. (1994). Identity salience and psychological centrality: Equivalent, overlapping, or complementary concepts? *Social Psychology Quarterly, 57*(1), 16–35.

Stryker, S., Serpe, R. T., & Hunt, M. O. (2005). Making good on a promise: The impact of larger social structures on commitments. In S. R. Thye & E. J. Lawler (Eds.), *Advances in group processes* (pp. 93–124). Oxford: Elsevier.

Wiley, N. (1988). The micro-macro problem in social theory. *Sociological Theory, 6*(2), 254–261.

Yarrison, F. W. (2013). *Normative vs. counter-normative identities: The structural identity model.* Unpublished master's thesis. Kent State University, Kent, OH.

Yarrison, F. W. (2016). Contextualizing proximate social structure in identity theory. In J. E. Stets & R. T. Serpe (Eds.), *New directions in identity theory and research* (pp. 343–365). New York, NY: Oxford University Press.

Yeager, D. S., Krosnick, J., Change, L., Javitz, H. S., Levendusky, M. S., Simpser, A., & Wang, R. (2011). Comparing the accuracy of RDD telephone survey and internet surveys conducted with probability and non-probability samples. *Public Opinion Quarterly*, *75*, 709–747.

OCCUPATIONAL STATUS, IMPRESSION FORMATION, AND CRIMINAL SANCTIONING: A VIGNETTE EXPERIMENT

Amy Kroska and Marshall R. Schmidt

ABSTRACT

Purpose – *We examine the effect of an offender's occupational status on criminal sentencing recommendations using a vignette experiment that crosses the offender's occupational status (white-collar vs blue- or pink-collar) and the crime label, with one label (overcharging) associated with white-collar offenders and the other (robbery) associated with lower-status offenders. We expect negative and potent post-crime impressions of the offender and the crime to increase perceptions of criminality and, in turn, the recommended sentence. We term these negative and potent impressions "criminality scores." Drawing on affect control theory (ACT) impression formation equations, we generate criminality scores for the offenders and the crimes in each condition and, using those scores as a guide, predict that white-collar offenders and offenders described as "robbing" will receive a higher recommended sentence. We also expect eight perceptual factors central to theories of judicial sentencing mediate these relationships.*

Methodology – *We test these hypotheses with a vignette experiment, administered to female university students, that varies a male offender's occupation and the word used to describe his crime.*

Findings – *Consistent with our ACT-derived predictions, white-collar offenders and offenders described as robbing received a higher recommended sentence. But, contrary to predictions, only one perceptual factor, crime seriousness, mediated these effects, and the mediation was partial.*

Advances in Group Processes, Volume 35, 103–128
Copyright © 2018 by Emerald Publishing Limited
All rights of reproduction in any form reserved
ISSN: 0882-6145/doi:10.1108/S0882-614520180000035005

Research Implications — *Our findings suggest the perpetrator's post-crime appearance of negativity and power offer a valuable supplement to theories of judicial sentencing.*

Originality — *This study is the first to test the hypothesis that sentencing disparities may be due to the way the perpetrators' sociodemographic attributes shape their post-crime appearance of negativity and power.*

Keywords: Affect control theory; criminal sanctioning; impression formation; judicial sentencing; occupational status; vignette experiment

The criminal justice system in the United States is designed to mete out punishments in a consistent manner, assigning sanctions based solely on legally relevant factors such as the seriousness of the crime and the offender's history of offenses. Yet, decades of research suggest that extralegal factors, such as race, ethnicity, gender, age, and citizenship status, affect prosecutorial and sanctioning outcomes (e.g., Bontrager, Bales, & Chiricos, 2005; Johnson, 2003, 2005; Kramer & Ulmer, 2002; Kutateladze, Andiloro, Johnson, & Spohn, 2014; Light, Massoglia, & King, 2014; Steen, Engen, & Gainey, 2005; Steffensmeier & Demuth, 2000; van Wingerden, van Wilsem, & Johnson, 2016) and that guidelines designed to eliminate these disparities have failed to do so (e.g., Johnson, 2005; Ulmer, 1997).

Two theories of sentencing decisions, focal concerns (Steffensmeier, Ulmer, & Kramer, 1998) and uncertainty avoidance (Albonetti, 1986, 1991), explain many of these patterns by illuminating the thought processes underlying judicial decisions. Yet, these theories offer little insight into how some sociodemographic factors, particularly those tied to socioeconomic class, trigger these thought processes. Therefore, we use affect control theory (ACT) (Heise, 2007), a theory of impression formation processes, as a supplement to these theoretical perspectives. ACT explains how the affective sentiments tied to each element of an event (actor, behavior, and object) jointly shape impressions of both the actor and the actor's behavior after the event. We draw on both ACT and the two primary theories of sentencing decisions to develop hypotheses regarding the impression formation processes behind punishment decisions for two interrelated factors: (1) the offender's occupational prestige and (2) the word used to describe the crime, with one word (overcharging) linked to white-collar crime and the other word (robbery) linked to lower-status street crime. We test the hypotheses with a vignette experiment, allowing us to determine the unique and joint effects of offender occupation and offense labeling on the recommended sentences rendered by undergraduate, graduate, and law students.

FOCAL CONCERNS AND UNCERTAINTY AVOIDANCE PERSPECTIVES

Both the focal concerns perspective (Steffensmeier et al., 1998) and the uncertainty avoidance perspective (Albonetti, 1991) explain the thought processes underlying judicial decision-makers' (i.e., judges' and prosecutors') sanctioning recommendations and decisions. According to the focal concerns perspective, three focal concerns shape their decisions: the offender's blameworthiness, protecting the community, and the practical implications of a decision. According to the perspective, two of these concerns – offender blameworthiness and concerns for protecting the community – are affected by the offender's connection to stereotypes of criminality and dangerousness, with males, African Americans, Hispanics, non-citizens, and young adults perceived as more criminal than their counterparts. Thus, according to this perspective, legal decision-makers are expected to give individuals in each of those groups harsher penalties than their counterparts.

The uncertainty avoidance perspective (Albonetti, 1991) offers a related account of this decision-making process. According to this perspective, judicial decision-makers seek to minimize risks to the community by selecting sentencing penalties that are punitive enough to deter future criminality. But, given their limited information, they tend to meet this goal by relying on stereotypes of criminality and on the precedents set in past sentencing decisions. Therefore, this perspective leads to largely the same predictions: legal decision-makers will give offenders with attributes linked to stereotypes of criminality (males, African Americans, Hispanics, non-citizens, and young adults) harsher penalties. Numerous studies provide support for both perspectives, showing that African Americans, and Hispanics receive heavier sentences than whites, men receive heavier sentences than women, young adults receive heavier sentences than teens and older adults, and non-citizens receive heavier sentences than citizens (e.g., Albonetti, 1991; Johnson, 2003, 2005; Kramer & Ulmer, 2002; Light et al., 2014; Steen et al., 2005; Steffensmeier & Demuth, 2000; Ulmer & Bradley, 2006; van Wingerden et al., 2016).

Although both perspectives offer predictions regarding the way that an offender's gender, race, ethnicity, citizenship status, and age affect judicial outcomes, they offer less insight into how socioeconomic status influences these outcomes. Both theories rely on stereotype studies to determine which attributes will elicit the strongest perceptions of criminality and danger, and researchers testing these theories have not – from what we can see in this literature – identified studies consistently linking SES with those perceptions, leaving them with little basis for predicting how offender SES will affect sentence severity. We explore one way to address this theoretical gap. We draw on ACT, a theory of impression formation processes, to develop hypotheses regarding the way that one SES-related factor, occupational status, will affect sentence severity. Because occupational status and crime-type are often confounded, we cross occupational status with crime label in our experiment, allowing us to isolate the unique effects of offender status and crime label. And we use ACT to develop predictions regarding how those labels, operationalized with a single word ("rob" vs "overcharge"), will affect sentence severity. Our study participants are not judges, so our results are not directly indicative of the decisions of judges. However, we do see our study as indicative of how person perception shapes punishment decisions among educated people, findings that may have implications for judicial sentencing.

Next, we review empirical work on the role of occupational status in sentencing outcomes. Our review includes research on the effects of socioeconomic status and education, given their close connection to occupational status.

OCCUPATIONAL STATUS AND SENTENCING: MIXED FINDINGS

Research on the effect of occupational status on sentencing outcomes shows mixed results. Several studies show that white-collar offenders receive lighter sentences than comparable lower-status offenders (e.g., Hagan, Nagel, & Albonetti, 1980). These studies show, for example, that auto thieves are more likely to receive a prison sentence and are given longer sentences than embezzlers (Maddan, Hartley, Walker, & Miller, 2012) and that grand theft offenders are more likely to be incarcerated than healthcare providers convicted of Medicaid fraud (Tillman & Pontell, 1992). Similar patterns have been identified for SES and education, with studies showing that those with ownership of the organization (e.g., executives, presidents) and con-artists who feign such a position receive lighter sanctions for fraud than middle-level managers (Eitle, 2000) and that offender education reduces sentence length (Johnson & Betsinger, 2009; Mustard, 2001) and the likelihood of a prison sentence (Griffin & Wooldredge, 2006; Johnson & Betsinger, 2009).

Yet, other studies suggest the reverse pattern — that higher status offenders receive *heavier* penalties than lower-status offenders who commit similar offenses. These studies show, for example, that high SES increases the odds of imprisonment among white-collar offenders (Weisburd, Wheeler, Waring, & Bode, 1991) and among those who commit a white-collar crime (Wheeler, Weisburd, & Bode, 1982), that physicians and psychiatrists are more likely than nurses and aides to go to prison if prosecuted by a Medicaid Fraud Control Unit (Payne, Dabney, & Ekhomu, 2011), and that a high school degree increases the prison sentence length in Ohio (Griffin & Wooldredge, 2006).

And still other studies show no significant differences in the sentencing outcomes for high- and low-status offenders (e.g., Nagel & Hagan, 1982). These studies show, for instance, that SES is unrelated to the likelihood of incarceration (Benson & Walker, 1988; Gottschalk & Rundmo, 2014) and sentence length (Benson & Walker, 1988), that education is unrelated to the likelihood of incarceration and sentence length (Blowers & Doerner, 2015), and that education and firm position are unrelated to fraud sanctioning (Holtfreter, 2013).

These mixed findings are likely due, in part, to variability in the extent to which differences between high- and low-status offenders are controlled in these analyses. Most of the studies aimed at identifying the effect of SES-related factors on sentencing outcomes use statistical controls to create comparability between the high- and low-status offenders. Yet, such analyses rarely include all of the variables that might differentiate a high status offender from a low-status offender (e.g., type of offense, quality of the defense team), leaving them unable to fully establish nonspuriousness. And establishing nonspuriousness is critical, given that occupational and socioeconomic clout are correlated with a host of variables that can affect sentencing outcomes, including offense type, quality of the defense team, and the dollar amount of the crime.

The mixed findings may also reflect changes over time in attitudes toward white-collar criminals. Indeed, many of the early studies suggest that white-collar and high SES offenders receive lighter sentences, while three of the most recent studies suggest that they receive heavier penalties (Payne et al., 2011) or that their high SES does not benefit them (Gottschalk & Rundmo, 2014; Holtfreter, 2013). In addition, recent opinion polls suggest that Americans today consider many white-collar crimes more serious than street crimes (Piquero, Carmichael, & Piquero, 2008), favor tougher penalties for corporate criminals (Unnever, Benson, & Cullen, 2008), and feel that white-collar criminals deserve equal or greater punishment than street criminals (Schoepfer, Carmichael, & Piquero, 2007). As Cullen, Hartman, and Jonson (2009) note, the US may now be in a period of "transformed attention" to white-collar crime. If so, judges and prosecutors today may give harsher penalties to white-collar offenders than in the past.

OUR VIGNETTE EXPERIMENT

We attempt to address both the methodological and attitudinal change issues that may underlie these mixed findings. We address the methodological issue using a vignette experiment that allows us to isolate the effect of the offender's occupational clout and the word used to describe his crime. We contrast two common and familiar white-collar occupations (executive and physician) with two common and familiar lower-class occupations, one blue-collar (handyman) and one pink-collar (shop clerk). We also contrast two familiar crime labels: rob and overcharge. Robbery, which the US Department of Justice defines as taking or attempting to take anything of value by force or threat of force or violence, is associated with low socioeconomic street crime offenders, whereas overcharging, a word often used to describe fraud, is more closely linked to white-collar offenders. Thus, we cross two crime words with the two occupation groups (white- and blue- or pink-collar) in the vignettes, allowing us to separate the status of the offender from the implicit status of the crime. All else is the same across the vignettes, including the dollar amount that is stolen. We also explicitly state the offender's gender (male), race (white), and age (35) to reduce the extent to which implicit assumptions about the offender shape recommendations.

We address the possibility that attitudes on these issues have changed recently by collecting new data from undergraduate, graduate, and law students at a public university, people likely to be well enculturated and knowledgeable about contemporary cultural sentiments (Heise, 2010), occupational prestige, and crime seriousness (Rossi & Berk, 1985). Next, we describe the theoretical perspective undergirding our hypotheses.

AFFECT CONTROL THEORY

ACT (Heise, 1979, 2007; MacKinnon, 1994; Smith-Lovin & Heise, 1988) offers a way to understand the impression formation processes underlying punishment decisions. The theory begins with the premise that cognitions about all social concepts — identities, behaviors, settings, emotions — have a relatively fixed affective connotation that varies along the three universal dimensions of meaning identified by Osgood and his colleagues in their cross-cultural research (e.g., Osgood, May, & Miron, 1975): evaluation, potency, and activity (EPA). Using the semantic differential scale, affect control theorists have collected EPA profiles for thousands of social concepts in several cultures.

ACT's main proposition is that individuals construct and cognitively reconstruct events to confirm the fundamental sentiments evoked by their definition of a situation; that is, they create and perceive events in ways that maintain their preexisting impressions of themselves, their interactants, and other elements of the situation. For instance, people who see themselves as good try to direct positive actions toward good people; powerful people maintain an impression of potency through powerful actions; and lively people sustain their image of expressivity with noisy, frenetic behaviors. The theory is based on empirically-derived impression formation equations that predict the way interactions affect observers' impressions of actors, behaviors, and objects (i.e., those who receive an action) (Heise, 2007). These equations are made accessible through *Interact*, a computer program that simulates social interaction using ACT principles (Heise, 1997).

Although the theory proposes that individuals try to confirm their fundamental sentiments, sometimes an interaction makes some element of the situation (e.g., actor, object) seem more or less good, potent, or active than expected by its fundamental sentiments. This nonconfirmation is quantified in the theory with a deflection score, with high scores indicating that the event seems unlikely or uncanny and low scores indicating the reverse — that the event seems likely or highly plausible (Heise & MacKinnon, 1987). High deflection is expected to motivate the people in the event to behave in ways that bring the transient impressions (the momentary impressions created by the event) into line with the fundamental sentiments. High deflection is also expected to motivate observers to redefine the event in ways that bring the transient impressions closer to the fundamentals. The observers' redefinition can involve modifying the actor's or the object's identity with an attribute (e.g., angry, cheerful) or a new identity, or it can involve redefining the behavior.

An *Interact* simulation between a physician and a client illustrates these principles. *Interact* simulates interaction using either a female or a male perspective, with the perspective determining whether the fundamental sentiments and impression formation equations are derived from female or male respondents. We use the most recent (2001–2003) US female sentiments and equations for this illustration (Francis & Heise, 2006; Heise, 2004). According to college females, a physician is quite good, extremely powerful, and slightly active (2.48, 2.74, 1.49), and a client is slightly good, slightly powerful, and slightly active

(1.29, 0.70, 0.52).[1] If the physician warns the client, the deflection score is low (1.8), because the act of warning – an action considered quite nice, quite powerful, and slightly active (2.02, 1.54, 1.25) – validates the meanings tied to both interactants' identities. But, if the physician robs the client, the deflection is considerably higher (17.5), because robbing – an extremely bad, neutral in power, and slightly active action (−2.84, −0.04, 0.68) – is not positive or potent enough for a physician interacting with a client. The event gives the physician a transient impression that is far less positive and somewhat less powerful than usual (−1.02, 1.92, 1.72), and it gives the client a transient impression that is also less positive and powerful than usual (0.25, −0.62, 0.29). Observers could try to make sense of the event by attributing a quite negative, slightly powerful, and quite active trait (−1.56, 1.08, 1.54) to the client, such as ruthless or reckless, or by attributing an infinitely bad, extremely weak, and neither active nor inactive trait (−4.01, −2.95, 0.33) to the physician. The interactants themselves could also try to reduce the deflection through their behavior toward each other. The physician would need a reparative behavior that is extremely good, quite potent, and neutral in activity (3.24, 2.14, −0.04), such as hug or comfort, while the client would need an action that is slightly good, slightly powerful, and neutral in activity (1.01, 0.92, 0.18), such as laud or excuse. Either action would move the transient impressions closer to the fundamental sentiments and begin to repair the damage done to the interactants' identities.

CRIMINALITY SCORES

We expect the post-event, or transient, evaluation and potency impressions of the vignette character and his crime to affect sentencing judgments, with bad and powerful impressions increasing perceptions of criminality and the recommended sentence. These expectations are rooted in observations that the most obviously criminal identities and actions in the *Interact* dictionaries are consistently rated as bad and powerful (Heise, 2007, pp. 67–68; also see Kroska, Lee, & Carr, 2017a, 2017b). For example, females consider a murderer infinitely bad (−3.67) and slightly powerful (1.42) and a mobster extremely bad (−2.53) and quite powerful (2.16), and they consider the act of murder infinitely bad (−4.06) and slightly powerful (1.37) and the act of torture extremely bad (−3.15) and slightly powerful (1.26). We create a perceptions of criminality score that sums those two components (negativity and potency) for the actor and the behavior. We do not include activity in the score, because it generally increases with potency among deviant identities (Heise, 2007, p. 67) and, therefore, may not independently shape perceptions of criminality. Thus, the actor criminality score is the sum of the additive inverse of the actor's transient evaluation and the actor's transient potency: actor criminality = (−1 × transient actor evaluation) + transient actor potency. The same formula is used for behavior criminality: behavior criminality = (−1 × transient behavior evaluation) + transient behavior potency.

IMPRESSION FORMATION HYPOTHESES

We draw on *Interact* simulations to determine the criminality scores for the occupational identities and crime words in each vignette. We then use those scores to develop predictions regarding the way that occupational clout and crime words will affect recommended sentences, predicting that perceptions of criminality will increase the recommended sentence. We use the female US 2001−2003 *Interact* data and equations to run the simulations.

Occupational status. We expect occupational status to affect recommended sentence through its effect on the impressions of criminality for both the offender and his behavior. Table 1 displays three types of scores for the four identities used in the vignettes: the fundamental evaluation and potency, the transient (i.e., post-event) evaluation and potency, and the criminality score. As shown, the white-collar actors have, on an average, higher fundamental evaluation and potency ratings than do the blue- and pink-collar actors (0.34 units higher for evaluation and 1.94 units higher for potency). But, these gaps decline after the actors enact the crimes, largely because good and powerful actors receive an extra evaluative and potency penalty when they direct bad actions at good objects, such as a client (client fundamental evaluation = 1.29) (Heise, 2007; Smith-Lovin, 1987). As shown, the evaluation gap is essentially eliminated (differences of only 0.08 after robbing and 0.10 after overcharging), and the potency gap is smaller, though still substantial, with white-collar offenders appearing 1.15 units more powerful after robbing and 1.11 units more powerful after overcharging. Together, these changes give the white-collar actors a criminality score that exceeds the blue- and pink-collar actors' criminality score by 1.07 units after robbing and by 1.01 units after overcharging.

The offender's occupational status also shapes the way his crime is perceived. Table 2 displays the same sets of numbers for the two crime words used in the vignettes. According to ACT's impression formation effects, the actor's fundamental evaluation and potency increase the potency of the actor's behavior (Heise, 2007; Smith-Lovin, 1987). Consistent with these effects, both robbing and overcharging seem more powerful when enacted by white- rather than blue- or pink-collar actors, with differences of 0.31 for both crime words. Consequently, the criminality scores for the behaviors are higher when enacted by the higher status offenders (0.30 units higher for robbing and 0.29 units higher for overcharging).

Together these simulation results suggest that the white-collar offenders *and* the white-collar offenders' crimes will seem more criminal than the blue- and pink-collar counterparts, predictions consistent with the studies suggesting that occupational status increases the severity of sentencing outcomes (e.g., Gottschalk & Rundmo, 2014; Holtfreter, 2013; Payne et al., 2011). Thus, we predict the following:

Occupational Status Hypothesis: Participants will recommend a heavier sentence for the white-collar offenders (executive and physician) than they do for the blue- and pink-collar offenders (handyman and shop clerk).

Table 1. Fundamental Sentiments, Transient Impressions, and Criminality Scores for Occupational Identities Used in Vignettes.

Actor Identities	Fundamental Sentiments		After Robbing a Client			Transient Impressions After Overcharging a Client		
	Evaluation	Potency	Evaluation	Potency	Criminality Score	Evaluation	Potency	Criminality Score
White-collar								
Executive	1.38	2.75	−1.26	1.94	3.20	−0.60	1.94	2.54
Physician	2.48	2.74	−1.02	1.92	2.94	−0.27	1.93	2.20
Average	1.93	2.75	−1.14	1.93	3.07	−0.44	1.94	2.37
Blue- and pink-collar								
Handyman	2.08	1.26	−1.11	1.04	2.15	−0.39	1.08	1.47
Shop clerk	1.11	0.35	−1.32	0.53	1.85	−0.68	0.58	1.26
Average	1.60	.81	−1.22	0.79	2.00	−0.54	0.83	1.37
Difference in averages	0.34	1.94	0.08	1.15	1.07	0.10	1.11	1.01

Notes: The evaluation and potency values and simulation results were taken from *Interact*, using the 2001–2003 US female dictionary (Francis & Heise, 2006). Criminality score = (−1 × transient evaluation) + transient potency. We used the actual values rather than the rounded values reported in the table to compute the difference in averages (bottom row).

Table 2. Fundamental Sentiments, Transient Impressions, and Criminality Scores for the Crime Words Used in Vignettes.

Crime Words	Fundamental Sentiments	Transient Impressions						Difference in Averages
		White-collar Actor			Blue- or Pink-collar Actor			
		Executive	Physician	Average	Handyman	Shop Clerk	Average	
Rob								
Evaluation	−2.84	−2.04	−2.00	−2.02	−2.01	−2.05	−2.03	0.01
Potency	−0.04	0.89	0.86	0.88	0.63	0.51	0.57	0.31
Criminality score		2.93	2.86	2.90	2.64	2.56	2.60	0.30
Overcharge								
Evaluation	−1.78	−1.26	−1.19	−1.23	−1.21	−1.28	−1.25	0.02
Potency	0.41	1.04	1.02	1.03	0.79	0.66	0.73	0.31
Criminality score		2.30	2.21	2.26	2.00	1.94	1.97	0.29
Difference in averages				0.64			0.63	

Notes: The evaluation and potency values and simulation results were taken from *Interact*, using the 2001–2003 US female dictionary (Francis & Heise, 2006). Criminality score = (−1 × transient evaluation) + transient potency. We used the actual values rather than the rounded values reported in the table to compute the difference in averages (bottom row and far right column).

Crime word. As shown in Table 2, the act of robbing someone is evaluated more negatively than the act of overcharging someone, a difference that persists after enactment by either type of offender. Robbing is also given a lower fundamental potency score than overcharging someone – perhaps because it is seen as an especially ineffectual or cowardly way to acquire money – and that potency difference persists after enactment. But, the potency difference is offset by the larger evaluation difference; consequently, the average criminality scores for robbing (2.90 and 2.60) are 0.64 and 0.63 units higher than the average criminality scores for overcharging (2.26 and 1.97). Therefore, we expect participants to give heavier sentences to offenders who are described as "robbing" rather than "overcharging" their clients:

Crime Word Hypothesis: Participants will recommend a heavier sentence for offenders who are described as "robbing" rather than "overcharging" their clients.

Note in Table 1 that the average difference in criminality scores by worker type for the two crimes is very similar, with differences of 1.07 for robbing and 1.01 for overcharging. The same similarity is evident in Table 2, with the behavior criminality score differences of 0.30 for robbing and 0.29 for overcharging. Consequently, we do not expect occupation to moderate the effect of the crime word on sentencing recommendations. Nonetheless, we do explore that possibility in our analyses.

MEDIATION HYPOTHESES

According to both the focal concerns and the uncertainty avoidance perspectives, a perpetrator's crime and demographic attributes (e.g., gender, race, age) shape a decision maker's impressions of the defendant's criminality, blameworthiness, and dangerousness, and those impressions then shape the decision maker's sentencing recommendations and decisions. Thus, we explore the extent to which those types of perceptions mediate the hypothesized relationship between the offender's occupational status and the recommended sentence. We examine four criminal perceptions of the offender (likely to recidivate, often committed the crime in the past, dangerous, and blameworthy), two noncriminal perceptions of the offender (law-abiding and moral), and two criminal perceptions of the crime (bad and serious). In line with the hypotheses outlined above, we expect white-collar offenders and the crime word "rob" to increase the criminal perceptions, and we expect the criminal perceptions to then increase the recommended sentence. Thus, our eight hypotheses – six for offender perceptions and two for crime perceptions – are as follows:

Offender Perception Mediation Hypotheses 1–6: Perceptions of the offender ((1) likely to recidivate, (2) often committed the crime in the past, (3) law-abiding, (4) moral, (5) dangerous, and (6) blameworthy) will mediate the positive effect of white-collar status on recommended sentence severity.

Crime Perception Mediation Hypotheses 1–2: Perceptions of the crime ((1) bad and (2) serious)) will mediate the positive effect of describing the crime as "robbing" (rather than "overcharging") on recommended sentence severity.

IMPRESSIONS OF CRIMINALITY HYPOTHESIS

The assumption underlying our hypotheses is that impressions of criminality, defined as the sum of the negative and powerful transient impressions of both the offender and his behavior, will increase the recommended sentence. Therefore, we examine that hypothesis directly by using the criminality scores for the actor and the behavior in each condition (displayed in Tables 1 and 2) as the predictors. Thus, our final two hypotheses are:

Impressions of Criminality Hypothesis 1—2: Criminality scores of the (1) offender and the (2) crime will increase the recommended sentence.

METHODS

Sample

We collected data with an online survey distributed to students at a large southern university in the fall of 2014. All students — undergraduate, graduate, and law students — who were registered for classes in the fall semester were invited to participate through a mass email. We incentivized participation by offering participants the option of being included in a drawing for one of five US$30 Target gift cards. We used the female *Interact* data and equations to develop our hypotheses, so we use only female participants (who were the majority (69%) of the sample) for the analyses. Research comparing sentencing recommendations across different sampling groups (college students, members of the general population, and prison inmates) shows considerable overlap in recommendations across these groups (Steffensmeier & Kramer, 1982), suggesting that results from our convenience sample of females have implications for the larger adult population in the United States. In addition, the high education of our sample (one-third of the participants are working on a graduate or law degree) is beneficial, given that educated individuals are likely to have greater commonality with the culture at large regarding occupational prestige and criminal seriousness (Rossi & Berk, 1985) and could, in the future, even serve as prosecutors or judges.

Experimental Design

We use a vignette experiment with a 2 × 2 design that varies the broad occupational category (white- vs blue- or pink-collar) and the crime word (rob vs overcharge) and randomly places participants in conditions. Each condition includes only one vignette, and we collapse the four occupational conditions into two categories. Thus, the *white-collar* condition includes vignettes with an offender who is either an executive or a physician, and the *blue- and pink-collar* condition includes vignettes with an offender who is either a handyman or a shop clerk. We chose these occupations because they are familiar and common and have fairly similar within-group EPA scores.[2] The vignette explicitly notes the age (35) and race (white) of the actor to reduce the effect of implicit age- or race-based stereotypes. The name of the character, Matthew, is one of the names most commonly given to white boys born between 1974 and 1979 (Bertrand & Mullainathan, 2004), close to the time that the vignette character would have been born. The full vignette is as follows:

> Matthew Barker is a thirty-five year old white male [executive/physician/handyman/shop clerk] who works in a major city for a subsidy of a much larger corporation. Matthew has been a(n) [executive/physician/handyman/shop clerk] in his position for six years and as a result has much freedom in what he does at work and is able to work without direct supervision or approval for work related tasks. He previously held this position at another company before his current organization hired him. Matthew earns enough money through his income that he is able to live comfortably within his means and provide for his family. He is in charge of invoicing, billing, and collecting fees for services provided. He knows that his work will only be checked and questioned if there is a major issue with his work. Over the course of four years, Matthew was able to [rob/overcharge] clients by billing them for services they did not receive. Matthew did not do this at his former job, but realizes he can do this under his current employer with little chance of anyone noticing. As a result of his actions Matthew was able to personally profit $50,000 over a four-year period, and clients suffer small personal financial losses, though no more than $200 dollars. The company does not suffer as a direct result of his actions, but they do lose clients who go elsewhere for services feeling that they can pay less.

Note that the crime word (rob or overcharge) is mentioned only once in the vignette. However, as we explain below, the crime seriousness question, which is the last question before the instructions for the dependent variable measure, asked participants to report their perceptions of the seriousness of either robbery or overcharging, with the crime in the question matching the crime in the vignette. Therefore, this crime seriousness question should have reminded participants of the crime in the vignette, thereby contributing to the crime word manipulation.

Although our focal analyses use condition dummy variables (white- vs blue- or pink-collar and rob vs overcharge) as predictors, when we assess the impressions of criminality hypotheses, we use the actor and behavior criminality scores for each condition (displayed in Tables 1 and 2) as predictors.

Dependent Variable

Recommended sentence is the penalty participants recommend for the character in the vignette. Participants were asked what sentence they would recommend, and they were given 10 response options: misdemeanor fine, no prison term; probation with no prison term; 5 years imprisonment with opportunity for parole; 10 years imprisonment with opportunity for parole; 15 years imprisonment with opportunity for parole; 20 years imprisonment with opportunity for parole; 25 years imprisonment with opportunity for parole; life imprisonment with opportunity for parole; life imprisonment without parole; and death penalty. The variable is right skewed, so we log it. This reduces but does not eliminate the skew (after logging, the chi-square for the joint test of skewness and kurtosis = 20.38, $p < 0.001$). Table 3 lists the descriptive statistics for this and the other variables in the analyses. Because the lowest sentence available was a misdemeanor fine rather than nothing, we also analyzed the data using a left limit Tobit. Those results are highly similar to the OLS results that we report.

Table 3. Descriptive Statistics for Variables in Analyses ($N = 557$).

	Mean	SD	Min	Max
Dependent variable				
Recommended sentence (logged)	0.95	0.41	0.00	2.20
Independent variables				
Conditions				
White-collar occupation[a]	0.52		0.00	1.00
Rob (0 = overcharge)	0.49		0.00	1.00
Perceptions of the offender				
Likely to recidivate	8.61	1.56	0.00	10.00
Often committed crime in the past	5.22	2.83	0.00	10.00
Law-abiding	5.61	2.28	0.00	10.00
Moral	2.03	1.73	0.00	8.40
Dangerous	3.66	2.44	0.00	10.00
Blameworthy	9.11	1.38	1.80	10.00
Perceptions of the crime				
Bad	8.53	1.44	2.00	10.00
Serious	7.57	1.96	0.00	10.00
Participant characteristics				
Age	25.31	9.19	18.00	65.00
Graduate or law student (0 = undergraduate student)	0.33		0.00	1.00
Race and ethnicity				
African American	0.05		0.00	1.00
American Indian	0.07		0.00	1.00
Asian American, Hawaiian, or Pacific Islander	0.09		0.00	1.00
Hispanic	0.06		0.00	1.00
Mixed race, international, or other	0.04		0.00	1.00
White (omitted)	0.70		0.00	1.00
Religious affiliation				
Catholic	0.11		0.00	1.00
Evangelical Protestant[b]	0.41		0.00	1.00
Mainline Protestant[c] (omitted)	0.08		0.00	1.00
No affiliation, agnostic, or atheist	0.27		0.00	1.00
Other[d]	0.13		0.00	1.00

Notes: All participants are females.
[a]1 = Executive or physician; 0 = handyman or shop clerk.
[b]Assembly of God, Baptist, Born Again Christian, Evangelical, Nondenominational Christian, Pentecostal, Seventh-day Adventist.
[c]Episcopalian, Lutheran, Methodist, or Presbyterian.
[d]Buddhist, Hindu, Jew, Mormon, Muslim, other, or multiple affiliations.

Mediators

We use measures of eight perceptions – six of the offender and two of the crime – to evaluate the two mediation hypotheses. These eight items followed the vignette but preceded the recommended sentence measure, and all were followed by a 101-point sematic differential slider. As shown in Table 3, we divided the values by 10 so the range is 0–10. In the Appendix, we list the eight items, the question used to measure each item, and the anchors at each end of each slider. The focal words in each item were bolded (e.g., "generally obeys the laws" was bolded in the law-abiding item). Note that the seriousness question was somewhat separated from the vignette, because it asked participants to rate the seriousness of robbery or overcharging rather than asking them to rate the seriousness of the crime in the vignette.

Participant Attributes

Participant attributes are also included in the final models. *Graduate or law student* is dichotomous, with undergraduate student status omitted. *Age* is continuous. *Race and ethnicity* includes six categories, with white omitted. Given the link between religious beliefs and punitiveness (e.g., Unnever, Cullen, & Applegate, 2005), we control for religious affiliation. The *religious affiliation* question offered participants eighteen options, including an "other" write-in option, and allowed them to select all that apply. We collapsed the 18 and the various combinations into five categories, as shown in Table 3, which lists the most common affiliations in each category. Our categorization scheme is a variation on Steensland and colleagues' (2000) scheme that excludes the Black Protestant category and puts the denominations from that category in their respective Protestant categories (Evangelical or mainline).

RESULTS

Table 4 shows the OLS regressions of recommended sentence on the conditions, possible mediators, and participant attributes. Model 1 provides support for our first two hypotheses. As predicted in the Occupational Status Hypothesis, participants recommend a heavier sentence for white-collar offenders (executive and physician) than they do for the blue- or pink-collar offenders (handyman and shop clerk). And, as predicted in the Crime Word Hypothesis, participants recommend a heavier sentence for offenders who are described as "robbing" rather than "overcharging" their client. We also examined the interaction between occupation and crime word. As anticipated, the difference in slopes is not significant ($b = 0.064$, $p = 0.345$, not shown), suggesting that the effect of these crime words on the recommended sentence does not differ by the occupational status of the offender.

Models 2 and 3 add the perceptual factors that are needed to assess the eight mediation hypotheses. Because the wording of the crime seriousness question was distinct, we first introduce a model that includes all of the perceptual factors except that one. As shown in Model 2, participants who consider the offender

Table 4. OLS Regressions of Recommended Sentence on Conditions and Controls among Females ($N = 557$).

Model	Recommended Sentence (Logged)			
	1	2	3	4
Conditions				
White-collar occupation[a]	0.107**	0.088**	0.073*	0.072*
	(0.034)	(0.033)	(0.033)	(0.033)
Rob (0 = overcharge)	0.113***	0.113***	0.081*	0.080*
	(0.034)	(0.033)	(0.034)	(0.033)
Perceptions of the offender				
Likely to recidivate		−0.007	−0.005	−0.008
		(0.011)	(0.011)	(0.011)
Often committed crime in the past		0.001	0.002	0.004
		(0.006)	(0.006)	(0.006)
Law-abiding		−0.008	−0.008	−0.007
		(0.008)	(0.008)	(0.008)
Moral		−0.028**	−0.026*	−0.027*
		(0.011)	(0.011)	(0.011)
Dangerous		0.034***	0.028***	0.027***
		(0.007)	(0.008)	(0.008)
Blameworthy		−0.008	−0.015	−0.019
		(0.013)	(0.013)	(0.013)
Perceptions of the crime				
Bad		0.009	−0.009	−0.007
		(0.014)	(0.015)	(0.015)
Serious			0.037***	0.039***
			(0.010)	(0.010)
Participant characteristics				
Graduate, law, or medical student (0 = undergraduate student)				−0.035
				(0.043)
Age				−0.032**
				(0.012)
Age^2				0.0005**
				(0.0002)
Race and ethnicity				
African American (0 = white)				−0.045
				(0.076)
American Indian (0 = white)				0.080
				(0.066)
Asian, Hawaiian, or Pacific Islander (0 = white)				−0.065
				(0.059)

Table 4. (*Continued*)

Model	Recommended Sentence (Logged)			
	1	2	3	4
Hispanic (0 = white)				0.114
				(0.073)
Mixed race, international, or other (0 = white)				−0.049
				(0.088)
Religious affiliation				
Catholic (0 = mainline Protestant)				−0.220**
				(0.075)
Evangelical Protestant (0 = mainline Protestant)				−0.138*
				(0.062)
No affiliation, agnostic, or atheist (0 = mainline Protestant)				−0.133*
				(0.064)
Other (0 = mainline Protestant)				−0.071
				(0.073)
Intercept	0.841	0.887	0.834	1.470
	(0.030)	(0.167)	(0.166)	(0.238)
R^2	0.036	0.115	0.136	0.180
Adjusted R^2	0.033	0.100	0.120	0.146

Notes: Unstandardized coefficients; standard errors in parentheses; †$p < 0.10$; *$p < 0.05$; **$p < 0.01$; ***$p < 0.001$ (two-tailed tests).
[a]1 = executive or physician; 0 = handyman or shop clerk.

moral recommend a lighter sentence, and those who see him as dangerous recommend a heavier sentence. But, despite the significance of these effects, the condition coefficients change very little. Model 3 adds crime seriousness. As shown, perceptions of crime seriousness increase the recommended sentence, and the condition coefficients decline considerably. Thus, Model 3 suggests, consistent with the Crime Perception Mediation Hypothesis 2, that crime seriousness partially mediates the effect of the offender's occupation and the crime word. We conducted formal mediation assessments using the Sobel test, and those results support that conclusion. High occupational status increases the perceived seriousness of the crime ($b = 0.395$, $se = 0.139$, $p = 0.005$, not shown), and, as shown in Model 3 of Table 4, crime seriousness then increases the recommended sentence. This mediation effect reduces the occupational status coefficient by 16.7% ($p = 0.025$). In addition, using the word "rob" rather than "overcharge" increases the perceived seriousness of the crime ($b = 0.865$, $se = 0.137$, $p < 0.001$, not shown), and crime seriousness then increases the recommended sentence. This mediation effect reduces the rob coefficient by 28.4% ($p = 0.002$). None of the other mediation effects reach significance.

We conducted two checks to evaluate the robustness of the mediation results. First, we considered the possibility that the perceptual factors were too highly correlated to create significant independent mediator effects. However, the mean variance inflation factor (VIF) for Model 3 is 1.27, below the common cut-off of 2 for the mean VIF, and the individual VIFs range from 1.05 to 1.73, well below the cut-off of 10 for individual VIFs. Second, because the crime seriousness measure was somewhat separated from the vignette, we considered the possibility that this one perceptual factor consumed variance that might have been explained by other perceptual factors – ones that *did* focus directly on the vignette. However, when the Sobel analyses are run on the other perceptual factors with crime seriousness excluded, the results are the same. None of the other perceptual factors even approach a significant level of mediation. Thus, the results support none of the six offender perception mediation hypotheses and only one of the two crime perception mediation hypotheses.

In Model 4 of Table 4, we add controls for the participants' demographic attributes. As expected in an experiment with random assignment, these controls have little effect on the condition coefficients. But, a few of the attributes reach significance. Age has a curvilinear effect on the recommended sentence: it reduces the recommended sentence until age 35 and increases the recommended sentence after that point. In addition, Catholics, Evangelical Protestants, and those with no religious affiliation recommend lighter sentences than do mainline Protestants.

Impressions of Criminality Hypotheses

Table 5 reports results relevant to the two impressions of criminality hypotheses. Due to high collinearity (average VIF = 3.34) between the actor and behavior criminality scores, we could not include both in the same model; thus, we use separate models for each predictor. The coefficients for the controls in Table 5 are highly similar to the coefficients for the controls in Table 4, so we display only the focal coefficients in Table 5. The results support our hypotheses. Model 1 shows, as predicted in the first of these hypotheses, that negative and potent impressions of the offender after the crime increase the recommended sentence. And Model 5 shows, as predicted in the second of these hypotheses, that negative and potent impressions of the offender's behavior after he enacts the behavior also increase the recommended sentence. Models 2–3 and 6–7 show that these effects hold after controlling for the mediators, while Models 4 and 8 show that these effects hold after controlling for participant attributes.

DISCUSSION AND CONCLUSION

Equality in judicial decision-making was the goal underlying the criminal justice system reforms of the past few decades (Ulmer, 1997). Yet, as numerous studies suggest, extralegal factors, including race, ethnicity, gender, age, and citizenship status, continue to affect sanctioning outcomes. The primary theories of

Table 5. Coefficients from OLS Regressions of Recommended Sentence on Criminality Scores and Controls among Females ($N = 557$).

	Recommended Sentence (Logged)							
Model	1	2	3	4	5	6	7	8
Actor criminality score	0.108***	0.097***	0.074**	0.071**				
	(0.027)	(0.026)	(0.027)	(0.027)				
Behavior criminality score					0.201***	0.190***	0.141**	0.137**
					(0.049)	(0.047)	(0.048)	(0.048)
R^2	0.028	0.107	0.132	0.176	0.030	0.111	0.133	0.177
Adjusted R^2	0.026	0.093	0.118	0.143	0.028	0.098	0.119	0.145

Notes: Unstandardized coefficients; standard errors in parentheses; **$p < 0.01$; ***$p < 0.001$ (two-tailed tests); Models 2 and 6 control for all the perceptual factors except crime seriousness; Models 3 and 7 control for all the perceptual factors; and Models 4 and 8 control for all the perceptual factors and all the participant attributes.

sentencing decisions, the focal concerns perspective (Steffensmeier et al., 1998) and the uncertainty avoidance perspective (Albonetti, 1991), help account for these persisting patterns, explaining the thought processes and perceptions that lead judicial decision-makers to give or recommend giving heavier sentences to African American men than white men (e.g., Johnson, 2003), to Hispanic men than white men (e.g., Ulmer & Bradley, 2006), to noncitizens than citizens (e.g., Light et al., 2014), and to males than females (e.g., Griffin & Wooldredge, 2006). But, the linkage between offenders' attributes and judicial decision-makers' perceptions in these theories is unclear if no stereotype studies link the attributes to perceptions of criminality. Therefore, we drew on a theory of impression formation, ACT (Heise, 2007), in an effort to develop predictions for one such attribute, occupational prestige.

We developed these predictions using *Interact*, the computerized version of ACT. We simulated eight events, varying the actor (executive and physician for white-collar actors and handyman and shop clerk for blue- and pink-collar actors) and the action (rob a client and overcharge a client) to explore how these two interrelated factors jointly shape the transient impressions of the offender and his crime. Given that the sentiments tied to the most obviously criminal identities and behaviors are bad and powerful (Heise, 2007, pp. 67–68; Kroska et al., 2017a, 2017b), we expected bad and powerful post-event, or transient, impressions of the offender and his crime to increase the recommended sentence. After enacting the crimes, the two sets of actors appeared equally bad, but the white-collar actors appeared more powerful than their blue- and pink-collar counterparts. Similarly, after enacting the crimes, the two criminal actions (rob and overcharge) seemed similarly bad, but the white-collar actors' criminal actions seemed more powerful than the blue- and pink-collar actors' criminal actions. Consequently, both the white-collar actors and the white-collar actors' crimes had larger criminality scores than did their counterparts, leading us to predict that participants would recommend a heavier sentence for the white-collar criminals. The simulation results also showed that the transient impressions of robbing were more negative and only slightly less powerful than the transient impressions of overcharging, giving robbing higher criminality scores than overcharging. Thus, we hypothesized that participants would recommend a heavier sentence for offenders described as "robbing" rather than "overcharging." We also hypothesized that eight perceptions central to the focal concerns and uncertainty avoidance perspectives would mediate these effects. Finally, we advanced a hypothesis focused on the assumption underlying our hypotheses – that negativity and potency in the transient impressions of offenders and their crimes would increase the punishment response.

We tested these hypotheses with the vignette experiment that varied the offender's occupation and the word used to describe his crime. The results showed, as predicted, that participants recommended heavier sentences for the white-collar offenders and for the offenders described as "robbing" their clients. In addition, crime seriousness mediated these effects, providing support for one of the two crime perception mediation hypotheses. But, contrary to the six offender perception mediation hypotheses, none of the offender perceptions functioned as mediators. We also found support for our impressions of criminality hypotheses: negative and potent transient impressions of both the offenders and the crimes increased the recommended sentence. Below we discuss the implications of these findings and highlight fruitful avenues for future research.

Empirical Implications: Occupational Status

Previous studies of the effect of occupational and socioeconomic status on sentencing outcomes show mixed results, with some suggesting that high occupational and socioeconomic status offenders receive heavier sentences (e.g., Maddan et al., 2012), others showing the reverse (e.g., Payne et al., 2011), and still others showing no differences (e.g., Gottschalk & Rundmo, 2014). Some of the mixed findings may be rooted in incomplete and/or variable controls for the factors that differentiate high- and low-status offenders and their crimes, while the other differences may reflect changes across time, with judges and prosecutors developing in recent years a less tolerant attitude toward white-collar crime. We attempt to address the methodological issue by using a vignette experiment, allowing us to isolate the effect of occupational status and a factor that may be correlated with occupational status: the word used to describe the offender's crime. We address the possibility of changing attitudes by collecting new data from people likely to reflect contemporary attitudes: undergraduate, graduate, and law students at a public university. Our findings show, consistent with our ACT-based predictions, that participants recommended a heavier penalty for the white-collar offenders, suggesting that when all else is equal, individuals today favor giving white-collar criminals a heavier sentence than comparable blue- or pink-collar criminals.

Our findings may reflect a new sentiment driven by the increased attention given to white-collar crime (Cullen et al., 2009) or a long-held sentiment masked in analyses that could not fully control for differences between high- and low-status offenders and their crimes. These possibilities suggest several promising avenues for future research. One possibility is a vignette experiment conducted as a repeated cross-sectional study, a design that would allow researchers to track changes over time in reactions to white-collar vs lower-status offenders. Other possibilities include more elaborate experimental designs that vary the occupation and/or crime words in additional ways or that vary additional factors, such as the gender, race, age, or emotional displays of the offender and/or the victim. These additional manipulations would illuminate more fully when and how occupational status shapes observers' recommended punishment.

Empirical Implications: Crime Word

As predicted, offenders who were described as "robbing" rather than "overcharging" their clients were given a heavier sentence. This is not especially surprising, given that robbery, as we noted earlier, is defined by the Department of Justice as a violent crime. But, the vignette did not reference violence, and the amount of money stolen and the mechanism of theft was uniform across vignettes, so this effect came solely from the word — a word that was used only once in the vignette and once in the context of a question that followed the vignette. This finding suggests that the informal use of violent crime words in a trial may subtly shape jurors' impressions of a defendant, possibly conjuring up images of aggression or street crime, even when those words do not accurately describe the crime. It also suggests that the inaccurate use of violent crime words in media depictions of a crime could give prospective jurors an aggressive image of the defendant, thus underscoring the importance of courtroom policies that mandate accuracy in attorneys' and others' word choices and that limit the use of jurors who have had intense exposure to media descriptions of the crime in question.

Yet, it is possible that participants in our "rob" condition assumed that violence or a threat of violence was used even though it was not mentioned; therefore, follow-up studies could explicitly state that the offender did not use violence or threats of violence to determine if a violent crime word has an effect even when violence is explicitly dissociated from the crime. Follow-up studies could also build on these findings by using a range of crime words or by varying the details of the crime, including its financial consequences or the sociodemographic attributes of the victim.

Theoretical Implications

Perceptions of crime seriousness mediated the effect of occupational status and the crime word, providing partial support for the focal concerns and the uncertainty avoidance perspectives. Yet, the other seven perceptual factors did not function as mediators. These non-findings may be rooted in the hypothetical nature of the task, so researchers using this method in the future could attempt to heighten realism with a cover story designed to persuade participants of the importance of their judgments for the development of judicial policies, or they could follow the lead of other researchers who have used descriptions of actual court cases as stimuli (e.g., Tsoudis & Smith-Lovin, 1998) or framed the stimuli as transcripts from a videotaped confession (e.g., Robinson, Smith-Lovin, & Tsoudis, 1994). The non-findings could also be linked to our sample of university students, so future researchers could target for their sample only students who are likely to play a pivotal role in courtroom decisions, such as law students.

Yet, the results also suggest that these mediators may offer limited explanatory power for some extralegal factors. Our overarching hypothesis – that negative and potent impressions of the offender and the offender's crime increase the punishment response – received support in all of our analyses, suggesting that these broad and universally applicable affective sentiments may function as valuable supplements to the largely cognitive perceptual mediators in sentencing theories. Future work could examine this proposition using *Interact* to simulate events in crime databases to determine if sentencing penalties are associated with transient impressions in the way we propose. If they are, our hypothesis may explain why some groups (e.g., African Americans, Hispanic, men, young adults, and non-citizens) are routinely given harsher penalties than their counterparts. Indeed, our hypothesis, if supported in additional research, has the potential to illuminate in a broader way the factors that unite those who are at heightened risk for harsher penalties in the court system and in their contacts with the police.

Future studies could also explore other EPA formulas for operationalizing perceptions of criminality. In our initial operationalization effort, we gave transient impressions of negativity and potency equal weight in the criminality score, but a differential weighting scheme may improve the score's explanatory power, a possibility that could be explored in future studies. In this initial effort, we also did not include impressions of activity in our criminality score, because activity generally increases with potency among deviant identities. But, this correlation is only partial, so future studies could also explore the usefulness of activity for distinguishing between high and low perceptions of criminality.

NOTES

1. The *Interact* data were collected online with semantic differential slider scales (Heise, 2010, pp. 51–54) from undergraduate students at the Indiana University between 2001 and 2003 (Heise, 2004). EPA profiles are interpreted as follows: −4.3 is the worst/most impotent/most inert that anything can be; −3.0 is extremely bad/powerless/quiet; −2.0 is quite bad/powerless/quiet; −1.0 is slightly bad/powerless/quiet; 0.0 is neutral; neither bad nor good/powerless nor powerful/quiet nor active; +1.0 is slightly good/powerful/active; +2.0 is quite good/powerful/active; +3.0 is extremely good/powerful/active; +4.3 is the best/most potent/most active that anything can be.

2. The survey included two other occupation conditions, an attorney and a nurse, which we did not include, because we sought to group together occupations that shared a similar EPA profile, and the EPA profiles for those occupations are highly distinctive for their categories. The evaluation of an attorney (0.30) is considerably lower than the evaluation for other white-collar workers, and both the evaluation (2.86) and the potency (1.51) of a nurse are considerably higher than other pink-collar workers. These

occupations could be examined in future work, exploring contrasts between affectively typical and affectively atypical white- and pink-collar occupations.

ACKNOWLEDGMENTS

The authors thank Rob Clark and Sam Perry for very helpful suggestions.

REFERENCES

Albonetti, C. A. (1986). Criminality, prosecutorial screening, and uncertainty: Toward a theory of discretionary decision making in felony case processing. *Criminology, 24*, 623–644.
Albonetti, C. A. (1991). An integration of theories to explain judicial discretion. *Social Problems, 38*, 247–266.
Benson, M., & Walker, E. (1988). Sentencing the white-collar offender. *American Sociological Review, 53*, 294–302.
Bertrand, M., & Mullainathan, S. (2004). Are Emily and Greg more employable than Lakisha and Jamal? A field experiment on labor market discrimination. *American Economic Review, 94*, 991–1013.
Blowers, A. N., & Doerner, J. K. (2015). Sentencing outcomes of the older prison population: An exploration of the age leniency argument. *Journal of Crime and Justice, 38*, 58–76.
Bontrager, S., Bales, W., & Chiricos, T. (2005). Race, ethnicity, threat and the labeling of convicted felons. *Criminology, 43*, 589–622.
Cullen, F. T., Hartman, J. L., & Jonson, C. L. (2009). Bad guys: Why the public supports punishing white-collar offenders. *Crime, Law and Social Change, 51*, 31–44.
Eitle, D. J. (2000). Regulatory justice: A re-examination of the influence of class position on the punishment of white-collar crime. *Justice Quarterly, 17*, 809–839.
Francis, C., & Heise, D. R. (2006). Mean affective ratings of 1,500 concepts by Indiana University undergraduates in 2002–3 [Computer file]. Distributed at Affect Control Theory Website, Program Interact. Retrieved from http://www.indiana.edu/~socpsy/ACT/interact.htm.
Gottschalk, P., & Rundmo, T. (2014). Crime: The amount and disparity of sentencing – A comparison of corporate and occupational white collar criminals. *International Journal of Law, Crime and Justice, 42*, 175–187.
Griffin, T., & Wooldredge, J. (2006). Sex-based disparities in felony dispositions before versus after sentencing reform in Ohio. *Criminology, 44*, 893–923.
Hagan, J., Nagel, I. H., & Albonetti, C. (1980). The differential sentencing of white-collar offenders in ten federal district courts. *American Sociological Review, 45*, 802–820.
Heise, D. R. (1979). *Understanding events: Affect and the construction of social action*. New York, NY: Cambridge University Press.
Heise, D. R. (1997). INTERACT: Introduction and software. Affect Control Theory website, University of Indiana. Retrieved from http://www.indiana.edu/~socpsy/ACT/interact.htm.
Heise, D. R. (2004). Project notes on the EPA dictionary compiled at Indiana University, 2001–3. Retrieved from http://www.indiana.edu/~socpsy/ACT/PDF/ProjectNotes.pdf.
Heise, D. R. (2007). *Expressive order: Confirming sentiments in social actions*. New York, NY: Springer.
Heise, D. R. (2010). *Surveying cultures: Discovering shared conceptions and sentiments*. Hoboken, NJ: John Wiley & Sons.
Heise, D. R., & MacKinnon, N. J. (1987). Affective bases of likelihood judgments. *Journal of Mathematical Sociology, 13*, 133–151.
Holtfreter, K. (2013). Gender and "other people's money": An analysis of white-collar offender sentencing. *Women and Criminal Justice, 23*, 326–344.
Johnson, B. D. (2003). Racial and ethnic disparities in sentencing departures across modes of conviction. *Criminology, 41*, 449–489.

Johnson, B. D. (2005). Contextual disparities in guideline departures: Courtroom social contexts, guidelines compliance, and extralegal disparities in criminal sentencing. *Criminology, 43*, 761−796.
Johnson, B. D., & Betsinger, S. (2009). Punishing the "model minority": Asian−American criminal sentencing outcomes in federal district courts. *Criminology, 47*, 1045−1090.
Kramer, J. H., & Ulmer, J. T. (2002). Downward departures for serious violent offenders: Local court "corrections" to Pennsylvania's sentencing guidelines. *Criminology, 40*, 897−932.
Kroska, A., Lee, J. D., & Carr, N. T. (2017a). Juvenile delinquency and self-sentiments: Exploring a labeling theory proposition. *Social Science Quarterly, 98*, 73−88.
Kroska, A., Lee, J. D., & Carr, N. T. (2017b). Juvenile delinquency and stigma sentiments: Exploring a modified labeling theory proposition. *Advances in Group Processes, 34*, 21−47.
Kutateladze, B. L., Andiloro, N. R., Johnson, B. D., & Spohn, C. C. (2014). Cumulative disadvantage: Examining racial and ethnic disparity in prosecution and sentencing. *Criminology, 52*, 514−551.
Light, M. T., Massoglia, M., & King, R. D. (2014). Citizenship and punishment: The salience of national membership in U.S. criminal courts. *American Sociological Review, 79*, 825−847.
MacKinnon, N. J. (1994). *Symbolic interactionism as affect control*. Albany, NY: SUNY Press.
Maddan, S., Hartley, R. D., Walker, J. T., & Miller, J. M. (2012). Sympathy for the devil: An exploration of federal judicial discretion in the processing of white-collar offenders. *American Journal of Criminal Justice, 37*, 4−18.
Mustard, D. B. (2001). Racial, ethnic, and gender disparities in sentencing: Evidence from the U.S. federal courts. *Journal of Law and Economics, 44*, 285−314.
Nagel, I. H., & Hagan, J. (1982). The sentencing of white-collar criminals in federal courts: A sociolegal exploration of disparity. *Michigan Law Review, 80*, 1427−1465.
Osgood, C. E., May, W. H., & Miron, M. S. (1975). *Cross-cultural universals of affective meaning*. Urbana, IL: University of Illinois Press.
Payne, B. K., Dabney, D. A., & Ekhomu, J. L. (2011). Sentencing disparity among upper and lower class and health care professional convicted of misconduct. *Criminal Justice Policy Review, 24*, 353−369.
Piquero, N. L., Carmichael, S., & Piquero, A. R. (2008). Research note: Assessing the perceived seriousness of white-collar and street crimes. *Crime and Delinquency, 54*, 291−312.
Robinson, D. T., Smith-Lovin, L., & Tsoudis, O. (1994). Heinous crime or unfortunate accident? The effects of remorse on responses to mock criminal confessions. *Social Forces, 73*, 175−190.
Rossi, P. H., & Berk, R. A. (1985). Varieties of normative consensus. *American Sociological Review, 50*, 333−347.
Schoepfer, A., Carmichael, S., & Piquero, N. L. (2007). Do perceptions of punishment vary between white-collar and street crimes? *Journal of Criminal Justice, 35*, 151−163.
Smith-Lovin, L. (1987). Impressions from events. *Journal of Mathematical Sociology, 13*, 35−70.
Smith-Lovin, L., & Heise, D. R. (Eds.). (1988). *Analyzing social interaction: Advances in affect control theory*. New York, NY: Gordon and Breach.
Steen, S., Engen, R. L., & Gainey, R. R. (2005). Images of danger and culpability: Racial stereotyping, case processing, and criminal sentencing. *Criminology, 43*, 435−468.
Steensland, B., Park, J. Z., Regnerus, M. D., Robinson, L. D., Wilcox, W. B., & Woodberry, R. D. (2000). The measure of American religion: Toward improving the state of the art. *Social Forces, 79*, 291−318.
Steffensmeier, D., & Demuth, S. (2000). Ethnicity and sentencing outcomes in U.S. federal courts: Who is punished more harshly? *American Sociological Review, 65*, 705−729.
Steffensmeier, D., & Kramer, J. H. (1982). Sex-based differences in the sentencing of adult criminal defendants: An empirical test and theoretical overview. *Sociology and Social Research, 66*, 289−304.
Steffensmeier, D., Ulmer, J., & Kramer, J. (1998). The interaction of race, gender, and age in criminal sentencing: The punishment cost of being young, black, and male. *Criminology, 36*, 763−798.
Tillman, R., & Pontell, H. N. (1992). Is justice "collar-blind"?: Punishing Medicaid provider fraud. *Criminology, 30*, 547−574.

Tsoudis, O., & Smith-Lovin, L. (1998). How bad was it? The effects of victim and perpetrator emotion on responses to criminal court vignettes. *Social Forces, 77*, 695–722.

Ulmer, J. T. (1997). *Social worlds of sentencing: Court communities under sentencing guidelines.* Albany, NY: SUNY Press.

Ulmer, J. T., & Bradley, M. S. (2006). Variation in trial penalties among serious violent offenses. *Criminology, 44*, 631–670.

Unnever, J. D., Benson, M. L., & Cullen, F. T. (2008). Public support for getting tough on corporate crime: Racial and political divides. *Journal of Research in Crime and Delinquency, 45*, 163–190.

Unnever, J. D., Cullen, F. T., & Applegate, B. K. (2005). Turning the other cheek: Reassessing the impact of religion on punitive ideology. *Justice Quarterly, 22*, 304–339.

van Wingerden, S., van Wilsem, J., & Johnson, B. D. (2016). Offender's personal circumstances and punishment: Toward a more refined model for the explanation of sentencing disparities. *Justice Quarterly, 33*, 100–133.

Weisburd, D., Wheeler, S., Waring, E., & Bode, N. (1991). *Crimes of the middle classes: White-collar offenders in the federal courts.* New Haven, CT: Yale University Press.

Wheeler, S., Weisburd, D., & Bode, N. (1982). Sentencing the white-collar offender: Rhetoric and reality. *American Sociological Review, 47*, 641–659.

APPENDIX: MEASURE AND ANCHORS FOR THE EIGHT PERCEPTUAL VARIABLES

Variable Name	Wording and Anchors
Perceptions of the offender	
Likely to recidivate	"How likely is it that the offender will commit this same crime in the future?" (very unlikely/very likely)
Often committed crime in the past	"How often do you think the offender has committed this crime before?" (very rarely/very often)
Law-abiding	"In your opinion, how likely is it that the offender generally obeys the law?" (very unlikely/very likely)
Moral	"In your opinion, how moral is the offender?" (very immoral/very moral)
Dangerous	"In your opinion, how dangerous is the offender?" (not dangerous/very dangerous)
Blameworthy	"In your opinion, how blameworthy is the offender?" (not blameworthy/very blameworthy)
Perceptions of the crime	
Bad	"In your opinion, what the offender did was [...]" (good, nice/bad, awful)
Serious	"How serious of a crime do you think robbery/overcharging is?" (not at all/extremely), with the crime word matching the crime word in the vignette

UNDERSTANDING WHITE AMERICANS' PERCEPTIONS OF "REVERSE" DISCRIMINATION: AN APPLICATION OF A NEW THEORY OF STATUS DISSONANCE

Deena A. Isom Scott

ABSTRACT

Purpose – *This chapter has two central goals: (1) to present a foundational argument for status dissonance theory and (2) to apply its central propositions to understanding why some White Americans perceive anti-White bias. Building upon status construction theory, status dissonance theory generally posits that one's overall status value determined by their combined status characteristics influences the degree they internalize normative referential structures. The salience of normative referential structures frames one's justice perceptions, which creates status dissonance that manifests as a positional lens through which individuals perceive and interact with the social world. In an application of this framework, it is hypothesized that among Whites, one's gender and class will impact one's perceptions of resource reallocation (i.e., racial equality), which in turn impacts the likelihood one perceives anti-White bias generally and personally.*

Design – *Using the Pew Research Center's Racial Attitudes in America III Survey, this study employs logistic and ordered probit regressions on a nationally representative sample of White Americans to assess the above propositions.*

Findings – *Among Whites, males, those whom self-identified as lower class, and the least educated have the highest odds of perceiving resource reallocation, and in turn all of these factors increased the odds of perceiving anti-White bias generally in society as well as perceiving personal encounters of "reverse" discrimination.*

Implications – *The findings and theoretical propositions provide a foundation for additional investigations into understanding the causes and consequences of within and between group variation in perceptions and responses to social inequality as well as mechanisms to counter status hierarchies.*

Keywords: Discrimination; White Americans; status characteristics; status construction; status dissonance; race; ethnicity; gender; social class

A surprising trend has emerged in the last few decades. Many in the racial majority now believe that White Americans face as much or more racial discrimination than people of Color, particularly Black Americans (Jones, 2008; Jones, Cox, Galston, & Dionne, 2011; Norton & Sommers, 2011). These perceptions are surfacing in a time when America has never been more equal (Anderson, 2016; Thernstrom & Thernstrom, 1998), with the gender wage gap being the smallest in history (Bureau of Labor Statistics, 2016) and Black college enrollment on the rise (National Center for Education Statistics, 2016). Though, White males still earn more than their similarly situated female and Black and Latinx counterparts (Bureau of Labor Statistics, 2016), and are still the majority seat holders in the corporate sector (McGirt, 2016; U.S. Equal Employment Opportunity Commission, 2016). Yet, the advances of marginalized populations toward equality leave some White Americans, about 30% (e.g., Isom Scott & Andersen, 2018; Jones, Cox, Cooper, & Lienesch, 2017; Pew Research Center, 2016),[1] feeling as if they are "the victims of government-sponsored racial discrimination" (Kimmel, 2013, p. 40).

Scholars argue that for some Whites, progress toward racial equality is perceived as a threat to their dominant status as the racial majority (Outten, Schmitt, Miller, & Garcia, 2012; Sidanius & Pratto, 1999), and often times Whites believe that equality for marginalized populations may only be achieved at their expense (Eibach & Keegan, 2006; Kimmel, 2013; Norton & Sommers, 2011). In other words, racial equality is a zero-sum game (Wilkins, Wellman, Babbitt, Toosi, & Schad, 2015).[2] "If one believes this story of Whites losing the presidency, losing cultural icons, losing college admission opportunities, and losing jobs […] (then they) feel like they have lost more than they actually have lost, because of the immense power and resources (Whites) had to begin with" (Hammon, 2013, p. 119). Therefore, "efforts to level the playing field may feel like water is rushing uphill, like it's reverse discrimination against (Whites). Meritocracy sucks when you are suddenly one of the losers and not the winners" (Kimmel, 2013, p. xiii). Many Whites, particularly men, perceive that the steps taken to remedy social inequality are taking away resources *they* are entitled to and are in turn *unfair to them*, leading to anger towards women and people of Color and feelings of loss and victimhood (Kimmel, 2013). Thus, some White Americans appear to believe that their social status is not only threatened, but already lost, and *they* are now the victims of a racially biased society.

The perceptions of others of those claiming anti-White bias is well-established in the literature (Blodorn & O'Brien, 2013; Unzueta, Everly, & Gutiérrez, 2014; Wilkins, Wellman, & Kaiser, 2013), and the various negative outcomes of Whites' perceived status threat, including political movements and negative racial attitudes (Abascal, 2015; Craig & Richeson, 2014a, 2014b; Enos, 2016; Willer, Feinber, & Watts, 2016), have been studied. What have not been assessed, however, are the potential underlying social psychological processes that lead to some Whites perceiving a shift, and even loss, in status, which in turn potentially result in perceptions of anti-White bias. This paper builds upon the mechanisms provided by status construction theory to present a new theory – status dissonance theory – to illuminate potential mechanisms that result in perceptions of anti-White bias.

Status construction theory (Ridgeway, 1991; Ridgeway & Balkwell, 1997; Ridgeway, Boyle, Kuipers, & Robinson, 1998; Ridgeway & Correll, 2006; Ridgeway & Erickson, 2000; Ridgeway & Glasgow, 1996; with elaborations by Hysom, 2009; Webster & Hysom, 1998) generally posits that the arbitrary associations between nominal characteristics, such as race/ethnicity and gender, and the distribution of resources, goal objects, power, and prestige, are reinforced and perpetuated through confirming social interactions until the value of some characteristics, such as being White and male, over others, such as being Black and female, becomes a cultural norm. Status construction theory and its extensions provide sufficient mechanisms for the creation, dissemination, and even de-generalization of status beliefs. Yet, how do we explain when some of those holding high-status states, such as White men, feel oppressed and targeted? Building upon the mechanisms proposed by status construction theory, I present a theory of status dissonance that posits a sufficient process for understanding the disconnect between one's believed deserved status value in social structure and how one perceives others to actually value people similar to themselves. In other words, how one believes things ought to be compared to how one thinks things are. This status dissonance then provides a lens through which the individual perceives and interacts with and behaves within the social world. This paper concludes with an application of status dissonance theory's central propositions to assess how some Whites compared to others come to perceive anti-White bias using a nationally representative sample of White Americans (Pew Research Center, 2017).

STATUS CONSTRUCTION THEORY

Drawing upon an expectation states tradition (Berger & Conner, 1974; Berger, Rosenholtz, & Zelditch, 1980; Ridgeway & Berger, 1986), status construction theory (Ridgeway, 1991) posits sufficient mechanisms by which structural conditions influence social interactions and in turn affect cultural norms and beliefs.

A nominal characteristic is an attribute that is commonly distinguishable and professed to categorize people, such as gender, race, or ethnicity. A characteristic has status value when cultural norms and beliefs suggest that one category (i.e., white skin or males) is more worthy than another (i.e., black skin or females).

Ridgeway (1991) makes four assumptions about the structural conditions of society, based on structuralist theory (Blau, 1977), which are sufficient, but not necessary, for a culture of status value to emerge. First, exchangeable resources must be unequally distributed across the population; thus, at the least, there is a dichotomous distinction in the population between those with abundant resources and those without. Second, this distinction between the resource rich and poor must be socially meaningful, so that individuals associate most with similar others. Third, the population is distinguishable on a characteristic which is socially salient (i.e., easily noticeable in society, such as race/ethnicity or gender), but does not have status value.[3] And lastly, there must be a correlation between the resource distribution and the nominal characteristic. Consequently, there is a structure of inequality in society such that resources are disproportionately associated with different categories of the nominal characteristic (Ridgeway, 1991). Thus, according to status construction theory, because the resource distribution of a society and the nominal characteristics of white skin and skin of color are associated, the links between status, resources, and race/ethnicity are made in a specific interaction. Race and ethnicity, therefore, along with resources, become categorical cues for performance expectations,[4] and thus, status (Berger & Conner, 1974; Ridgeway, 1991; Ridgeway et al., 1985).

Status value beliefs are reinforced through repeated interaction with dissimilar others, particularly with those that differ in both resources and the nominal characteristic. Beliefs gained in such interactions will be transferred to similar others and will be reinforced by similar outcomes; therefore, the status value of race/ethnicity, for example, becomes increasing salient and categorically meaningful. Race/ethnicity acquires independent status value, and categorical referential structures emerge (Ridgeway, 1991; Ridgeway & Berger, 1986). Referential structures are widely held, socially endorsed beliefs about what is assumed to be the relationship between remunerative distribution of resources and a nominal characteristic. As racialized referential structures are more commonly applied over time, they become legitimized rationales for racial inequality (Ridgeway & Berger, 1986).

Status construction theory has been extensively examined with experimental methods, supporting the posited mechanisms for the creation of status value (Ridgeway & Erickson, 2000; Ridgeway et al., 1998; Ridgeway & Glasgow, 1996) and their diffusion into social norms (Ridgeway & Correll, 2006; Ridgeway & Erickson, 2000; Ridgeway, Backor, Li, Tinkler, & Erickson, 2009). The posited processes have also been generalized beyond the lab with nationally representative (Brezina & Winder, 2003) and international (Brashears, 2008) survey data. Furthermore, scholars have expanded the mechanisms of status construction theory, finding the distribution of other valued things, such as honors, a better office, or praise (i.e., "goal objects"), create status value in addition to exchangeable resources, and things such as personal characteristics and behaviors may gain status value as well (Webster & Hysom, 1998). Much empirical work on status construction theory focuses on how the lower status actor comes to internalize status value beliefs about one's self and others and behaves in accordance with these norms. For instance, in an experiment, Ridgeway and Erickson (2000) found that repeatedly witnessing those like themselves treated as unworthy led subjects to believe that those like themselves have low status value, though subjects resisted evaluating themselves as such. Hysom (2009) also found that those arbitrarily given goal objects, such as an honorary title, were more resistant to influence from others and evaluated themselves as the most competent in the task group. Together these findings reinforce how referential structures differentially influence individual's perceptions of self and their beliefs about how others view people similar to one's self based on status value.

DEGENERALIZATION OF STATUS VALUE

Ridgeway suggests "for the status value of a nominal characteristic to be undermined in a sustainable way, resource differences between those who differ on the characteristics must be eliminated" (1991, p. 382), and one has to have numerous disconfirming interactions with dissimilar others to counteract assumptions and stereotypes about status value (Ridgeway, 1997). Extensive work has focused on decreasing status generalizations by countering normative referential structures, particularly in terms of race. For instance, in a review of the status generalization research, Webster and Driskell (1978) outlined the work of Katz, Cohen, and colleagues attempting to neutralize performance expectations in mixed-race task groups. Their interventions intended to promote equality, but were largely ineffective and arguably counterproductive. As Webster and Driskell summarize, "from the whites' point of view, the blacks behaved inappropriately, considering their low abilities; from the blacks' point of view the whites, refusing to acknowledge the blacks' equal abilities, behaved inappropriately" (1978, p. 227). Beyond the status struggle and increased hostility[5] (see Webster & Driskell, 1978), this statement also implies a racial variance in acceptance of normative referential structures. In other words, Whites believing in their superior abilities and competence generally over Blacks, and Blacks not internalizing the referential status beliefs about their assumed inferior status.

More recent work advancing these traditions find that racial inequality can be reduced in task-oriented groups. Using similar experimental designs, Goar and Sell (2005) found how a task is framed influenced Black women's group participation, and Walker, Doerer, and Webster (2014) found that increased participation by Black women increased their group influence. Though, neither experimental manipulation completely eliminated White dominance in the groups. Building upon their previous work, Cohen and colleagues (see Webster & Driskell, 1978) did achieve racially equality in interactions only by counteracting normative referential structures through teaching the Black participants to be assertive, giving the Black participants positive feedback during the task, designating the Black participants as leaders in the group, and providing the group with information on Blacks' superior knowledge for the task at hand. Thus, equality was only achieved when Blacks' superiority was demonstrated. In support of Ridgeway's claims (1991; 1997), these findings reinforce the notion that people of Color, particularly Blacks, have to work harder to neutralize normative referential structures in order to achieve the same respect and status as Whites.

Such extreme demonstrations of ability and worthiness are likely needed to surmount normative referential structures because they challenge the legitimated order. In other words, the status equality of Blacks with Whites contradicts cultural norms. "Given that individuals form expectations for valued status positions on the basis of these referential beliefs, this leads them to treat individuals who occupy high-status positions differently depending on their external status. Specifically, those with low external status may often be treated as normatively inappropriate occupants of high-status positions" (Berger & Webster, 2006, p. 281). Resistance is most likely from those in the highest status positions because they have the most to lose for legitimizing the rise in status of someone from a lower social order. Yet, *not all* of those holding the highest status positions resist or feel threatened by the advancement of lower status others. Furthermore, while everyone in society generally *knows* the normative referential structures, there is a large variation in the degree of influence status value beliefs have on individuals. Following a status construction theory tradition, status dissonance theory attempts to explain why and how those with similar status characteristics respond differently to changes in social inequality.

STATUS DISSONANCE THEORY

Status dissonance is the degree of discrepancy between where one believes those with similar characteristics should be positioned on the social hierarchy and where one believes others actually position people similar to themselves. In other words, where one believes they ought to be compared to where they believe they truly are. Similar to reflected appraisals[6] (Cooley, 1902; Felson, 1985; Mead, 1934), status dissonance gauges individual's perceptions about cultural norms and their social positions in relation to others, but not actually other's beliefs. Status dissonance theory generally posits that one's overall status value influences the degree they internalize normative referential structures. The salience of normative referential structures frames an individual's justice perceptions, which in turn create status dissonance that manifests as a positional lens through which individuals perceive and interact with the social world. The foundational arguments underlying these mechanisms are presented below.

Differential Roles of Status Characteristics

While other characteristics beyond the "big two" of gender and race, such as sexual orientation or being a doctor, may possess status value (e.g., Berger & Fisek, 2006; Walker, Webster, & Bianchi, 2011; Webster & Hysom, 1998), the degree and salience of the given characteristic often varies with the context (Berger, Fisek, Norman, & Zelditch, 1977). Despite variations in significance across situations, every individual still has a fundamental self that is the combination of all of their characteristics. People do not experience any characteristic in insolation, thus all individual understanding of any one characteristic is conditioned by all other embodied characteristics (Hill Collins & Bilge, 2016). Status dissonance theory argues that the combination of one's status characteristics determines one's overall status value. Taking into account the known variation in salience of given status characteristics, status dissonance theory further suggests that all status characteristics do not contribute equally to an individual's overall status value, but instead operate on a graduated scale.

Given the significance of easily recognizable differences to form fundamental schemas of self and others[7] (Fiske & Taylor, 2017), race and gender are posited to carry the most weight and operate as level-one status characteristics. Other characteristics have intrinsic value and these make up the second level of status characteristics. For instance, social class is fundamentally ordinal. The foundation of a class structure is the difference between those with resources and those without, the bourgeoisie and the proletariat, and the struggles for power that comes with such divides (Marx, 1867). The third level of status characteristics are those that must be disclosed in some way to others. One's sexual orientation or nonconforming gender identity are prime examples. All of these characteristics not only vary in importance to any individual's identity, but they also vary in significance for social standing and their degree of privateness. For instance, one may choose to disclose their sexual orientation or not, but one cannot easily hide their race in social settings (though their socially ascribed race may not align with their racial identity). Thus, status dissonance theory posits that one's combination of status characteristics, with each providing varying degrees of significance, determines one's overall status value in society.

Referential Structures

Building upon status construction theory, status dissonance theory posits that individuals understand their overall relative status in the social hierarchy based on normative referential structures determined by the combined status value of their held characteristics. For instance, a White woman knows that traditional society does not value her as much as a White man, but society does value her more than a Black woman. Furthermore, it is posited that one's combination of status value will impact the likelihood they generally internalize the normative referential structure, with the "big two" of race and gender being the primary drivers, followed by the other levels of status characteristics. Thus, White men should be the most likely to internalize normative referential structures because these beliefs reinforce their high status value in society. The impact of other status characteristics will follow the expected associations, with the higher valued status state being most likely to internalize normative referential structures. The degree of this association, however, is contingent upon one's racial and gender status. For instance, a working class, White man is still likely to internalize traditional status generalization because he has high status value based on his race and gender. An upper class, Black woman, however, is unlikely to internalize such normative beliefs to the same degree as her White male counterpart because despite her economic success, she still faces disadvantages based on her race and gender.

Contact with Dissimilar Others and "Broadcast Processes"

Referential structures, however, are posited to be conditioned by two factors: contact with dissimilar others and the "broadcast process" (Ridgeway & Balkwell, 1997). Ridgeway (1991) argues that status value spreads most rapidly through interactions with doubly dissimilar others. While such interactions spread normative referential structures, counter-normative interactions also degeneralize status beliefs (e.g., Goar & Sell, 2005; Ridgeway & Correll, 2006; Walker et al., 2014). Furthermore, interactions between dissimilar others has been found to reduce prejudicial beliefs, with the largest reductions occurring when people chose to interact with people of different races (Pettigrew & Tropp, 2006). Research, however, also finds that forced encounters, such as at work, sometimes increase discriminatory beliefs and behaviors (Pettigrew, Tropp, Wagner, & Christ, 2011). Thus, interaction with dissimilar others could dismantle or reinforce traditional referential structures, depending upon the nature of the interaction.

Furthermore, referential structures may be spread through other means besides face-to-face interactions. Ridgeway and Balkwell (1997) argue that a "broadcast process" of cultural diffusion may spread normative referential structures through means such as media consumption, interactions with institutions, and observing others' public social interactions. Therefore, the social messages one consumes will condition the degree they internalize normative referential structures. For instance, White Americans are consistently receiving messages about their dwindling status and value in American society, especially from conservative media (Mitchell, Gottfried, Kiley, & Masta, 2014; Resnick, 2017; Stern, 2016). With repeated messages about the advances of people of Color, particularly at what they perceive to be their expense, White Americans are more likely to believe not only that racial equality has been achieved, but also that they are now the disadvantaged.

Justice Perceptions

The degree of internalization of traditional referential structures in turn impacts one's perceptions of fair outcomes. Status construction theory (Ridgeway, 1991) posits that referential structures emerge due to the correlation between the distribution of resources and a nominal characteristic. Furthermore, this distribution is evaluated as just based on normative expectations of competence and worthiness. Status dissonance theory argues that one's referential structure provides the framework for evaluating the fairness of an outcome. Status construction theory assumes that status value is granted based on expectations and outcomes,

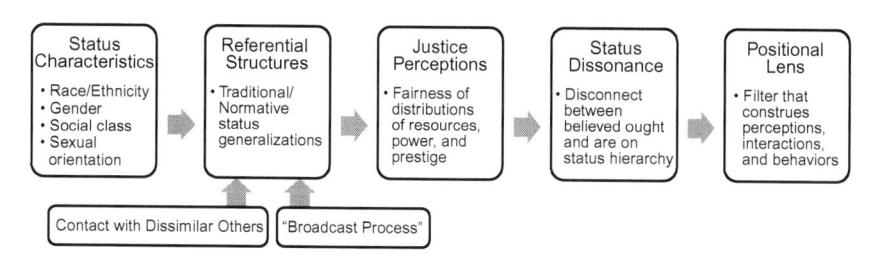

Fig. 1. Nomological Depiction of Status Dissonance Theory.

following the distributive justice principle of equity[8] (e.g., Adams, 1965; Cook & Hegtvedt, 1983; Folger, 1986; Jasso, 1980). Therefore, a fair outcome is based on one's status value. Thus, if one has internalized the normative referential structure, then they should believe that Whites, men, and the middle and upper classes rightfully deserve their place in the social structure because they are more worthy and qualified for the position, and in turn, social inequalities are justified. If one has not internalized the normative referential structures, they are likely to have a different justice framework and think changes are needed in terms of social policies and institutions to reduce social inequality.

Status Dissonance and a Positional Lens

One's justice perceptions then lead to the degree one experiences status dissonance. Status dissonance is the discrepancy between one's beliefs about how people with similar status characteristics to one's self should fall on the status hierarchy compared to how one believes others actually value similarly situated others generally. Such status dissonance arises from perceptions of injustice toward self or similar others based on one's held referential structure. Status dissonance provides a lens through which one interacts with the world. In other words, it shapes their perceptions of world events as well as interpersonal interactions and guides one's behaviors. Fig. 1 presents a nomological depiction of the foundational arguments for status dissonance theory.

THE CURRENT STUDY

Together these theoretical arguments and empirical findings provide a basis for understanding the recent emergence of perceptions of anti-White bias among some White Americans. The shift in the American economy has left many Americans, particularly rural, undereducated, working class people, many of whom are White, unable to make a living wage or provide a comfortable life for their families (Chen, 2015; Kimmel, 2013).[9] At the same time, numerous policies have been passed in recent decades to equalize the playing field for marginalized populations (Thernstrom & Thernstrom, 1998), leading to many social and economic advances for people of Color. While resources have not actually been re-distributed, some White Americans, particularly working class men, perceive the advancement of people of Color, especially Black Americans, as coming at their loss. Thus, they are likely to feel their status as Whites, and as men, are threatened. These beliefs may be reinforced further by the changing demographics in the workplace which they may perceive as unjust and underserved, especially if people of Color are being hired for new positions, being promoted, or replacing former White employees. Additionally, their formerly segregated neighborhoods may now be racially integrated with shifts in the housing market.[10]

Status dissonance theory would posit lower class, White men have likely internalized a normative referential structure that places them, as White men, high on the social hierarchy. Especially since, "White men of all classes benefit from a system based on racial and gender inequality" (Kimmel, 2013, p.xii). This framework informs their justice perceptions of changes in society, thus leading them to perceive the advancement of women and people of Color as undeserved and illegitimate. These feelings result in status dissonance as they believe that society does not value them as White men to the degree they deserve. This status dissonance results in a positional lens that informs their perceptions and interactions with the social world, leading them to perceive encounters that reinforce their feelings of status dissonance, (e.g., the promotion of a Black man over himself, as anti-White bias). Following a status dissonance theory framework, this leads to the following hypotheses:

H1. Among Whites, being male and lower social class increase the likelihood one believes that Black Americans have achieved equal status with White Americans (i.e., perceptions of resource reallocation).

H2. Among Whites, being male and lower social class increase the likelihood one perceives anti-White bias generally and personally.

H3. Perceptions of resource reallocation increase the likelihood one perceives anti-White bias generally and personally controlling for status characteristics.

H4. Frequency of contact with Black Americans will condition the association of perceptions of resource reallocation with perceptions of anti-White bias generally and personally for White Americans.

These hypotheses are assessed below with a nationally representative sample of White Americans collected by the Pew Research Center (2017).

METHOD

Data and Sample

Data for the present study are taken from the 2016 Racial Attitudes in America III Survey (Pew Research Center, 2017). Collected via telephone between February 29, 2016 and May 8, 2016, the full dataset includes a nationally representative sample of 3,769 adults. The aim of the survey was to gauge racial differences in attitudes and perceptions about inequality in America. The sampling procedure included a disproportionately-stratified sample of Blacks and Latinxs to ensure representativeness. The final data include probability weights for statistical analysis to account for this sampling strategy, which are implemented in the present study. Data were made publicly available July 27, 2017 and obtained from the Pew Research Center website (Pew Research Center, 2017).[11] The current study utilizes the non-Hispanic White sample. Relevant variables were selected and analyzed for systematic and randomly missing data patterns prior to measure creation.[12] The final data include 1,750 White adults, and is 56% male with a mean age of 53 years old and an average annual income of approximately US$50,000.

Measures

Dependent Variables

Participants were asked, "Thinking about our country [...] Overall, would you say that Blacks are treated less fairly than Whites, Whites are treated less fairly than Blacks, or both are treated about equally in [...]" six different situations: the workplace, in stores and restaurants, when applying for a mortgage or a loan, when dealing with the police, when dealing with the courts, and in voting elections. Items were recoded to receive a value of 1 if the respondent said Whites were treated less fairly than Blacks in any of the presented situations. The items were then totaled to create a measure of general perceptions of anti-White bias, however, this count outcome was highly skewed ($sk_p = 8.427$, sd $= 0.059$). Therefore, the final measure of *General Anti-White Bias* perceptions is a dichotomous indicator of White participants ever reporting thinking that Whites were treated less fairly than Blacks.

Participants were also asked about their personal experiences with racial discrimination. The measure of "reverse" discrimination perceptions comes from the question, "Have you ever personally experienced discrimination or been treated unfairly because of your race or ethnicity, or not?" If the participant answered yes, they were asked if it was a regular experience, only occurred from time to time, or rarely. Responses were recoded as 0 = no/never, 1 = rarely, 2 = from time to time, and 3 = frequently. The resulting outcome is an ordered indicator of perceived frequency of *Personal Anti-White Bias* experiences.

Independent Variables

The status characteristic of gender is dummy coded as *Male* = 1, thus females serve as the reference category. The second-level status characteristic of social class is not solely about economic divisions, but about culture, values, and morals (Bourdieu, 1987; Lamont, 1992). While there are reasonably established objectives based upon wealth, income, educational attainment, and occupation of who classifies as upper, middle, working, and lower class (Newman, 2010), most Americans do not classify themselves in these terms. Instead, they see themselves as some degree of "middle" class, either out of modesty or self-promotion (Ortner, 1998). Thus, objective and subjective indicators of social class are included. Participants were asked, "If you were asked to use one of these commonly used names for the social classes, which would you say you belong in?," and self-classified as lower class, lower middle class, middle class, upper middle class, and upper class. These *Socioeconomic Class* categories were coded into a series of dummy variables with upper class as the reference category. The initial survey also asked several questions about educational experiences. The original researchers (Pew Research Center, 2017) combined these indicators to classify people as having a high school diploma or less, an Associate's degree or some college experience, or a Bachelor's degree or more. These *Education* categories were coded into a series of dummy variables with a Bachelor's degree or higher as the reference category. *Income* comes from the question, "Last year, that is in 2015, what was your total family income from all sources, before taxes?," with responses ranging from less than US$10,000 to US$150,000 or more.[13] Together, socioeconomic class, education, and income provide indicators for the status characteristic of social class.

Participants were asked, "Which of these two statements comes closer to your own views – even if neither is exactly right. Our country has made the changes needed to give Blacks equal rights with Whites. Our country needs to continue making changes to give Blacks equal rights with Whites." Responses were recoded into a dichotomous indicator where 1 indicates participants most support the first statement (i.e., US racial equality has been achieved), providing a measure of perceptions of *Resource Reallocation* and racial equality.

Frequency of interracial interactions comes from the question, "In your daily life, how much contact do you, personally, have with people who are [self-reported White respondents were asked "Black"] – would you say a lot, some, only a little or no contact at all?" Responses were reverse coded so 1 = no contact at all and 4 = a lot of contact, providing a measure of frequency of *Contact with Blacks*.

Control Variables
Age is self-reported age at the time of survey administration. *Marital Status* is a dichotomous variable (1 = currently married). Lived experiences impact one's perceptions and worldview; thus, recent financial hardships are controlled for. Participants were asked if they had experienced being laid off, having trouble paying bills, having to borrow money, or having to get food from a food bank during the last year, with positive responses = 1. Items were totaled to create a count measure of *Recent Financial Hardships*. Research also suggests that perceived threats to Whites' social status, such as Black Americans achieving racial equality, are associated with stronger conservative political ideologies (Forscher & Kteily, 2017; Mayrl & Saperstein, 2013; Willer et al., 2016). Furthermore, one's political leadings likely reflect their media consumption and internalization of various cultural values (e.g., Müller et al., 2017); in other words, their "broadcast process." Thus, *Political Ideology* is controlled for by a set of dummy variables recoded from an indicator categorizing participants as conservatives, moderate conservatives, moderates, moderate liberals, and

liberals, with liberals serving as the reference category.[14] Table 1 provides the sample demographics and variable correlations.

Analytical Strategy

The current study utilizes logistic and ordered probit regression analyses. A series of stepwise binary logistic regressions are reported for the regression of status characteristics on resource reallocation as well as status characteristics and resource reallocation on general perceptions of anti-White bias. Odds ratios (ORs) are presented for ease of interpretation, with higher odds indicated when the ORs are above one and lower odds if the ORs are below one. Ordered probit regressions are employed to assess the regression of status characteristics and resource reallocation on frequency of perceptions of personally experienced anti-White bias. Positive coefficients indicate a greater likelihood of perceiving anti-White bias personally, whereas negative coefficients indicate a lower likelihood. The coefficients, however, do not provide an easily understood indicator of the degree of the assessed effects. Thus, the predicted probabilities of each level of assessed frequency of perceived personal encounters of anti-White bias were analyzed with the margins command in Stata14. Data were cleaned in SPSS23 and all analyses were finalized with Stata14. As directed by Pew Research Center (2017), probability weights were employed for all statistical models to best match the American population. Weighted results are presented, but unweighted results are available upon request.

RESULTS

Hypothesis one predicts that among Whites, being male and lower social class increase the likelihood one believes that Black Americans have achieved equal status with White Americans (i.e., perceptions of resource reallocation). Table 2 presents the logistic regressions of status characteristics on perceptions of resource reallocation. Surprisingly, few status characteristics are significantly associated with perceptions of racial equality (i.e., resource reallocation). However, the resulting directionality generally supports the hypothesis. First, Model 1 reveals that males have greater odds of perceiving racial equality than females, though not significantly. The associations with social class, however, are a bit more complicated. Those who self-classified as lower class do have greater odds of perceiving racial equality than those who self-identified as upper class; however, those in the middle class categories have lower odds comparatively, though again not significantly.

The same curvilinear pattern emerges with the other social class indicators. Whites with a high school diploma or less have marginally significant greater odds of perceiving racial equality than those with a bachelor's degree or more. Though again, Whites with only some college credit have lower odds compared to college graduates, but not significantly. Income is significantly associated with perceptions of racial equality, with those making US$150,000 or more annually having 8.98 times higher odds than those making less than US$10,000 a year.

Table 1. Correlation Matrix and Descriptive Statistics ($N = 1,750$).

	A	B	C	D	E	F	G	H	I	J	K	L	M	N	O	P	Q	R	S	T	U	V
A General perceptions of anti-White bias	1																					
B Perceived personal experiences of anti-White bias	0.105**	1																				
C Male	0.061*	0.094**	1																			
Socioeconomic class																						
D Lower class	0.028	0.058*	−0.037	1																		
E Lower middle class	0.033	0.116**	0.019	−0.121**	1																	
F Middle class	0.005	−0.052*	−0.034	−0.256**	−0.506**	1																
G Upper middle class	−0.057*	−0.066**	0.028	−0.127**	−0.250**	−0.530**	1															
H Upper class	0.007	−0.042	0.044	−0.039	−0.078**	−0.164**	−0.081**	1														
Education																						
I High school of less	0.050*	0.003	0.039	0.154**	0.115**	−0.044	−0.120**	−0.067**	1													
J Associate's degree or some college	0.023	0.035	−0.029	0.036	0.112**	0.028	−0.146**	−0.050*	−0.339**	1												
K Bachelor's degree or higher	−0.063**	−0.033	−0.009	−0.166**	−0.198**	0.014	0.231**	0.102**	−0.575**	−0.574**	1											
L Income	−0.034	−0.043	0.134**	−0.347**	−0.351**	0.076**	0.393**	0.143**	−0.368**	−0.104**	0.411**	1										
M Resource reallocation	0.288**	0.090**	0.075**	−0.007	−0.021	0.024	−0.005	−0.001	0.041	−0.049*	0.007	0.051*	1									
N Contact with Blacks	0.043	0.183**	0.057*	0.016	0.025	0.010	−0.042	−0.009	−0.037	0.003	0.030	0.050*	0.048*	1								
O Recent financial hardships	0.017	0.171**	−0.027	0.253**	0.270**	−0.159**	−0.196**	−0.040	0.137**	0.056**	−0.168**	−0.358**	−0.024	0.129**	1							
P Age	0.013	−0.112**	−0.079**	−0.016	−0.121**	0.059*	0.061*	−0.019	0.022	−0.029	0.006	−0.060*	−0.034	−0.209**	−0.220**	1						
Q Marital status	0.038	−0.053*	0.048*	−0.146**	−0.164**	0.096**	0.117**	0.021	−0.159**	−0.029	0.164**	0.431**	0.057*	0.014	−0.183**	0.138**	1					
Political ideology																						
R Conservative	0.071**	0.021	0.078**	−0.065**	−0.070**	0.060*	0.022	0.024	−0.001	0.029	−0.025	0.068**	0.140**	0.009	−0.108**	0.080**	0.106**	1				
S Moderate conservative	0.027	0.018	0.001	−0.024	−0.041	0.019	0.024	0.015	0.057*	0.011	−0.059*	0.050*	0.023	0.020	−0.033	0.032	0.015	−0.184**	1			
T Moderate	0.012	0.062**	0.079**	0.107**	−0.029	−0.099**	−0.041	0.017	0.018	−0.030	0.026	−0.113**	−0.051*	0.019	0.070**	−0.112**	−0.044	−0.412**	−0.274**	1		
U Moderate liberal	−0.036	−0.065**	−0.067**	0.030	−0.028	−0.049*	−0.036	0.053*	0.008	−0.113**	−0.071**	−0.076**	−0.160**	−0.034	0.024	0.109**	−0.020	−0.194**	−0.129**	−0.288**	1	
V Liberal	−0.083**	−0.062**	−0.107**	−0.037	−0.004	−0.095**	0.124**	0.044	−0.113**	−0.071**	0.160**	0.095**	−0.160**	−0.022	0.035	−0.062**	−0.054*	−0.242**	−0.161**	−0.360**	−0.170**	1
Mean	0.038	0.621	0.559	0.193	0.518	0.207	0.254	0.025	0.254	0.253	0.493	5.890	0.189	2.140	0.530	52.800	0.587	0.217	0.109	0.380	0.119	0.175
Standard deviation	0.191	0.946	0.497	0.233	0.394	0.406	0.435	0.155	0.435	0.435	0.500	2.350	0.391	0.873	0.906	17.800	0.493	0.412	0.312	0.486	0.324	0.380

Notes: $*p < 0.05$; $**p < 0.01$.

Table 2. Status Characteristics on Resource Reallocation (i.e., Racial Equality).[a,b]

Variables	Model 1 OR	Lower	Upper	Model 2 OR	Lower	Upper
		95% Confidence Interval			95% Confidence Interval	
Male	1.15	0.83	1.57	1.03	0.74	1.43
Socioeconomic class						
Lower class	1.16	0.36	3.80	1.00	0.29	3.40
Lower middle class	0.87	0.31	2.41	0.74	0.26	2.06
Middle class	0.90	0.35	2.35	0.73	0.28	1.89
Upper middle class	0.72	0.27	1.92	0.66	0.25	1.78
Education						
High school or less	1.46^	0.99	2.15	1.32	0.89	1.97
Associate's degree or some college	0.79	0.53	1.18	0.71	0.47	1.07
Income	1.12**	1.03	1.22	1.07	0.97	1.17
Controls						
Contact with Blacks	—	—	—	1.12	0.93	1.35
Recent financial hardships	—	—	—	0.94	0.76	1.17
Age	—	—	—	0.99	0.98	1.00
Marital status	—	—	—	1.32	0.90	1.94
Political ideology	—	—	—			
Conservative	—	—	—	6.57**	3.21	13.45
Moderate conservative	—	—	—	3.68**	1.65	8.20
Moderate	—	—	—	4.17**	2.05	8.47
Moderate liberal	—	—	—	3.30**	1.44	7.56
Constant	0.12**	0.04	0.37	0.05**	0.01	0.22
Wald χ^2	15.94*			46.25**		

Notes: ^$p < 0.10$; *$p < 0.05$; **$p < 0.01$.
[a]Probabiltiy weighted results presented, unweighted results available upon request.
[b]"Upper class," "bachelor's degree or higher," and "liberal" are the reference categories for socioeconomic status, education, and political ideology, respectively.

Overall, Model 1 finds only very modest support for the first hypothesis as status characteristics generally are not significant predictors of perceptions of resource reallocation, even though males and those holding the lowest social class status do have the highest odds of perceiving racial equality.

Model 2 adds the controls of contact with Blacks, age, marital status, recent financial hardships, and political ideology. While the directionality holds, the status indicators of education and income are no longer significant, and political ideology solely is significantly associated with perceptions of racial equality with the inclusion of the controls. The more conservative one leans politically, the greater their odds of perceiving racial equality compared to liberals. Again, while not statistically significant, all associations are generally in the predicted directions, lending some support to the present hypotheses.

Hypothesis two predicts that among Whites, being male and lower social class increase the likelihood one perceives anti-White bias generally and personally. Table 3 presents the binary logistic regressions of status characteristics and resource reallocation on perceptions of anti-White bias generally. Model 1 reveals that males are significantly more likely to perceive anti-White bias generally, with 2.25 times greater odds than females. In terms of social class, the same general patterns emerge as those in relation to perceptions of resource reallocation. Those that self-identify as lower class and those that have a high school education or less have the greatest odds of perceiving anti-White bias generally, though not or only marginally significantly. Those who self-identify in the middle classes and had some college-level education, however, have lower odds compared to the upper class and those with a college degree, but not significantly. The same patterns hold for income, but the association is not significant. As with resources, status characteristics are generally associated with general perceptions of anti-White bias in the hypothesized directions, but with only marginal significance, thus providing only modest support to the current hypothesis.

Hypothesis three predicts that perceptions of resource reallocation increase the likelihood one perceives anti-White bias generally and personally controlling for status characteristics. Model 2 of Table 3 finds that Whites who believe America has achieved racial equality have 9.8 times greater odds of perceiving anti-White bias generally compared to Whites who do not ascribe to such beliefs. The significant associations between gender and self-identified social class also generally remain unchanged. Those with less than a college degree are also marginally significantly more likely to perceive anti-White bias generally than those with a college degree.

The final hypothesis predicts that the frequency of contact with Black Americans will condition the association of perceptions of resource reallocation with perceptions of anti-White bias generally and personally for White Americans. Model 3 of Table 3 finds that the frequency of contact with Black Americans does not significantly impact the odds of general anti-White bias perceptions, though they are positively associated. Model 4 finds that contact with Black Americans does not condition the effect of resource reallocation as hypothesized. Finally, comparing Table 3's Model 5 and Model 3 shows that the associations for gender, social class, education, and resource reallocation remain essentially unchanged when the controls are added to the model. Furthermore, unlike with resource reallocation, none of the controls including politically ideology, significantly impact general anti-White bias perceptions, but they are positively associated.

Tables 4 and 5 assess if the same associations found for general anti-White bias hold for the associations with perceptions of frequency of personal experiences with "reverse" discrimination as hypothesized. Table 4 presents the ordered probit regressions of status characteristics and resource reallocation on perceptions of frequency of personal experiences with anti-White bias. As hypothesized, Model 1 reveals that males and self-identified lower class and middle lower class Whites have significantly higher likelihoods of frequently perceiving "reverse"

Table 3. Status Characteristics and Resource Reallocation on General Perceptions of Anti-White Bias.[a,b]

Variables	Model 1 OR	Model 1 95% CI Lower	Model 1 95% CI Upper	Model 2 OR	Model 2 95% CI Lower	Model 2 95% CI Upper	Model 3 OR	Model 3 95% CI Lower	Model 3 95% CI Upper	Model 4 OR	Model 4 95% CI Lower	Model 4 95% CI Upper	Model 5 OR	Model 5 95% CI Lower	Model 5 95% CI Upper
Male	2.25*	1.12	4.55	2.17*	1.04	4.52	2.11*	1.01	4.41	2.11*	1.01	4.41	2.19*	1.05	4.58
Socioeconomic class															
Lower class	1.44	0.15	14.12	1.53	0.16	14.84	1.42	0.15	13.52	1.42	0.15	13.47	1.28	0.13	12.51
Lower middle class	0.83	0.11	6.45	1.04	0.15	7.28	0.96	0.14	6.66	0.96	0.14	6.57	0.87	0.12	6.17
Middle class	0.58	0.09	3.83	0.69	0.12	3.99	0.66	0.12	3.71	0.66	0.12	3.67	0.54	0.09	3.20
Upper middle class	0.14^	0.02	1.07	0.17^	0.02	1.22	0.17^	0.02	1.18	0.17^	0.02	1.17	0.16^	0.02	1.13
Education															
High school or less	2.25^	0.98	5.15	1.98	0.85	4.60	1.95	0.84	4.54	1.94	0.84	4.49	1.86	0.80	4.30
Associates degree or some college	1.90	0.82	4.37	2.19^	0.96	5.00	2.16^	0.95	4.91	2.15^	0.95	4.90	2.21^	0.95	5.17
Income	1.12	0.95	1.33	1.06	0.88	1.29	1.06	0.87	1.28	1.05	0.87	1.28	1.03	0.82	1.29
Resource reallocation	—	—	—	9.80**	4.70	20.41	9.56**	4.59	19.94	7.70*	1.36	43.68	9.00**	4.70	17.24
Contact with Blacks	—	—	—	—	—	—	1.19	0.84	1.70	1.12	0.64	1.99	1.19	0.82	1.72
Resource reallocation × contact with Blacks	—	—	—	—	—	—	—	—	—	1.10	0.54	2.26	—	—	—
Controls															
Recent financial hardships	—	—	—	—	—	—	—	—	—	—	—	—	1.15	0.74	1.79
Age	—	—	—	—	—	—	—	—	—	—	—	—	1.01	0.99	1.03
Marital status	—	—	—	—	—	—	—	—	—	—	—	—	1.68	0.78	3.62

Table 3. (Continued)

Variables	Model 1 OR	Model 1 95% CI Lower	Model 1 95% CI Upper	Model 2 OR	Model 2 95% CI Lower	Model 2 95% CI Upper	Model 3 OR	Model 3 95% CI Lower	Model 3 95% CI Upper	Model 4 OR	Model 4 95% CI Lower	Model 4 95% CI Upper	Model 5 OR	Model 5 95% CI Lower	Model 5 95% CI Upper
Political ideology															
Conservative	—	—	—	—	—	—	—	—	—	—	—	—	4.92	0.56	42.89
Moderate conservative	—	—	—	—	—	—	—	—	—	—	—	—	6.51	0.61	69.04
Moderate	—	—	—	—	—	—	—	—	—	—	—	—	3.67	0.41	32.77
Moderate liberal	—	—	—	—	—	—	—	—	—	—	—	—	2.31	0.21	26.11
Constant	0.02**	>0.00	0.11	0.01**	>0.00	0.05	>0.00**	>0.00	0.04	>0.00**	>0.00	0.06	>0.00**	>0.00	0.03
Wald χ^2	21.67**			88.26**			88.21**			89.41**			88.14**		

Notes: ^$p < 0.10$; *$p < 0.05$; **$p < 0.01$.
[a]Probabiltiy weighted results presented, unweighted results available upon request.
[b]"Upper class," "bachelor's degree or higher," and "liberal" are the reference categories for socioeconomic status, education, and political ideology, respectively.

Table 4. Status Characteristics and Resource Reallocation on Frequency of Perceived Personal Experiences of Anti-White Bias.[a,b]

Variables	Model 1 Coeff	Model 1 RSE	Model 2 Coeff	Model 2 RSE	Model 3 Coeff	Model 3 RSE	Model 4 Coeff	Model 4 RSE	Model 5 Coeff	Model 5 RSE
Male	0.22**	0.08	0.21**	0.08	0.19*	0.08	0.19*	0.08	0.18*	0.08
Socioeconomic class										
Lower class	0.78**	0.30	0.79**	0.30	0.68*	0.28	0.69*	0.28	0.57*	0.29
Lower middle class	0.68**	0.26	0.70**	0.26	0.62*	0.25	0.62*	0.25	0.59*	0.25
Middle class	0.37	0.25	0.38	0.25	0.33	0.24	0.33	0.23	0.39	0.24
Upper middle class	0.26	0.26	0.28	0.26	0.28	0.25	0.28	0.25	0.36	0.25
Education										
High school or less	−0.01	0.10	−0.02	0.10	−0.01	0.10	−0.01	0.10	−0.01	0.10
Associate's degree or some college	0.04	0.09	0.05	0.09	0.06	0.09	0.06	0.09	0.05	0.09
Income	0.02	0.02	0.01	0.02	>0.00	0.02	>0.00	0.02	0.03	0.02
Resource reallocation	—	—	0.23*	0.09	0.19*	0.09	0.01	0.33	0.19*	0.10
Contact with Blacks	—	—	—	—	0.32**	0.05	0.30**	0.05	0.28**	0.05
Resource reallocation × contact with Blacks	—	—	—	—	—	—	0.08	0.13	—	—
Controls										
Recent financial hardships	—	—	—	—	—	—	—	—	0.21**	0.04
Age	—	—	—	—	—	—	—	—	<0.00	>0.00
Marital status	—	—	—	—	—	—	—	—	−0.06	0.09
Political ideology										
Conservative	—	—	—	—	—	—	—	—	0.21^	0.13
Moderate conservative	—	—	—	—	—	—	—	—	0.06	0.15
Moderate	—	—	—	—	—	—	—	—	0.19^	0.11
Moderate liberal	—	—	—	—	—	—	—	—	0.01	0.16
Wald χ^2	27.13**		33.47**		76.23**		77.07**		99.87**	

Notes: ^$p < 0.10$; *$p < 0.05$; **$p < 0.01$.
[a] Probability weighted results presented, unweighted results available upon request.
[b] "Upper class," "bachelor's degree or higher," and "liberal" are the reference categories for socioeconomic status, education, and political ideology, respectively,

Table 5. Predicted Probabilities at Each Level of Frequency of Perceived Personal Experiences of Anti-White Bias[a,b].

Variables	Never PP	SE	Rarely PP	SE	Time to Time PP	SE	Frequently PP	SE
Male	−0.06*	0.03	0.01*	0.003	0.05*	0.02	0.01*	0.003
Socioeconomic class								
Lower class	−0.21^	0.11	0.01**	0.004	0.16^	0.08	0.04	0.028
Lower middle class	−0.21*	0.10	0.02**	0.005	0.16*	0.07	0.03	0.020
Middle class	−0.13^	0.08	0.01^	0.008	0.10^	0.06	0.02	0.010
Upper middle class	−0.13	0.09	0.01^	0.006	0.10	0.07	0.02	0.016
Education								
High school or less	>0.00	0.04	<0.00	0.003	<0.00	0.03	<0.00	0.004
Associates degree or some college	−0.02	0.03	>0.00	0.003	0.01	0.03	>0.00	0.004
Income	−0.01	0.01	>0.00	0.001	0.01	0.01	>0.00	0.001
Resource reallocation	−0.07^	0.03	0.01*	0.003	0.05^	0.03	0.01^	0.005
Contact with Blacks	−0.10**	0.02	0.01**	0.002	0.08*	0.01	0.01**	0.003
Controls								
Recent financial hardships	−0.07**	0.01	0.01**	0.002	0.06*	0.01	0.01**	0.002
Age	>0.00	>0.00	<0.00	>0.000	<0.00	>0.00	<0.00	>0.000
Marital status	0.02	0.03	<0.00	0.003	−0.02	0.02	<0.00	0.004
Political ideology								
Conservative	−0.08	0.05	0.01^	0.004	0.06	0.04	0.01	0.007
Moderate conservative	−0.02	0.05	>0.00	0.005	0.02	0.04	>0.00	0.007
Moderate	−0.07^	0.04	0.01^	0.004	0.05^	0.03	0.01	0.005
Moderate liberal	<0.00	0.06	>0.00	0.005	>0.00	0.04	>0.00	0.006

Notes: ^$p < 0.10$; *$p < 0.05$; **$p < 0.01$.
[a]Probabiltiy weighted results presented, unweighted results available upon request.
[b]"Upper class", "bachelor's degree or higher", and "liberal" are the reference categories for socioeconomic status, education, and political ideology, respectively.

discrimination. Model 2 finds that perceiving racial equality also significantly increases the likelihood one perceives personal anti-White bias. Unlike general perceptions of anti-White bias in America, Model 3 reveals that frequent contact with Black Americans increases the likelihood Whites perceive personal anti-White bias. Model 4 shows, however, that contact with Black Americans does not condition the effect of resource allocation on one's perceptions of personal anti-White bias as hypothesized. Finally, the effects of gender, social class, resource reallocation, and contact with Black Americans hold controlling for age, marital status, recent financial hardships, and political ideology.

Table 5 presents the predicted probabilities of each level of frequency of perceived personal encounters with "reverse" discrimination. Lending additional support to the hypotheses, Table 5 reveals that males have a 0.06 lower probability of never experiencing, and a 0.05 and 0.01 greater probability of experiencing anti-White bias personally from time to time or frequently, respectively, than females. The differences in perceptions of frequency of personal encounters across status characteristics are additionally supported looking at the probabilities for social class. Those in the lower class and lower middle class have significantly lower probabilities than the upper class to never experience "reverse" discrimination as well as a higher probability, though not significantly, of frequently experiencing anti-White bias. Those that perceive racial equality also have a marginally significant lower probability of never encountering anti-White bias, and a marginally significant greater probability of frequently encountering "reverse" discrimination. The same significant pattern emerges for frequent contact with Black Americans, with the more interracial contact the lower the probability of never and the higher the probability of frequently perceiving "reverse" discrimination. While generally not significant, the patterns also hold for political ideology with higher levels of conservativeness having lower probabilities of never and higher probabilities of frequently encountering anti-White bias.

DISCUSSION

This chapter set out to achieve two central goals: present a foundational argument for status dissonance theory and apply its central propositions to understanding why some White Americans perceive anti-White bias. Building upon status construction theory (Ridgeway, 1991), status dissonance theory generally argues that one's overall status value will influence the degree they internalize normative referential structures, which provides the framework for their justice perceptions. One's feelings of injustice then create status dissonance, which results in a positional lens through which individuals perceive and interact with the social world. In an application of this logic, it was generally posited that White, lower class men are likely to believe that enough has been done to give Blacks equal rights with Whites due to their internalization of normative referential structures and resulting justice framework. In turn, these beliefs were posited to create status dissonance, increasing their likelihood of perceiving anti-White bias.

Overall, the present findings, particularly the consistent directionality, lend modest support to the status dissonance theory inspired hypotheses. Among Whites, males, those who self-identified as lower class, and the least educated have the highest odds of perceiving resource reallocation, and in turn, all of these factors increased the odds of perceiving anti-White bias generally in society as well as perceiving personal encounters of "reverse" discrimination. Furthermore, while the theorized associations between contact with dissimilar others and "broadcast processes" could not be directly assessed, the positive associations revealed in terms of frequency of contact with Blacks and political ideology lend additional modest support to status dissonance theory.

Yet, while the most disadvantaged did have the strongest odds of holding these perceptions, those holding the most advantaged statuses (i.e., the most educated, the highest income, and self-identified upper class status) had higher odds of holding these perceptions than the middle social class categories. This curvilinear association between social class indicators and perceptions of racial equality and anti-White bias align, though not presently hypothesized, with the propositions of status dissonance theory. Status dissonance theory would suggest that those in the higher classes are also highly likely to internalize normative referential structures and feel status dissonance as lower status others advance. Though, their status dissonance may not be as severe as lower class individuals due to their higher overall status that comes with wealth. As Kimmel suggests, "working-class White men my experience that sense of entitlement differently from upper-class White men, but there are also many commonalities, many points of contact" (2013, p. xii). Furthermore, this curvilinear association aligns with previous research that finds higher education, conservative ideologies, and higher incomes are positively associated with perceptions of "reverse" discrimination among Whites, particularly for males (Lynch, 1989; Mayrl & Saperstein, 2013; Pincus, 2000).

Status dissonance theory provides a framework for understanding associations such as this as well as other variations between and within different groups of people. In other words, why similarly situated people may perceive and respond differently to shifts in the social hierarchy. Overall, while the effects were not always significant or large, the directional associations presently found have significant theoretical implications as well as provide a firm empirical foundation for additional research into these proposed mechanisms.

The new status dissonance theory and the current findings begin to fill a void in the status literature. Extensive research on status threat (Blalock, 1967; Blumer, 1958; Bobo & Hutchings, 1996; Bobo, 1999) finds perceptions of increases in the proportion of people of Color and/or their influence impacts Whites' voting behaviors, political alignment, and racial attitudes (Abascal, 2015; Andrews & Seguin, 2015; Craig & Richeson, 2014a, 2014b; Enos, 2014, 2016; Outten et al., 2012; Willer et al., 2016) as well as are associated with the increased use of direct social control, such as arrests rates of people of Color (Eitle, D'Alessio, & Stolzenberg, 2002; Parker, Stults, & Rice, 2005). Yet, "status threat" is always assumed, leaving the underlying social psychological processes that lead to these feelings and their potential outcomes unassessed. The present findings and theoretical propositions provide a bridge between these literatures and lay a foundation for additional investigations into unpacking the causes and consequences of perceptions of anti-White bias as well as mechanisms to counter status hierarchies.

Furthermore, while status dissonance theory is presently presented in the context of understanding anti-White bias, it potentially has much broader implications. The same processes may explain the variations in people of Color's perceptions of and responses to experienced racial discrimination. For instance, a young, lower-class, Black man likely knows the stereotypical beliefs associated with his embodied status characteristics. Then who he associates with, the nature of those associations, and the general messages he consumes from society impact his likelihood of internalizing those stereotypes (i.e., normative referential structures). These beliefs will then impact his justice perceptions and determine his degree of status dissonance, leading him to either believe that he belongs in his current social position or not. This in turn provides his positional lens through which he sees and interacts with the world. If he has not internalized the normative referential structure and judges his opportunities in life as unjust, then he is likely to feel a status dissonance and perceive more discrimination, from microaggressions to institutional racism, in society. Whereas, if he does internalize normative referential structures, he may interpret and respond to the same discriminatory encounters differently.[15] In other words, such processes may explain variations in experiences and responses to different types of discriminatory encounters between people of Color as well.

While status dissonance theory has significant potential, this initial application suffers from several limitations, particularly from the use of secondary data. First, while the present study was able to assess associations between status characteristics, perceptions of resource reallocation, and "reverse" discrimination, it is still not a true test of status dissonance theory. The 2016 Racial Attitudes in America III Survey (Pew Research Center, 2017) has many strengths, including being a recent nationally representative survey. However, it was not developed for the present study, thus can only approximate measures of the theoretical constructs needed to fully assess the proposed propositions. While the results provide modest support for the associations between status characteristics and anti-White bias, the proposed underlying processes driving these associations may only be assumed. Future research needs primary data, from lab experiments (to establish referential structures), vignette studies (to assess justice perceptions), and primary survey data (to determine status dissonance and assess causal associations), to fully test status dissonance theory. Furthermore, this is only a foundational argument for status dissonance theory, and its propositions need further refining in conjunction with empirical evidence. Nevertheless, the present study is the first of its kind and lends support for the need for additional research with primary data into the relationships between status and various social outcomes that perpetuate and counter social inequality.

Investigations into the effects of whiteness and White privilege are becoming more prominent in the literature (e.g., McDermott, 2015; Rothenberg, 2016; Tran & Paterson, 2015), and research on the associations between "reverse" discrimination and social ills for Whites are beginning to emerge (e.g., Isom Scott & Andersen, 2018; Kendzor et al., 2014). While it is important to understand the impacts of anti-White bias, it is also important to understand where these perceptions arise from as well. This study and status dissonance theory begin to fill that gap. In general, it is vital to understand all the factors that lead to and result from social inequality. Until we understand the processes we cannot do anything effective to counter them, and the racial tensions and tribulations that result will endure. It is my hope that status dissonance theory may provide another tool to aid in that understanding.

NOTES

1. Each of these studies finds that 30–36% of their White respondents report experiencing racial discrimination.

2. Zero-sum beliefs are the perspective that gains of one group can only come at the expense of another (see Wilkins et al., 2015 for a detailed discussion).

3. Race has never been without status value in America (see Anderson, 2016 for a critique of America's racial history). The argument presented by status construction theory (Ridgeway, 1991), however, is that the theorized conditions are sufficient, but only one potential mechanism of how status value may be attached to a nominal characteristic.

4. Status construction theory (Ridgeway, 1991) draws upon reward expectations theory (Ridgeway & Berger, 1986) to provide the method by which a nominal characteristic gains status value initially. Reward expectations theory suggests when people differ in resources, these differences are used to form performance expectations (Berger et al., 1980; Ridgeway & Berger, 1986). Performance expectations are generalized beliefs about one's and others' ability to meaningfully contribute to a task. Performance expectations may be based on assumptions about one's specific capability on a given task or general stereotypes about one's group affiliation (Berger et al., 1980; Ridgeway & Berger, 1986). Thus, a resource rich actor is assumed to be more competent and capable of performing a task than a resource poor actor. This assumption is made even if the actors are equal on all fronts expect for resource allocation (e.g., both are White). Resources, thus, act as a categorical cue that informs performance expectations (Ridgeway, Berger, & Smith, 1985). Higher resources lead to higher performance expectations for the resource rich by the resource poor and the actor their self. In turn, the opposite is also true in relation to the resource poor. The performance expectations influence each actor to either participate more or less and in turn affect the perceptions of each actor as competent and/or influential. In the end, the resource rich is viewed as a worthy and competent member responsible for the accomplishment of the task. The resource poor are judged as less competent and worthy, but likely a likeable supporter of the group. The resource rich, therefore, gain high status and the resource poor gain low status in a specific social interaction (Berger & Conner, 1974; Ridgeway, 1991; Ridgeway & Berger, 1986). For a thorough overview of status construction theory, see Ridgeway (2015).

5. For instance, Katz and Cohen (1962) put their Black participants through assertion training to try to reduce White dominated mixed-race group interaction. While the intervention did increase Blacks' participation, it also evoked hostility and derogatory behavior from Whites. See Webster and Driskell (1978) for a review of this research agenda and related works as well as their citations.

6. Reflected appraisals is a concept from symbolic interactionism and suggests that our sense of self is based on how we believe others see us. See Cooley (1902) and Mead (1934) for foundational works as well as Felson (1985).

7. Research on social cognition demonstrates that people use easily recognizable differences between people, such as race, to categorize people and formulate schemas about one's self and others. See Fiske and Taylor (2017) for a comprehensive overview of these processes.

8. Distributive justice posits perceived fairness of outcomes are based on the principles of equality, equity, and need. See Adams (1965), Cook and Hegtvedt (1983), Folger (1986), and Jasso (1980) as examples of foundational works in this expansive literature. Furthermore, see Hegtvedt and Isom (2014) for an overview for the relationship between justice and inequality.

9. For instance, the shift from a manufacturing economy to a service economy, and the changes that arise in employment opportunity, earning potential, and skills needed (see Chen, 2015 for discussion).

10. For instance, Blacks moving into a formerly all-White neighborhood as they acquire more wealth. This may lead some White residents to want to move, but they may be unable to because of their financial circumstances. The situations proposed are meant to represent forced interactions between dissimilar others, which have been shown to

increase prejudicial beliefs and behaviors (Pettigrew et al., 2011). However, research also finds that amiable interactions can reduce such beliefs (Pettigrew & Tropp, 2006). Given that the present measure can only capture frequency of interactions and not nature (see Method section), the current hypothesis is presented in neutral terms.

11. http://www.pewsocialtrends.org/dataset/2016-racial-attitudes-in-america-survey/; additional details about the original study are also available at this web address.

12. The initial White subsample included 1,799 participants. Missingness of selected variables ranged from 0% to 10.5%, with the majority missing none or less than 1% of responses. Missing values for income (10.5%) and political ideology (6.6%) were replaced using multiple imputation (Rubin, 1987; van Burren, 2012) in SPSS23, which utilizes Markov chain Monte Carlo techniques to simulate random draws from nonstandard distributions (for a detailed discussion of multiple imputation using Markov chains see Gilks, Richardson, & Spiegelhalter, 1996). Three additional variables were missing less than 2% of responses (i.e., age, highest education level, and self-report social class). Given the nature of these indicators and their limited missing, listwise deletion was implemented on these factors, resulting in a final sample size of 1,750 non-Hispanic White adults.

13. Response categories are 1 = less than US$10,000, 2 = 10 to under US$20,000, 3 = 20 to under US$30,000, 4 = 30 to under US$40,000, 5 = 40 to under US$50,000, 6 = 50 to under US$75,000, 7 = 75 to under US$100,000, 8 = 100 to under US$150,000, and 9 = US $150,000 or more.

14. Interviewers asked several questions about the respondent's political affiliations and ideological leanings. From these questions, Pew researchers crafted a categorical variable labeled "Party and Ideology" that serves as the basis for the present political ideology measures. For more information on the original questionnaire and methodology, see http://www.pewsocialtrends.org/dataset/2016-racial-attitudes-in-america-survey/

15. This is not suggesting people of Color's experienced encounters with racial discrimination equate to White's perceptions of anti-White bias. Whites' privileged position in American society prohibits their *true* oppression, but many still *feel* that there is bias against them, whereas people of Color face true oppression from multiple points in society (Anderson, 2016; Hammon, 2013). Instead, I am suggesting that status dissonance theory may explain differences between people of Color recognizing different acts of discrimination and forms of oppression, the extent one is personally bothered or affected by discrimination, and how one responds to oppression. These are worthy lines of inquiry for future research.

REFERENCES

Abascal, M. (2015). Us and them: Black-White relations in the wake of Hispanic population growth. *American Sociological Review, 80*, 789–813.

Adams, J. S. (1965). Inequity in social exchange. *Advances in Experimental Social Psychology, 2*, 267–299.

Anderson, C. (2016). *White rage: The unspoken truth of our racial divide*. New York, NY: Bloomsbury.

Andrews, K. T., & Seguin, C. (2015). Group threat and policy change: The spatial dynamics of prohibition politics, 1890–19191. *American Journal of Sociology, 121*, 475–510.

Berger, J., & Conner, T. L. (1974). Performance expectations and behavior in small groups: A revised formulation. In J. Berger, T. L. Conner, & M. H. Fisek (Eds.), *Expectation States Theory: A Theoretical Program* (pp. 85–109). Cambridge: Winthrop.

Berger, J., & Fisek, M. H. (2006). Diffuse status characteristics and the spread of status value: A formal theory. *The American Journal of Sociology, 111*, 1038–1079.

Berger, J., Fisek, M. H., Norman, R. Z., & Zelditch, Jr., M. (1977). *Status characteristics and social interaction: An expectation states approach*. New York, NY: Elsevier.

Berger, J., Rosenholtz, S., & Zelditch, Jr., M. (1980). Status organizing process. *Annual Review of Sociology, 6*, 479–508.

Berger, J., & Webster, Jr., M. (2006). Expectations, status, and behavior. In P. J. Burke (Ed.), *Contemporary social psychological theories* (pp. 268–300). Palo Alto, CA: Stanford University Press.

Blalock, H. M. (1967). *Toward a theory of minority-group relations*. New York, NY: John Wiley & Sons.

Blau, P. M. (1977). A macrosociological theory of social structure. *The American Journal of Sociology*, *83*(1), 26–54.

Blodorn, A., & O'Brien, L. T. (2013). Evaluations of White American versus Black American discrimination claimants' political views and prejudicial attitudes. *Journal of Experimental Social Psychology*, *49*(2), 211–216.

Blumer, H. (1958). Race prejudice as a sense of group position. *The Pacific Sociological Review*, *1*, 3–7.

Bobo, L. D. (1999). Prejudice as group position: Microfoundations of a sociological approach to racism and race relations. *Journal of Social Issues*, *55*, 445–472.

Bobo, L., & Hutchings, V. L. (1996). Perceptions of racial group competition: Extending Blumer's theory of group position to a multiracial social context. *American Sociological Review*, *61*, 951–972.

Bourdieu, P. (1987). What makes a social class? On the theoretical and practical existence of groups. *Berkeley Journal of Sociology*, 1–17.

Brashears, M. E. (2008). Sex, society, and association: A cross-national examination of status construction theory. *Social Psychology Quarterly*, *71*(1), 72–85.

Brezina, T., & Winder, K. (2003). Economic disadvantage, status generalization, and negative racial stereotyping by White Americans. *Social Psychology Quarterly*, *66*(4), 402–418.

Bureau of Labor Statistics. (2016). *Highlights of Women's Earnings in 2015*. Retrieved from https://www.bls.gov/opub/reports/womens-earnings/2015/home.htm

Chen, V. T. (2015). *Cut loose: Jobless and hopeless in an unfair economy*. Oakland, CA: University of California Press.

Cook, K. S., & Hegtvedt, K. A. (1983). Distributive justice, equity, and equality. *Annual Review of Sociology*, *9*, 217–241.

Cooley, C. H. (1902[1922]). *Human nature and social order*. New York, NY: Scribner.

Craig, M. A., & Richeson, J. A. (2014a). More diverse yet less tolerant? How the increasingly diverse racial landscape affects White Americans' racial attitudes. *Personality and Social Psychology Bulletin*, *40*, 750–761.

Craig, M. A., & Richeson, J. A. (2014b). On the precipice of a "majority-minority" America: Perceived status threat from the racial demographic shift affects White Americans' political ideology. *Psychological Science*, *25*, 1189–1197.

Eibach, R. P., & Keegan, T. (2006). Free at last? Social dominance, loss aversion, and White and Black Americans' differing assessments of progress towards racial equality. *Journal of Personality and Social Psychology*, *90*, 453–467.

Eitle, D., D'Alessio, S., & Stolzenberg, L. (2002). Racial threat and social control: A test of the political, economic, and threat of Black crime hypotheses. *Social Forces*, *81*(2), 557–576.

Enos, R. D. (2014). Causal effect of intergroup contact on exclusionary attitudes. *Proceedings of the National Academy of Sciences*, *111*, 3699–3704.

Enos, R. D. (2016). What the demolition of public housing teaches us about the impact of racial threat on political behavior. *American Journal of Political Science*, *60*, 123–142.

Felson, R. B. (1985). Reflected appraisal and the development of self. *Social Psychology Quarterly*, *48*(1), 71–78.

Fiske, S. T., & Taylor, S. E. (2017). *Social cognition: From brains to culture* (3rd ed.). Thousand Oaks, CA: Sage.

Folger, R. (1986). Re-thinking equity theory: A referent cognitions model. In H. Bierhoff, R. L. Cohen, & J. Greenberg (Eds.), *Justice in social relations* (pp. 145–163). New York, NY: Plenum Press.

Forscher, P., & Kteily, N. S. (2017). A psychological profile of the alt-right. Preprint published online. Retrieved from https://psyarxiv.com/c9uvw

Gilks, W. R., Richardson, S., & Spiegelhalter, D. J. (1996). *Markov chain Monte Carlo in practice.* London: Chapman & Hall.
Goar, C., & Sell, J. (2005). Using task definition to modify racial inequality within task groups. *The Sociological Quarterly, 46,* 525–543.
Hammon, B. (2013). Playing the race card: White Americans' sense of victimization in response to affirmative action. *Texas Hispanic Journal of Law and Policy, 19,* 95–120.
Hegtvedt, K. A., & Isom, D. (2014). Inequality: A matter of justice? In J. D. McLeod, M. Schwalbe, & E. Lawler (Eds.), *Handbook of the social psychology of inequality* (pp. 65–94). New York, NY: Springer.
Hill Collins, P., & Bilge, S. (2016). *Intersectionality.* Malden, MA: Polity Press.
Hysom, S. J. (2009). Status valued goal objects and performance expectations. *Social Forces, 87*(3), 1623–1648.
Isom Scott, D., & Andersen, T. S. (2018). "Whitelash?" Investigating the links between perceived discrimination and crime for White Americans. Manuscript submitted for publication.
Jasso, G. (1980). A new theory of distributive justice. *American Sociological Review, 45,* 3–32.
Jones, J. M. (2008, August 4). Majority of Americans say racism against Blacks widespread. *Gallup.* Retrieved from http://www.gallup.com/poll/109258/Majority-Americans-Say-Racism-Against-Blacks-Widespread.aspx
Jones, R. P., Cox, D., Cooper, B., & Lienesch, R. (2017). *Majority of Americans oppose transgender bathroom restrictions.* Washington, DC: Public Religion Research Institute. Retrieved from http://www.prri.org/research/lgbt-transgender-bathroom-discrimination-religious-liberty/
Jones, R. P., Cox, D., Galston, W. A., & Dionne, Jr., E. J. (2011). *What it means to be American: Attitudes towards increasing diversity in America ten years after 9/11.* Washington, DC: Public Religion Research Institute. Retrieved from https://www.prri.org/research/what-it-means-to-be-american/
Katz, I., & Cohen, M. (1962). The effects of training Negros upon cooperative problem solving in biracial teams. *Journal of Abnormal and Social Psychology, 64,* 319–325.
Kendzor, D. E., Businelle, M. S., Reitzel, L. R., Rios, D. M., Scheuermann, T. S., Pulvers, K., & Ahluwalla, J. S. (2014). Everyday discrimination is associated with nicotine dependence among African American, Latino, and White smokers. *Nicotine & Tobacco Research, 16*(6), 633–640.
Kimmel, M. (2013). *Angry White men: American masculinity at the end of an era.* New York, NY: Nation Books.
Lamont, M. (1992). *Money, morals and manners: The culture of the French and the American upper-middle class.* Chicago, IL: The University of Chicago Press.
Lynch, F. (1989). *Invisible victims: White males and the crisis of affirmative action.* New York, NY: Greenwood.
Marx, K. (1867[2017]). *Capital (Volume 1: A critique of the political economy).* Overland Park, KS: Digireads.com Publishing.
Mayrl, D., & Saperstein, A. (2013). When White people report racial discrimination: The role of region, religion, and politics. *Social Science Research, 42*(3), 742–754.
McDermott, M. (2015). Color-blind and color-visible identity among American Whites. *American Behavioral Scientist, 59*(11), 1452–1473.
McGirt, E. (2016, February 1). An inside look at what's keeping Black men out of the executive suite. *Fortune.* Retrieved from http://fortune.com/black-executives-men-c-suite/
Mead, G. H. (1934[1967]). *Mind, self, and society from the standpoint of a social behaviorist.* Chicago, IL: The University of Chicago Press.
Mitchell, A., Gottfried, J., Kiley, J., & Masta, K. E. (2014). *Political polarization & media habits: From Fox News to Facebook, how liberals and conservatives keep up with politics.* Pew Research Center. Retrieved from http://www.journalism.org/2014/10/21/political-polarization-media-habits/
Müller, P., Schemer, C., Wettstein, M., Schulz, A., Wirz, D. S., Engesser, S., & Wirth, W.(2017). The polarizing impact of news coverage on populist attitudes in the public: Evidence from a panel study in four European democracies. *Journal of Communication, 67,* 968–992.

National Center for Education Statistics. (2016). *Table 326.10: Graduation rate from first institution attended for first-time, full-time bachelor's degree — Seeking students at 4-year postsecondary institutions, by race/ethnicity, time to completion, sex, control of institution, and acceptance rate: Selected cohort entry years, 1996 through 2009*. Washington, DC: National Center for Education Statistics. Retrieved from https://nces.ed.gov/programs/digest/d16/tables/dt16_326.10.asp

Newman, D. M. (2010). *Sociology: Exploring the architecture of everyday life*. Thousand Oaks, CA: Pine Forge Press.

Norton, M. I., & Sommers, S. S. (2011). Whites see racism as a zero-sum game that they are now losing. *Perspectives on Psychological Science, 6*(3), 215–218.

Ortner, S. B. (1998). Identities: The hidden life of class. *Journal of Anthropological Research, 54*, 1–17.

Outten, H. R., Schmitt, M. T., Miller, D. A., & Garcia, A. L. (2012). Feeling threatened about the future: Whites' emotional reactions to anticipated ethnic demographic changes. *Personality and Social Psychology Bulletin, 38*, 14–25.

Parker, K. F., Stults, B. J., & Rice, S. K. (2005). Racial threat, concentrated disadvantage and social control: Considering the macro-level sources of variation in arrests. *Criminology, 43*(4), 1111–1134.

Pettigrew, T. F., & Tropp, L. R. (2006). A meta-analytic test of intergroup contact theory. *Journal of Personality and Social Psychology, 90*(5), 751–783.

Pettigrew, T. F., Tropp, L. R., Wagner, U., & Christ, O. (2011). Recent advances in intergroup contact theory. *International Journal of Intercultural Relations, 35*, 271–280.

Pew Research Center. (2016, June 27). *On views of race and inequality, Blacks and Whites are worlds apart*. Retrieved from http://assets.pewresearch.org/wp-content/uploads/sites/3/2016/06/ST_2016.06.27_Race-Inequality-Final.pdf

Pew Research Center. (2017). *2016 Racial attitudes in America III Survey* [Data file]. Available from http://www.pewsocialtrends.org/dataset/2016-racial-attitudes-in-america-survey/

Pincus, F. L. (2000). Reverse discrimination vs. white privilege: An empirical study of alleged victims of affirmative action. *Race and Society, 3*, 1–22.

Resnick, B. (2017, January 28). White fear of demographic change is a powerful psychological force: Increasing diversity could make America a more hostile place. *Vox*. Retrieved from https://www.vox.com/science-and-health/2017/1/26/14340542/white-fear-trump-psychology-minority-majority

Ridgeway, C. (1991). The social construction of status value: Gender and other nominal characteristics. *Social Forces, 70*, 367–386.

Ridgeway, C. (1997). Interaction and the conservation of gender inequality: Considering employment. *American Sociological Review, 62*, 218–235.

Ridgeway, C., & Berger, J. (1986). Expectations, legitimation and dominance in task groups. *American Sociological Review, 51*, 603–617.

Ridgeway, C., Berger, J., & Smith, L. (1985). Nonverbal cues and status expectation states account. *American Journal of Sociology, 90*, 955–978.

Ridgeway, C., & Correll, S. J. (2006). Consensus and the creation of status beliefs. *Social Forces, 85*(1), 431–453.

Ridgeway, C., & Erickson, K. G. (2000). Creating and spreading status beliefs. *American Journal of Sociology, 106*, 579–615.

Ridgeway, C. L. (2015). Status construction theory. *The Blackwell Encyclopedia of Sociology*, online edition, doi:10.1002/9781405165518.wbeoss257.pub2

Ridgeway, C. L., Backor, K., Li, Y. E., Tinkler, J. E., & Erickson, K. G. (2009). How easily does a social difference become a status distinction? Gender matters. *American Sociological Review, 74*, 44–62.

Ridgeway, C. L., & Balkwell, J. W. (1997). Group processes and the diffusion of status beliefs. *Social Psychology Quarterly, 60*(1), 14–31.

Ridgeway, C. L., Boyle, E. H., Kuipers, K. J., & Robinson, D. T. (1998). How do status beliefs develop? The role of resources and interactional experience. *American Sociological Review, 63*, 331–350.

Ridgeway, C. L., & Glasgow, K. (1996). Creating and spreading status beliefs. *American Journal of Sociology, 106*, 579–615.
Rothenberg, P. S. (2016). *White privilege: Essential readings on the other side of racism* (5th ed.). New York, NY: Worth Publishers.
Rubin, D. B. (1987). *Multiple imputation for nonresponse in surveys.* New York, NY: Wiley & Sons.
Sidanius, J., & Pratto, F. (1999). *Social dominance: An intergroup theory of social hierarchy and oppression.* New York, NY: Cambridge University Press.
Stern, K. (2016, November 23). My descent into the right-wing media vortex. *Vanity Fair.* Retrieved from https://www.vanityfair.com/news/2016/11/my-descent-into-the-right-wing-media-vortex
Thernstrom, A., & Thernstrom, S. (1998). *Black progress: How far we've come, and how far we have to go.* Washington, DC: Brookings Institution. Retrieved from https://www.brookings.edu/articles/black-progress-how-far-weve-come-and-how-far-we-have-to-go/
Tran, N., & Paterson, S. E. (2015). "American" as a proxy for "whiteness": Racial color-blindness in everyday life. *Women & Therapy, 38*, 341–355.
Unzueta, M. M., Everly, B. E., & Gutiérrez, A. S. (2014). Social dominance orientation moderates reactions to Black and White discrimination claimants. *Journal of Experimental Social Psychology, 54*, 81–88.
U.S. Equal Employment Opportunity Commission. (2016). *2015 Job patterns for minorities and women in private industry.* Washington, DC: U.S. Equal Employment Opportunity Commission. Retrieved from https://www1.eeoc.gov/eeoc/statistics/employment/jobpat-eeo1/2015/index.cfm#select_label
van Buuren, S. (2012). *Flexible imputation of missing data.* Boca Raton, FL: Chapman & Hall/CRC.
Walker, L. S., Doerer, S. C., & Webster, Jr., M. (2014). Status, participation, and influence in task groups. *Sociological Perspectives, 57*(3), 364–381.
Walker, L. S., Webster, Jr., M., & Bianchi, A. J. (2011). Testing the spread of status value. *Social Science Research, 40*, 1652–1663.
Webster, Jr., M., & Driskell, Jr., J. E. (1978). Status generalization: A review and some new data. *American Sociological Review, 43*, 220–236.
Webster, Jr., M., & Hysom, S. J. (1998). Creating status characteristics. *American Sociological Review, 63*, 351–378.
Wilkins, C. L., Wellman, J. D., Babbitt, L. G., Toosi, N. R., & Schad, K. D. (2015). You can win but I can't lose: Bias against high-status groups increases their zero-sum beliefs about discrimination. *Journal of Experimental Social Psychology, 57*, 1–14.
Wilkins, C. L., Wellman, J. D., & Kaiser, C. R. (2013). Status legitimizing beliefs predict positivity toward Whites who claim anti-White bias. *Journal of Experimental Social Psychology, 49*(6), 1114–1119.
Willer, R., Feinber, M., & Watts, R. (2016). Threats to racial status promote tea party support among White Americans. Published online at http://dx.doi.org/10.2139/ssrn.2770

WHEN DO WE FEEL RESPONSIBLE FOR OTHER PEOPLE'S BEHAVIOR AND ATTITUDES?

Vanessa K. Bohns, Daniel A. Newark and Erica J. Boothby

ABSTRACT

Purpose — *We explore how, and how accurately, people assess their influence over others' behavior and attitudes. We describe the process by which a person would determine whether he or she was responsible for changing someone else's behavior or attitude, and the perceptual, motivational, and cognitive factors that are likely to impact whether an influencer's claims of responsibility are excessive, insufficient, or accurate.*

Methodology/approach — *We first review classic work on social influence, responsibility or blame attribution, and perceptions of control, identifying a gap in the literature with respect to understanding how people judge their own responsibility for other people's behavior and attitudes. We then draw from a wide range of social psychological research to propose a model of how an individual would determine his or her degree of responsibility for someone else's behavior or attitude.*

Practical implications — *A potential influencer's beliefs about the extent of his or her influence can determine whether he or she engages in an influence attempt, how he or she engages in such an attempt, and whether he or she takes responsibility for another person's behavior or beliefs.*

Originality/value of paper — *For decades, scholars researching social influence have explored how one's behavior and attitudes are shaped by one's social environment. However, amidst this focus on the perspective of the target of social influence, the perspective of the influencer has been ignored.*

This paper addresses the largely neglected question of how much responsibility influencers take for the impact their words, actions, and presence have on others.

Keywords: Influence; persuasion; social cognition; responsibility; attribution; attitudes

You made what you thought was a throwaway remark but, unbeknownst to you, it caused a colleague to reassess his career. You felt vindicated when your spouse finally heeded your pleas to start exercising, but in reality he began jogging because his doctor insisted on it. At graduation, you were both touched and surprised when a student you met only twice said she could not have graduated without your mentorship. These examples illustrate some common ways in which we may or may not influence other people's behavior and attitudes, and, moreover, ways in which we may misjudge that influence.

In this paper, we ask: How calibrated to reality are people's perceptions of their influence over others? We first motivate this research question by describing the unique perspective of a potential influencer and highlighting the importance of understanding the process of social influence from this perspective. We then differentiate the process of determining one's own responsibility for another person's behavior or attitude from outside observers' judgments of responsibility and from the process of determining one's own responsibility for chance outcomes – both questions that have been explored in other research.

Ultimately, we propose a model outlining the process by which – and the perceptual, motivational, and cognitive factors that are likely to impact when – people recognize, or fail to recognize, the extent of their influence over others' behavior and attitudes. Specifically, we identify factors that are likely to lead an influencer to (1) overclaim responsibility for a target's behavior or attitude; (2) underclaim responsibility for a target's behavior or attitude; or (3) accurately claim responsibility for a target's behavior or attitude.

WHY FOCUS ON THE PERSPECTIVE OF THE INFLUENCER?

For decades, social influence has been a central topic of study for social psychologists. As Crano and Prislin (2011) pointed out, "it could be argued that a history of social influence research is a history of social psychology" (p. 321). Similarly, Robert Zajonc (1965) claimed that "the main efforts of social psychology [are] the problem of how and why the behavior of one individual affects the behavior of another" (p. 269). As such, extensive work has been conducted on the topic of social influence, painting a rich portrait of the variety of ways – large and small – that we are influenced by the people around us. This wide-ranging body of research has demonstrated that we are influenced not only by others' overt persuasive appeals and requests (Bohns, Roghanizad, & Xu, 2014; Chaiken, 1980; Cialdini, 1987; Flynn & Lake (Bohns), 2008; Milgram, 1963; Petty & Cacioppo, 1986), but also by simply observing others' behavior (Asch,

1951; Bandura, 1961; Gino & Galinsky, 2012; Latané & Darley, 1969; Nolan, Schultz, Cialdini, Goldstein, & Griskevicius, 2008), by the subtle touch of another person (Jakubiak & Feeney, 2016, 2017; Levav & Argo, 2010), and by the mere presence of others (Bond, 1982; Boothby, Clark, & Bargh, 2014; Carver & Scheier, 1981; Zajonc, 1965, 1980). The upshot of decades of research is that our behaviors, thoughts, attitudes, beliefs, and decisions are undeniably shaped by our social environment.

However, this is only half of the social influence story. Not only are we influenced by others, but also we are a source of influence over others (Bohns, 2016). Our words, behaviors, and mere presence impact others just as others' words, behaviors, and mere presence impact us. Yet while there is extensive work on the consequences of social influence for the target of that influence, the influencer's perspective – in particular, his or her expectations and assumptions about his or her impact over others – has largely been neglected (for rare exceptions, see, Bohns, 2016; Gilbert, Pelham, & Krull, 1988; Johnson, Feigenbaum, & Weiby, 1964). In most studies of social influence, it is either taken for granted that the influencer intended to influence the target and is aware of his or her impact, or questions concerning the motivations and awareness of the influencer are ignored entirely. However, understanding influencers' beliefs about their own influence is essential to determining whether people are likely to engage in influence attempts, how they engage in such attempts, and when they take responsibility for another person's actions (accurately or not). If we think our boss is unlikely to implement a solution we propose, we are unlikely to speak up (Bohns, 2015; Milliken, Morrison, & Hewlin, 2003). If we fail to recognize the bad advice a student has derived from a misinterpretation of a comment we made, we will have no opportunity to remedy the situation.

Social influence requires at least two people. We cannot fully understand the process of social influence if we focus only on the motivations and perceptions of one.

TAKING VS ASSIGNING RESPONSIBILITY

The current paper is specifically concerned with how and when an individual takes or forsakes his or her own responsibility for another person's behavior or attitude. This is in contrast to research exploring how outside observers judge an individual's culpability for some action or consequence.

There has been a significant amount of research on this latter topic. Classic work by Heider (1958) outlined a series of conditions, adapted and modified by subsequent researchers (e.g., Cushman, 2008; Malle, Guglielmo, & Monroe, 2014; Shaver, 2012), under which an actor is likely to be deemed responsible for a given outcome. Such conditions vary by model, but include such considerations as agent causality, the foreseeability of a given outcome, the intentionality of the actor, and the seriousness of the outcome. Other work has identified additional factors that influence outside observers' attributions of an actor's responsibility for a given outcome, including the valence of the outcome (Knobe, 2003, 2004; Leslie, Knobe, & Cohen, 2006) and attributes of the potential influencer

(Gailey, 2013; Kennedy & Anderson, 2017; Leslie et al., 2006; Paharia, Kassam, Greene, & Bazerman, 2009; Sanders, Hamilton-Taylor, & Jones, 1996). For example, researchers have found that we are more likely to deem others responsible for unintended negative consequences than unintended positive ones (Knobe, 2003, 2004; Leslie et al., 2006). And research has found that the power and status of an influencer are positively correlated with whether outside observers assign responsibility for negative outcomes (Kennedy & Anderson, 2017; Sanders et al., 1996). That is, a CEO is typically judged to be more culpable for the unethical practices of his or her company than someone lower in the company's hierarchy.

While outside observers have their own cognitive biases and motivations, those biases and motivations likely diverge significantly from those of potential influencers. For example, while outside observers are more likely to judge an actor as responsible for a negative outcome than a positive one (Knobe, 2003, 2004; Leslie et al., 2006), a potential influencer will generally have the opposite inclination, being more motivated to judge him or herself responsible for a positive outcome than a negative one (Arkin, Appelman, & Burger, 1980; Bradley, 1978; Heider, 1958; Kelley, 1967; Markman & Tetlock, 2000). Similarly, while a CEO may appear to an outsider to be more culpable for organizational wrongdoing than one of his or her subordinates, the CEO is likely to see this situation differently (Fast & Tiedens, 2010). Thus, there is reason to doubt the generalizability of conclusions drawn from work on third parties assigning responsibility to others to the question of when people are likely to take or forsake responsibility for the behavior of another person they themselves may have influenced.

TAKING RESPONSIBILITY FOR OUTCOMES THAT INVOLVE HUMAN BEHAVIOR VS THOSE THAT DO NOT

Another difference between the focus of the current paper and previous research is the distinction between taking responsibility for another person's behavior or attitude and taking responsibility for an outcome that does not involve human behavior (e.g., a chance event). We are specifically interested in how individuals judge their influence over people, not random occurrences or consequences external to a person's attitudes or behaviors. Much work has explored how responsible people feel in these latter situations. For example, research on this topic has demonstrated how the fundamental human motivation to feel in control over one's environment (Fiske, 2002; Kelley, 1973) can lead to illusions of control over chance events such as coin tosses and lotteries (Langer, 1975; Langer & Roth, 1975).

This desire for control has also been used to explain self-serving biases, in which people are more willing to take responsibility for positive outcomes than negative outcomes (Arkin et al., 1980; Bradley, 1978; Heider, 1958; Kelley, 1967). For example, Markman and Tetlock (2000) found that participants who were informed that stocks they had chosen performed poorly as a result of unforeseen circumstances were more likely to deny responsibility for the outcome, claiming they "couldn't have known" about the unforeseen circumstance, than were those who were told their stocks had performed well as a result of unforeseen circumstances.

In each of these cases, however, the outcome over which an individual is claiming (or forsaking) responsibility is not another person's behavior or attitude. While some of the motivations identified by this research on claiming responsibility for such outcomes, such as a desire to feel in control of one's environment, are also likely to be pertinent when judging one's influence over another person, there are important differences between judging one's influence over a chance outcome such as a lottery or stock investment and another person's behavior or belief.

One notable difference is that the outcomes of chance events tend to be clear and conclusive. The result of a coin toss is heads or tails; a stock price either rises or falls. Thus, the only question a potential influencer must answer when considering what led to such an outcome is whether he or she caused it or could have foreseen it: Did I will that coin to come up heads? Could I have anticipated that the stock price would fall? Conversely, a change in a person's behavior or attitude is often ambiguous and uncertain. Attitudes and behaviors can change in myriad ways, making the variety of potential outcomes considerable. Moreover, targets of influence can downplay or exaggerate a change of heart or a change in behavior, making it more difficult for an influencer to accurately detect whether a given outcome has even occurred.

Further, the fact that people have intentionality means that judging whether one has influenced another person requires considering more than just one's own role in a given situation. It also requires a potential influencer to take another person's perspective and to judge how someone else's cognitions, motivations, and emotions have likely impacted his or her reaction to an influence attempt. People can be resistant or amenable to change, they can be selective in the ways they process and interpret information, and they can have emotional reactions in ways that coins and stocks cannot. Thus, determining whether one has caused another person's behavior draws from an entirely different set of social cognitive mental processes and aptitudes (e.g., perspective-taking, empathy, social prediction) than does determining whether one has caused a chance event or an outcome external to human behavior (cf. Malle et al., 2014).

HOW DO WE DETERMINE OUR RESPONSIBILITY FOR OTHERS' BEHAVIOR AND ATTITUDES?

Interpersonal influence occurs when one person changes[1] another person's attitude or behavior (Chaiken, Wood, & Eagly, 1996; Reardon, 1991). As such, for an individual to come to the conclusion that he or she influenced, and therefore is responsible for, another person's behavior or attitude, he or she must first come to the conclusion that a behavior or attitude change has taken place. If a potential influencer believes that there was no behavioral or attitudinal influence of any kind, then the matter is resolved – he or she has nothing for which to take responsibility. If, on the other hand, a potential influencer detects a behavior or attitude change, the next questions he or she must answer concern the root cause of the change. Does the potential influencer believe the other person's change in behavior or attitude is the result of some internal cause (i.e., the person herself) or some external force? And if the change is attributed to an external force, to which external force is it attributed (e.g., oneself, a different potential influencer, or other circumstances)? The answers to each of these questions will be impacted by various perceptual factors (e.g., whether the influence was immediately detectable) and motivational factors (e.g., whether the influence was intended or desirable). As such, the answers are susceptible to bias that may lead to inaccurate assessments of one's influence.

In the following sections, we organize the process of determining one's responsibility for another's behavior according to the three main questions a potential influencer must answer to arrive at the conclusion that he or she is in fact responsible: (1) Did a change occur? (2) Was the change extrinsically driven? (3) Was the change the result of something *I* said or did? For each question in the model, we describe the process involved in answering that question. We then present the perceptual, cognitive, and motivational factors that are likely to affect each of these processes and therefore moderate the potential influencer's answers. Our complete model is depicted in Fig. 1.

DID A CHANGE OCCUR? SIGNAL STRENGTH AND DETECTION OF CHANGE

Identifying a change in someone else's attitude or behavior is essentially a form of signal detection (Nevin, 1969; Wickens, 2002). That is, a potential influencer must decide whether a change is present or absent under conditions of ambiguity, which may result in the potential influencer correctly identifying a change (a "hit"), correctly assuming no change occurred (a "correct rejection"), missing a change that in fact occurred (a "miss"), or perceiving a change that was not in fact there (a "false alarm"). The accuracy with which an individual will perform this task depends on both the discriminability of the signals available that indicate a change has occurred (e.g., the observability of the influence act and/or the target's response to it), and anything that might cause the influencer to be generally more or less likely to perceive a change (e.g., self-serving motivations, cognitive limitations). Below we review the cognitive and motivational factors that are likely to moderate the strength, and resulting discriminability, of the signals arising from the influencer indicating that they have done something that could elicit a change, the signals arising from the target indicating that a change has actually taken place, as well as factors that are likely to moderate a potential influencer's bias towards detecting, or not detecting, a change.

Strength of the Influencer's Signals

One person's perceived responsibility for another person's behavior or attitude starts with an act of influence. This act can take various forms: a behavior, an argument, or even one's mere presence. Each of these forms of influence varies in terms of its signal strength, and may therefore signal a change in behavior or

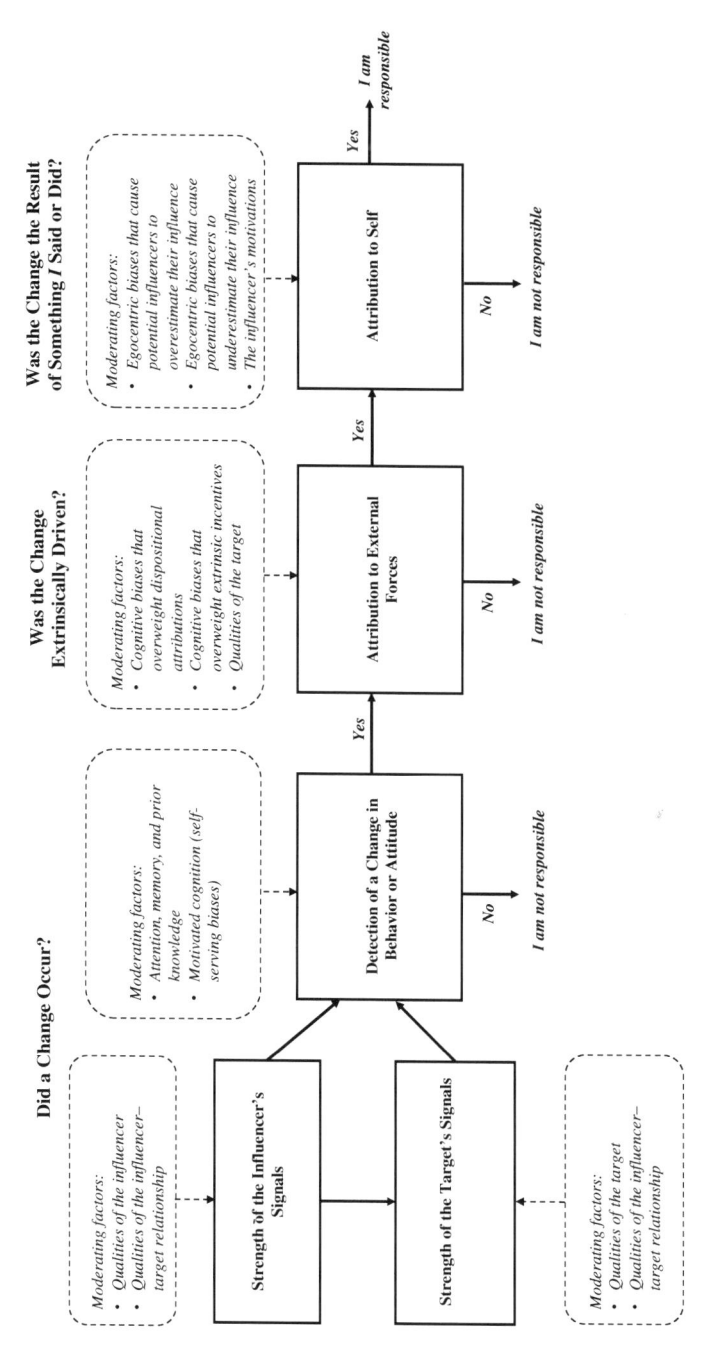

Fig. 1. A Model of How We Determine Whether We Are Responsible for Changing Someone Else's Behavior or Attitude.

attitude on the part of the influence target to varying degrees. For example, one's mere presence at an event may elicit a corresponding attitude change on the part of a target, but mere presence may be too subtle a behavior for a potential influencer to code as an act of influence, possibly causing the influencer to miss the target's resulting change in attitude. On the other hand, the act of crafting a long, carefully reasoned email is likely to be highly salient to a potential influencer and therefore coded as a clear act of influence (regardless of whether the target takes the time to read the email), potentially causing the influencer to falsely detect a change that did not occur.

Moderators of the Strength of the Influencer's Signals

Qualities of the Influencer
Some individuals may be generally predisposed to engage in clear, undeniable acts of influence. For example, individuals high on dispositional traits that entail the manipulation and influence of others, such as Machiavellianism (Jones & Paulhus, 2009; Paulhus & Williams, 2002), traits associated with an overblown sense of one's own self-importance, such as narcissism (Grijalva, Harms, Newman, Gaddis, & Fraley, 2015; Zitek & Jordan, 2016), and individuals high in trait dominance (Anderson & Kilduff, 2009) may be more likely to intentionally attempt to influence others and to do so forcefully and directly. Further, individuals who have general authority – generally higher power or status – may have a history of influencing others via direct requests and orders. Overall, these individual qualities may lead potential influencers to engage in influence acts that are easily coded as such, thus signaling the possibility of a corresponding change in attitude or behavior.

Qualities of the Influencer–Target Relationship
In addition to general authority, a potential influencer may have a specific, formal sort of authority over a target, as in the case of a professor and a student, or a boss and an employee. When the direction of influence seems one-sided, even if is not (see Bohns & Flynn, 2013; DeCremer & Tenbrunsel, 2012; Hollander & Webb, 1955), the authority figure may engage in more direct and intentional forms of influence (e.g., explicit advice, direct orders), while subordinates may engage in subtler, potentially even unintentional, forms of influence (e.g., suggesting, storytelling). Other relationship qualities, such as closeness and liking, frequency of interaction, and relationship type (e.g., hierarchical, romantic, friendship, familial), may similarly impact the form of the influence act in terms of its directness, forcefulness, and intentionality. For example, one may feel free to give direct, forceful advice to one's sibling in a way one would not to an acquaintance, and one's parents' presence or absence at an event is more likely to be coded as something that might impact a child's behavior than the presence or absence of a stranger. Overall, these qualities of the influencer–target relationship may affect the salience of the influence act and therefore whether it is coded as such.

Strength of the Target's Signals

Following an influence act is a target's response to it. A target can respond in a variety of ways to another person's influence. People can have immediate or delayed reactions to influence attempts, they can have one reaction immediately which can change with time (e.g., Cook & Flay, 1978), or they can have one reaction publicly and another privately (e.g., Wood, Lundgren, Ouellette, Busceme, & Blackstone, 1994). Relatedly, an attitude or behavior change may be small or large. All of these affect the discriminability of the change signal, making it more or less difficult for a potential influencer to detect. A change that happens an hour, a week, or a month following an influence act, or is subtle, such as a shift in attitude, will be less perceptible to the potential influencer. The extent to which an individual reacts in obvious ways (i.e., with large, immediate behavioral changes) to an influence attempt is moderated by various features of the target and his or her relationship to the influencer.

Moderators of the Strength of the Target's Signals

Qualities of the Target
Some individuals may be generally predisposed to react to influence acts in more obvious and immediate ways. For example, individuals high in trait agreeableness are motivated to maintain positive relationships (Graziano & Eisenberg, 1997). A corresponding component of agreeableness is a tendency to comply with and defer to others rather than resisting attempts at influence (Costa, McCrae, & Dye, 1991; Graziano, Jensen-Campbell, & Hair, 1996). Further, a target's preexisting attitudes and inclinations may interact with an influence act. For example, convincing someone to do the opposite of what he or she had previously intended is likely to lead to a larger and more perceptible change than just increasing slightly the person's confidence in the wisdom of what he or she already intended to do. Therefore, the first type of change should be easier to detect than the second.

Qualities of the Influencer–Target Relationship
In addition to genuinely reacting to an influence attempt to various degrees, a person may be motivated to hide or exaggerate the degree to which he or she was influenced by a particular influencer for self-presentational or relational reasons. For example, a child who follows her parents' advice may conceal that fact in order to protect her pride (Goldsmith & Fitch, 1997). Alternatively, an employee wanting to make a good impression on the boss may explicitly note or overplay the ways in which he or she has incorporated the boss's advice over the past week (Brooks, Gino, & Schweitzer, 2015). Thus, those who are influenced often have some control over how detectable any influence is to a potential influencer, and the strength of the target's signals can be impacted by motivations related to the influencer–target relationship.

Detection of a Change in Behavior or Attitude

As mentioned earlier, the accuracy with which an individual will detect a change in behavior or attitude depends both on the discriminability of the available signals (i.e., the influence act and a target's reaction to it) and any bias exhibited by the influencer that may lead him or her to be more or less sensitive to a change. Here we turn to this latter factor and review cognitive and motivational factors that may contribute to a given influencer's bias towards (or against) detecting a change in a target's behavior or attitude.

Attention, Memory, and Prior Knowledge

While there are features of the potential behavior or attitude change itself, such as its size and proximity, that make it more or less perceptible to a potential influencer, there are also features of the influencer's attention and memory that are likely to make him or her more or less attuned to potential changes. An influencer under heavy cognitive load may be less accurate in noticing a change, coding an influence attempt as such, or remembering whether an influence attempt was made. For example, a busy college professor meeting with multiple students a day may not have the cognitive resources to notice when a student seems to be particularly impacted by a piece of advice, causing her to underestimate the likelihood that an attitude change occurred. Alternatively, the same professor may not have the cognitive resources to notice when a particular student was not in class to hear a piece of advice she shared with everyone, causing her to overestimate the likelihood that an attitude change occurred in that student.

Further, memory effects may impact actual influence differently from perceived influence. For example, in a phenomenon known as the "sleeper effect," an argument made by an untrustworthy source, or an argument whose credibility is discounted in some other way, is only weakly persuasive at first, but tends to increase in persuasive strength over time as the poor credibility cue is forgotten while the content of the argument remains (Cook, Gruder, Hennigan, & Flay, 1979; Cook & Flay, 1978; Gruder et al., 1978; Hovland & Weiss, 1951; Pratkanis, Greenwald, Leippe, & Baumgardner, 1988). Thus, attitudinal change may increase with time, particularly with respect to weak initial arguments. However, a potential influencer is unlikely to understand this quirk of persuasion, and ultimately a time delay is more likely to decrease his or her memory and awareness of any attitudinal change that may have taken place.

In addition, a potential influencer may or may not be aware of a person's initial position or behavioral inclination (Rader, Soll, & Larrick, 2015). If a person already agreed with the influencer's stance on a given issue, or had already been planning to do what an influencer is trying to get him or her to do, the resulting behavior may appear to the influencer to represent a tangible change, when in fact there was no change at all.

Motivated Cognition
In addition to an influencer having limited cognitive resources, the resources he or she does have are likely to be influenced by various motivational biases. A long history of research on motivated cognition has demonstrated our tendency to see what we want to see (Kruglanski, 1996; Kruglanski et al., 2012). Thus, all else equal, an influencer who is motivated to perceive a behavior change is more likely to see one than an influencer who is motivated not to perceive a behavior change. Unlike a neutral observer, a potential influencer has a stake in the final attribution of influence that is made. This is likely to motivate the tendency to view a change for the self-serving reasons outlined earlier (Arkin et al., 1980; Bradley, 1978; Heider, 1958; Johnson et al., 1964; Kelley, 1967; Markman & Tetlock, 2000). If a potential influencer sees a behavior or attitude change as positive, she may be biased towards detecting such a change. If she sees it as negative, she may be biased towards missing it. Further, qualities of the influencer – for example, the traits of narcissism, Machiavellianism, and dominance discussed earlier – may bias a potential influencer towards detecting a change because of a general inclination to believe that one is highly influential.

WAS THE CHANGE EXTRINSICALLY DRIVEN? ATTRIBUTION TO EXTERNAL FORCES

If a behavior or attitude change is detected, the next question a potential influencer must answer concerns the root cause of the change. Does the potential influencer view the other person's change in behavior or attitude to be the result of some internal force? That is, did the target individual feel compelled to make a change for reasons stemming from *within*, or is this change attributable to some *external* cause? A potential influencer must determine whether it is likely that the target individual would have made this change on his or her own or whether there is a particularly compelling external explanation. As with the question of whether a change is detected in the first place, various cognitive and motivational factors are likely to affect the source to which a potential influencer attributes an identified attitude or behavior change.

Moderators of an Attribution to External Forces
Cognitive Biases That Overweight Dispositional Attributions
The question of whether a given behavior is attributed to internal or external forces has typically been asked with respect to the perceptions of outside observers, most notably in paradigms related to the fundamental attribution error (Jones & Harris, 1967) or correspondence bias (Gilbert & Malone, 1995). These paradigms have famously demonstrated that outside observers are more likely to say that another person's behavior is dispositionally driven than situationally driven. Indeed, these same factors are likely to play a role in the attributions made by a potential influence source; thus, one may assume that a potential influence source will be generally biased in the direction of assuming that others' actions are the result of internal factors. However, there are notable

motivational and perceptual differences between the perspectives of an outside observer and a potential influence source that may differentially affect their attributions. Thus, while outside observers are generally predisposed to assume others' behavior is internally driven, rather than externally driven, a potential influence source may not share this bias to the same degree. Considerations particular to the role of influence source will be discussed in the next section on determining the specific external source to which a behavior or attitude change is attributed.

Cognitive Biases That Overweight Extrinsic Incentives
Other research has found that outside observers tend to overweight extrinsic as opposed to intrinsic incentives when predicting and interpreting others' behavior (Heath, 1999; Miller & Ratner, 1998). For example, in a series of studies by Heath (1999), participants thought their peers' career choices were motivated primarily by pay and other extrinsic incentives (e.g., title, job security) rather than intrinsic incentives such as learning new things. And in other research, participants have been found to attribute others' prosocial actions (e.g., donating blood) to monetary incentives rather than intrinsic charitable motivations. Heath (1999) has argued that these findings differ from traditional actor–observer effects (e.g., Jones & Harris, 1967) in part because of the salient incentives, particularly money, used in such paradigms. For these reasons, the general bias towards dispositional explanations may in fact reverse when an influencer attempts to influence a target using salient extrinsic incentives. For example, someone who complies with a request in the absence of money may be viewed as doing so because of an internal desire to do so, but someone who complies with a request in exchange for a monetary incentive may be viewed as doing so because of external forces, i.e., to receive the payment (see also Bohns, Newark, & Xu, 2016).

Qualities of the Target
Finally, some targets, as a result of particular qualities they possess, are more likely to be viewed as acting of their own accord, and their behavior is therefore more likely to receive an internal attribution. For example, research has found that more powerful and/or high-status individuals are more likely to be viewed as acting of their own volition (Overbeck, Tiedens, & Brion, 2006). So, a higher status employee seen working late is more likely to be viewed as doing so because she wanted to, rather than because she has been asked. Similarly, targets who are more likely to be objectified and dehumanized, such as women and outgroup members, are perceived to possess less agency, leading perceived behavioral changes to be viewed as being more externally, rather than internally, caused (Bohns & Flynn, 2013; Gray, Knobe, Sheskin, Bloom, & Barrett, 2011; Gruenfeld, Inesi, Magee, & Galinsky, 2008).

WAS THE CHANGE THE RESULT OF SOMETHING *I* SAID OR DID? ATTRIBUTION TO SELF

Once a behavior or attitude change has been detected and it has been determined that the change was likely due to external (rather than internal) forces, the third and final question a potential influence source must answer is whether *oneself* is the specific external source responsible for the change. As with the preceding questions, various features of the interaction are likely to impact whether a potential influence source determines that he or she is ultimately responsible for the other person's behavior or attitude change.

Moderators of an Attribution to Self

Egocentric Biases That Cause Potential Influencers to Overestimate their Influence
In most cases of behavior and attitude change, there are multiple potential influence sources. A decision-maker will often consult with multiple friends and acquaintances for advice. An individual's attitudes are also shaped by things he or she reads or sees. In general, any interaction a person has is both preceded and followed by numerous interactions with other people and potential sources of information.

Nonetheless, a potential influence source may overestimate his or her influence on a target because he or she is not aware of these other potential sources of influence or does not fully consider the extent to which one of these other sources may have impacted a target. Furthermore, there are documented egocentric biases that are likely to cause potential influencers to overestimate the extent to which their actions are noticed by others – and may therefore lead them to overestimate the impact of their own influence on others. In particular, a bias known as the "spotlight effect" describes people's tendency to think others notice their behaviors and features to which they are particularly attuned, for example, tripping and falling or wearing an embarrassing outfit, more than others actually do (Epley, Savitsky, & Gilovich, 2002; Gilovich, Medvec, & Savitsky, 2000; Gilovich & Savitsky, 1999). Thus, one's own behavior – and its potential impact on others – may loom larger than the variety of alternative influencers. For example, a potential influencer may be more likely to think an embarrassing gaffe on his or her part is what ultimately caused an influencee to move away or switch seats.

Egocentric Biases That Cause Potential Influencers to
Underestimate Their Influence
On the other hand, there are documented egocentric biases that would make the opposite prediction – that we are likely to underestimate the extent to which others are attuned to our behavior, and therefore underestimate our influence. For example, research by Boothby, Clark, and Bargh (2017) has demonstrated that we tend to assume that others are paying *less* attention to us than they in fact are, a bias they describe as akin to believing one is wearing an "invisibility cloak." In these studies, participants, whether in a bustling dining hall or a quiet

waiting room with just one other person, believed that they were being noticed and observed less than they actually were. These researchers have reconciled their findings with the spotlight effect by demonstrating that people tend to overestimate the extent to which a particularly embarrassing behavior or feature is noticed by others, but underestimate the extent to which they are generally noticed by others when going about their daily lives. Thus, while we may overestimate the extent to which our embarrassing gaffes influence others, we may underestimate the effect of more subtle, everyday forms of influence, such as one's mere presence, or brief, seemingly insignificant interactions with strangers.

A different, but related, kind of bias finds that people generally underestimate the role of social factors in determining others' behaviors. Nolan and colleagues (2008) showed this with respect to outside observers who tended to discount the effectiveness of normative social influence (as opposed to informational influence; Deutsch & Gerard, 1955; Rader, Larrick, & Soll, 2017) on targets' behavior. While information about their neighbors' behavior had a larger impact on participants' actual energy consumption than information about the link between energy consumption and climate change, participants expected the latter information to be more effective at motivating others' energy consumption. Notably, Flynn and Lake (Bohns) (2008) found a similar bias on the part of influencers. In these studies, participants consistently and substantially underestimated the likelihood that others would comply with their direct, face-to-face requests, because they underestimated the power of the strong social forces that drive people to say "yes" (by making it awkward and uncomfortable to say "no") in these situations. These findings have since been replicated and extended in numerous follow-up studies (Bohns et al., 2011, 2016, 2014; Newark, Bohns, & Flynn, 2017; Newark, Flynn, & Bohns, 2014; Roghanizad & Bohns, 2017). This underestimation-of-compliance effect, like the invisibility cloak, would predict an overall tendency to underestimate one's influence over others.

The Influencer's Motivations
A variety of motivations on the part of the influencer can play a role in determining whether he or she attributes a behavior or attitude to his or her own influence. Unlike an outside observer, an influence source is an active participant in the very situation they are interpreting (Neisser, 1980). This unique perspective means that influence sources are more "cognitively busy" managing their own impressions and other aspects of the situation than an outside observer would be (Gilbert et al., 1988). It also means that they have a stake in the final attribution that is made, e.g., deciding they are responsible for someone else's positive attitude change, or their bad behavior, which is likely to motivate their attributions for the self-serving reasons described earlier (Arkin et al., 1980; Bradley, 1978; Heider, 1958; Johnson et al., 1964; Kelley, 1967; Markman & Tetlock, 2000). If the behavior, attitude, or decision change in question is positive, a potential influence source may be motivated to view him or herself as the primary contributor to the change, whereas if it is negative, a potential influence

source may be motivated to attribute the change, if not to internal factors, to another external factor (e.g., another person, stressful circumstances).

Other motivations on the part of the influencer include the control motivations described earlier. People are generally motivated to believe that they have control over their environment (Fiske, 2002; Kelley, 1973). As such, they claim to have more control than they can realistically have over chance outcomes (Langer, 1975; Langer & Roth, 1975) and collectively derived outcomes (Kruger & Savitsky, 2009). These same motivations are likely to play a role when claiming responsibility for others' behavior, particularly when an influence attempt is intentional and noticeable (Schaerer, Tost, Huang, Gino, & Larrick, 2018). In such circumstances, a potential influencer may therefore over-claim responsibility for another person's behavior or attitude.

On the other hand, research on politeness and "face" (e.g., Brown & Levinson, 1978; Goffman, 1971) suggests that people prefer to feel as if they are not pressuring others. To preserve face for oneself and one's interaction partner, the expectation is that we should take pains to maintain at least the appearance that the other party has autonomy and is complying with any request we make of his own accord. For this reason, a request such as "Can you please close the door?" is considered more polite than a directive such as "Close the door." In fact, perhaps for this reason, Flynn and Lake (Bohns) (2008) have shown that when making a request, people believe that their indirect requests (e.g., hints) will be more effective at garnering compliance when in fact direct requests are far more effective. This desire to feel one is not pressuring others may override, or at least attenuate, the desire to feel one is in control of one's environment when it comes to determining one's responsibility over human, rather than non-human, outcomes.

DISCUSSION

We have proposed a model of how a potential influencer is likely to determine whether he or she is responsible for another person's change in behavior or attitude. As part of this model, we have reviewed a series of perceptual, motivational, and cognitive factors that we argue are likely to impact when people recognize, or fail to recognize, the extent of their influence over others' behavior and attitudes. These factors can be used to determine when an influencer is likely to overclaim, underclaim, or accurately claim responsibility for a target's behavior or attitude, which in turn could impact an influencer's choice of influence tactic. Here we turn to a discussion of some ancillary factors that are also likely to affect how accurately an individual perceives his or her influence, as well as discussion of the cumulative context within which any single influence attempt occurs, and what it means to be "accurate" about one's influence over another person.

Ancillary Modes of Influence and Ancillary Outcomes

Throughout this paper, we have focused on primary modes of influence such as direct requests, intended hints, imploring gestures, or imploring facial expressions. But in addition to the things we explicitly say and do to try to influence others, there are numerous more subtle forms of potential influence of which we may be less cognizant. These include our physical beauty and other physical traits, dress, voice attributes, odor, and mannerisms. When considering the impact of our words, we may be inclined to think that what we say is all that matters, forgetting that how we say it – with what tone of voice, with what facial expression, from what physical distance – may matter a great deal.

Just as there are more minor modes of influence, there are also secondary outcomes of influence. When we ask a seated passenger to give up his subway seat we are on the lookout for whether our request caused him to give up his subway seat, and so we may be less attuned to the fact that our request may have caused him to experience certain emotions (e.g., guilt for saying no). Attempts to influence behaviors may inadvertently influence attitudes, and vice versa. Attempts to influence attitudes or behaviors may inadvertently increase or decrease emotions and affective states, such as stress. The full web of modes and outcomes of influence is considerably complex.

Cumulative Influence

For the sake of simplicity, our theory has focused on potential influencers' interpretations of single influence attempts or events: Did my friend take the advice I gave her last week? Did my impassioned speech change my mentee's opinion? However, actual influence is often more complex than a single response to a single event. Many forms of attitude or behavior change take place within a broader social context and may result from an accumulation of influence attempts over time. A person may not change her deeply held beliefs following a single conversation; however, she might change her beliefs after hearing the same message repeatedly from multiple influence sources.

Potential influencers, as well, may perceive their own attempts at influence as a cumulative process: Has my son finally listened to what I've been telling him all along? Was the tenth appeal for more staff the one that finally led my boss to this hiring decision? Thus, a question for future research and theorizing is whether potential influencers accurately perceive how influence accumulates over time.

What Does It Mean to Be "Accurate" about One's Influence over Another Person?

Inherent to a discussion of "accurate" and "inaccurate" perceptions of the effectiveness of one's influence is an assumption that there is some true, objective understanding of what influenced another person. However, what actually influenced someone and by how much is rarely clear, sometimes even to the person whose attitude or behavior has changed. Someone who experiences a change of heart or a behavioral shift cannot always clearly dole out responsibility for that shift. For example, the same motivations that might lead a target to conceal the impact of a given piece of advice from a potential influencer might similarly lead a target to conceal the impact of that same piece of advice from him or herself. Thus, while we refer to the "accuracy" of influencers' judgments of their own influence, in many cases we can really only compare one person's (the influencer's) perception to another's (the target's) perception, not to some objective reality.

CONCLUSION

We regularly try to determine the impact of our words, actions, and presence on other people: Did he notice that I wasn't there today? Was she offended by my comment? Did he take my advice to heart? Yet, how people go about making such determinations has largely been neglected, despite extensive literatures on social influence and responsibility or blame attribution. On the other hand, we regularly impact people in ways we are not aware of. Yet, there is little if any literature addressing the question of when we are likely to recognize or fail to recognize the influence we have on others. This paper offers a starting point for exploring these questions. We have proposed a model of how an individual is likely to determine his or her degree of responsibility for someone else's behavior or attitude, which includes a series of cognitive, motivational, and perceptual considerations that we believe to be both unique and critical to the process of determining or recognizing one's influence over, and responsibility for, others' behavior and attitudes.

NOTE

1. We note that "changes" here includes "strengthens" and "enforces," not merely "reverses" or "alters."

REFERENCES

Anderson, C., & Kilduff, G. J. (2009). The pursuit of status in social groups. *Current Directions in Psychological Science*, 18(5), 295–298.

Arkin, R. M., Appelman, A. J., & Burger, J. M. (1980). Social anxiety, self-presentation, and the self-serving bias in causal attribution. *Journal of Personality and Social Psychology*, 38(1), 23.

Asch, M. J. (1951). Nondirective teaching in psychology: An experimental study. *Psychological Monographs: General and Applied*, 65(4), 23–35.

Bandura, A. (1961). Psychotherapy as a learning process. *Psychological Bulletin*, 58(2), 143.

Bohns, V. K. (2015). You're already more persuasive than you think. *Harvard Business Review*.

Bohns, V. K. (2016). (Mis) Understanding our influence over others: A review of the underestimation-of-compliance effect. *Current Directions in Psychological Science*, 25(2), 119–123.

Bohns, V. K., & Flynn, F. J. (2013). Underestimating our influence over others at work. *Research in Organizational Behavior*, 33, 97–112.

Bohns, V. K., Handgraaf, M. J., Sun, J., Aaldering, H., Mao, C., & Logg, J. (2011). Are social prediction errors universal? Predicting compliance with a direct request across cultures. *Journal of Experimental Social Psychology*, 47(3), 676–680.

Bohns, V. K., Newark, D. A., & Xu, A. Z. (2016). For a dollar, would you…? How (we think) money affects compliance with our requests. *Organizational Behavior and Human Decision Processes*, 134, 45–62.

Bohns, V. K., Roghanizad, M. M., & Xu, A. Z. (2014). Underestimating our influence over others' unethical behavior and decisions. *Personality and Social Psychology Bulletin, 40*(3), 348–362.
Bond, C. F. (1982). Social facilitation: A self-presentational view. *Journal of Personality and Social Psychology, 42*(6), 1042.
Boothby, E. J., Clark, M. S., & Bargh, J. A. (2014). Shared experiences are amplified. *Psychological Science, 25*(12), 2209–2216.
Boothby, E. J., Clark, M. S., & Bargh, J. A. (2017). The invisibility cloak illusion: People (incorrectly) believe they observe others more than others observe them. *Journal of Personality and Social Psychology, 112*(4), 589.
Bradley, G. W. (1978). Self-serving biases in the attribution process: A reexamination of the fact or fiction question. *Journal of Personality and Social Psychology, 36*(1), 56.
Brooks, A. W., Gino, F., & Schweitzer, M. E. (2015). Smart people ask for (my) advice: Seeking advice boosts perceptions of competence. *Management Science, 61*(6), 1421–1435.
Brown, P., & Levinson, S. C. (1978). Universals in language usage: Politeness phenomena. In *Questions and politeness: Strategies in social interaction* (pp. 56–311). Cambridge: Cambridge University Press.
Carver, C. S., & Scheier, M. F. (1981). Self-consciousness and reactance. *Journal of Research in Personality, 15*(1), 16–29.
Chaiken, S. (1980). Heuristic versus systematic information processing and the use of source versus message cues in persuasion. *Journal of Personality and Social Psychology, 39*(5), 752.
Chaiken, S., Wood, W., & Eagly, A. H. (1996). Principles of persuasion. In E. T. Higgins & A. W. Kruglanski (Eds.), *Social psychology: Handbook of basic principles* (pp. 702–742). New York, NY: Guilford Press.
Cialdini, R. B. (1987). *Influence* (Vol. 3). Port Harcourt: A. Michel.
Cook, T. D., & Flay, B. R. (1978). The persistence of experimentally induced attitude change. In *Advances in experimental social psychology* (Vol. 11, pp. 1–57). New York, NY: Academic Press.
Cook, T. D., Gruder, C. L., Hennigan, K. M., & Flay, B. R. (1979). History of the sleeper effect: Some logical pitfalls in accepting the null hypothesis. *Psychological Bulletin, 86*(4), 662.
Costa, Jr, P. T., McCrae, R. R., & Dye, D. A. (1991). Facet scales for agreeableness and conscientiousness: A revision of the NEO Personality Inventory. *Personality and Individual Differences, 12*(9), 887–898.
Crano, W. D., & Prislin, R. (Eds.). (2011). *Attitudes and Attitude Change*. London: Psychology Press.
Cushman, F. (2008). Crime and punishment: Distinguishing the roles of causal and intentional analyses in moral judgment. *Cognition, 108*(2), 353–380.
De Cremer, D., & Tenbrunsel, A. E. (Eds.). (2012). *Behavioral business ethics: Shaping an emerging field*. New York, NY: Routledge.
Deutsch, M., & Gerard, H. B. (1955). A study of normative and informational social influences upon individual judgment. *The Journal of Abnormal and Social Psychology, 51*(3), 629.
Epley, N., Savitsky, K., & Gilovich, T. (2002). Empathy neglect: Reconciling the spotlight effect and the correspondence bias. *Journal of Personality and Social Psychology, 83*(2), 300.
Fast, N. J., & Tiedens, L. Z. (2010). Blame contagion: The automatic transmission of self-serving attributions. *Journal of Experimental Social Psychology, 46*(1), 97–106.
Fiske, A. P. (2002). Using individualism and collectivism to compare cultures – A critique of the validity and measurement of the constructs: Comment on Oyserman et al. (2002). *Psychological Bulletin, 128*(1), 78–88.
Flynn, F. J., & Lake (Bohns), V. K. B. (2008). If you need help, just ask: Underestimating compliance with direct requests for help. *Journal of Personality and Social Psychology, 95*(1), 128–143.
Gailey, J. A. (2013). Attribution of responsibility for organizational wrongdoing: A partial test of an integrated model. *Journal of Criminology, 2013*, 1–10.
Gilbert, D. T., & Malone, P. S. (1995). The correspondence bias. *Psychological Bulletin, 117*(1), 21.
Gilbert, D. T., Pelham, B. W., & Krull, D. S. (1988). On cognitive busyness: When person perceivers meet persons perceived. *Journal of Personality and Social Psychology, 54*(5), 733.

Gilovich, T., Medvec, V. H., & Savitsky, K. (2000). The spotlight effect in social judgment: An egocentric bias in estimates of the salience of one's own actions and appearance. *Journal of Personality and Social Psychology*, 78(2), 211.
Gilovich, T., & Savitsky, K. (1999). The spotlight effect and the illusion of transparency: Egocentric assessments of how we are seen by others. *Current Directions in Psychological Science*, 8(6), 165–168.
Gino, F., & Galinsky, A. D. (2012). Vicarious dishonesty: When psychological closeness creates distance from one's moral compass. *Organizational Behavior and Human Decision Processes*, 119(1), 15–26.
Goffman, E. (1971). *Relations in public: Microstudies of the public order*. New York, NY: Basic Books.
Goldsmith, D. J., & Fitch, K. (1997). The normative context of advice as social support. *Human Communication Research*, 23(4), 454–476.
Gray, K., Knobe, J., Sheskin, M., Bloom, P., & Barrett, L. F. (2011). More than a body: Mind perception and the nature of objectification. *Journal of Personality and Social Psychology*, 101(6), 1207.
Graziano, W. G., & Eisenberg, N. (1997). Agreeableness: A dimension of personality. In *Handbook of personality psychology* (pp. 795–824). New York, NY: Elsevier Academic Press.
Graziano, W. G., Jensen-Campbell, L. A., & Hair, E. C. (1996). Perceiving interpersonal conflict and reacting to it: The case for agreeableness. *Journal of personality and social psychology*, 70(4), 820.
Grijalva, E., Harms, P. D., Newman, D. A., Gaddis, B. H., & Fraley, R. C. (2015). Narcissism and leadership: A meta-analytic review of linear and nonlinear relationships. *Personnel Psychology*, 68(1), 1–47.
Gruder, C. L., Cook, T. D., Hennigan, K. M., Flay, B. R., Alessis, C., & Halamaj, J. (1978). Empirical tests of the absolute sleeper effect predicted from the discounting cue hypothesis. *Journal of Personality and Social Psychology*, 36(10), 1061.
Gruenfeld, D. H., Inesi, M. E., Magee, J. C., & Galinsky, A. D. (2008). Power and the objectification of social targets. *Journal of Personality and Social Psychology*, 95(1), 111.
Heath, C. (1999). On the social psychology of agency relationships: Lay theories of motivation overemphasize extrinsic incentives. *Organizational Behavior and Human Decision Processes*, 78(1), 25–62.
Heider, F. (1958). *The psychology of interpersonal relations*. New York, NY: John Wiley & Sons.
Hollander, E. P., & Webb, W. B. (1955). Leadership, followership, and friendship: An analysis of peer nominations. *The Journal of Abnormal and Social Psychology*, 50(2), 163.
Hovland, C. I., & Weiss, W. (1951). The influence of source credibility on communication effectiveness. *Public Opinion Quarterly*, 15(4), 635–650.
Jakubiak, B. K., & Feeney, B. C. (2016). Keep in touch: The effects of imagined touch support on exploration and pain. *Journal of Experimental Social Psychology*, 65, 59–67.
Jakubiak, B. K., & Feeney, B. C. (2017). Affectionate touch to promote relational, psychological, and physical well-being in adulthood: A theoretical model and review of the research. *Personality and Social Psychology Review*, 21, 228–252.
Johnson, T. J., Feigenbaum, R., & Weiby, M. (1964). Some determinants and consequences of the teacher's perception of causation. *Journal of Educational Psychology*, 55(5), 237.
Jones, D. N., & Paulhus, D. L. (2009). Machiavellianism. In M. R. Leary & R. H. Hoyle (Eds.), *Handbook of individual differences in social behavior* (pp. 93–108). New York, NY: Guilford Press.
Jones, E. E., & Harris, V. A. (1967). The attribution of attitudes. *Journal of Experimental Social Psychology*, 3(1), 1–24.
Kelley, H. H. (1967). Attribution theory in social psychology. In *Nebraska symposium on motivation*. Lincoln, NE: University of Nebraska Press.
Kelley, H. H. (1973). The processes of causal attribution. *American Psychologist*, 28(2), 107.
Kennedy, J. A., & Anderson, C. (2017). Hierarchical rank and principled dissent: How holding higher rank suppresses objection to unethical practices. *Organizational Behavior and Human Decision Processes*, 139, 30–49.

Knobe, J. (2003). Intentional action and side effects in ordinary language. *Analysis, 63*(279), 190–194.
Knobe, J. (2004). Intention, intentional action and moral considerations. *Analysis, 64*(282), 181–187.
Kruger, J., & Savitsky, K. (2009). On the genesis of inflated (and deflated) judgments of responsibility. *Organizational Behavior and Human Decision Processes, 108*(1), 143–152.
Kruglanski, A. W. (1996). *Motivated social cognition: Principles of the interface*. New York, NY: Guilford Press.
Kruglanski, A. W., Bélanger, J. J., Chen, X., Köpetz, C., Pierro, A., & Mannetti, L. (2012). The energetics of motivated cognition a force-field analysis. *Psychological Review, 119*(1), 1.
Langer, E. J. (1975). The illusion of control. *Journal of Personality and Social Psychology, 32*(2), 311.
Langer, E. J., & Roth, J. (1975). Heads I win, tails it's chance: The illusion of control as a function of the sequence of outcomes in a purely chance task. *Journal of Personality and Social Psychology, 32*(6), 951–955.
Latané, B., & Darley, J. M. (1969). Bystander "apathy". *American Scientist, 57*(2), 244–268.
Leslie, A. M., Knobe, J., & Cohen, A. (2006). Acting intentionally and the side-effect effect: Theory of mind and moral judgment. *Psychological Science, 17*(5), 421–427.
Levav, J., & Argo, J. J. (2010). Physical contact and financial risk taking. *Psychological Science, 21*, 804–810.
Malle, B. F., Guglielmo, S., & Monroe, A. E. (2014). A theory of blame. *Psychological Inquiry, 25*(2), 147–186.
Markman, K. D., & Tetlock, P. E. (2000). 'I couldn't have known': Accountability, foreseeability and counterfactual denials of responsibility. *British Journal of Social Psychology, 39*(3), 313–325.
Milgram, S. (1963). Behavioral study of obedience. *The Journal of Abnormal and Social Psychology, 67*(4), 371.
Miller, D. T., & Ratner, R. K. (1998). The disparity between the actual and assumed power of self-interest. *Journal of Personality and Social Psychology, 74*(1), 53.
Milliken, F. J., Morrison, E. W., & Hewlin, P. F. (2003). An exploratory study of employee silence: Issues that employees don't communicate upward and why. *Journal of Management Studies, 40*(6), 1453–1476.
Neisser, U. (1980). On "social knowing". *Personality and Social Psychology Bulletin, 6*(4), 601–605.
Nevin, J. A. (1969). Signal detection theory and operant behavior: A review of David M. Green and John A. Swets' signal detection theory and psychophysics. *Journal of the Experimental Analysis of Behavior, 12*(3), 475–480.
Newark, D. A., Bohns, V. K., & Flynn, F. J. (2017). A helping hand is hard at work: Help-seekers' underestimation of helpers' effort. *Organizational Behavior and Human Decision Processes, 139*, 18–29.
Newark, D. A., Flynn, F. J., & Bohns, V. K. (2014). Once bitten, twice shy: The effect of a past refusal on expectations of future compliance. *Social Psychological and Personality Science, 5*(2), 218–225.
Nolan, J. M., Schultz, P. W., Cialdini, R. B., Goldstein, N. J., & Griskevicius, V. (2008). Normative social influence is underdetected. *Personality and Social Psychology Bulletin, 34*, 913–923.
Overbeck, J. R., Tiedens, L. Z., & Brion, S. (2006). The powerful want to, the powerless have to: Perceived constraint moderates causal attributions. *European Journal of Social Psychology, 36*(4), 479–496.
Paharia, N., Kassam, K. S., Greene, J. D., & Bazerman, M. H. (2009). Dirty work, clean hands: The moral psychology of indirect agency. *Organizational Behavior and Human Decision Processes, 109*(2), 134–141.
Paulhus, D. L., & Williams, K. M. (2002). The dark triad of personality: Narcissism, Machiavellianism, and psychopathy. *Journal of Research in Personality, 36*(6), 556–563.
Petty, R. E., & Cacioppo, J. T. (1986). The elaboration likelihood model of persuasion. *Advances in Experimental Social Psychology, 19*, 123–205.
Pratkanis, A. R., Greenwald, A. G., Leippe, M. R., & Baumgardner, M. H. (1988). In search of reliable persuasion effects: III. The sleeper effect is dead: Long live the sleeper effect. *Journal of Personality and Social Psychology, 54*(2), 203.

Rader, C. A., Larrick, R. P., & Soll, J. B. (2017). Advice as a form of social influence: Informational motives and the consequences for accuracy. *Social and Personality Psychology Compass, 11*(8), 26–43.

Rader, C. A., Soll, J. B., & Larrick, R. P. (2015). Pushing away from representative advice: Advice taking, anchoring, and adjustment. *Organizational Behavior and Human Decision Processes, 130*, 26–43.

Reardon, K. K. (1991). *Persuasion in practice*. Newbury Park, CA: Sage.

Roghanizad, M. M., & Bohns, V. K. (2017). Ask in person: You're less persuasive than you think over email. *Journal of Experimental Social Psychology, 69*, 223–226.

Sanders, G., Hamilton-Taylor, J., & Jones, K. C. (1996). PCB and PAH dynamics in a small rural lake. *Environmental Science & Technology, 30*(10), 2958–2966.

Schaerer, M., Tost, L. P., Huang, L., Gino, F., & Larrick, R. (2018). Advice giving: A subtle pathway to power. in *Personality and Social Psychology Bulletin, 44*(5), 746–761.

Shaver, K. (2012). *The attribution of blame: Causality, responsibility, and blameworthiness*. New York, NY: Springer Science & Business Media.

Wickens, T. D. (2002). *Elementary signal detection theory*. New York, NY: Oxford University Press.

Wood, W., Lundgren, S., Ouellette, J., Busceme, S., & Blackstone, T. (1994). Minority influence: A meta-analytic review of social influence processes. *Psychological Bulletin, 115*, 323–345.

Zajonc, R. (1965). Social Facilitation. *Science, 149*(3681), 269–274.

Zajonc, R. B. (1980). Feeling and thinking: Preferences need no inferences. *American Psychologist, 35*(2), 151.

Zitek, E. M., & Jordan, A. H. (2016). Narcissism predicts support for hierarchy (at least when narcissists think they can rise to the top). *Social Psychological and Personality Science, 7*(7), 707–716.

EXPECTATIONS AND COORDINATION IN SMALL GROUPS

Antonio D. Sirianni

ABSTRACT

Purpose – *Expectations ostensibly lead to the formation of hierarchies, and hierarchies are thought to improve coordination. A simulation model is introduced to determine whether expectations directly improve coordination.*

Methodology/approach – *Agent-based simulations of small group behavior are used to determine what rules for expectation formation best coordinate groups. Within groups of agents that have differing but unknown task abilities, pairs take turns playing a coordination game with one another. The group receives a positive payoff when one agent chooses to take a high-importance role (leader) and the other chooses a low-importance role (follower), where the payoff is proportional to the ability of the "leader." When both individuals vie to be leader, a costly conflict gives the group information about which agent has a higher task-ability.*

Findings – *The rules governing individuals' formation of expectations about one another often lead to coordination that is suboptimal: They do not capitalize on the differential abilities of group members. The rules do, however, minimize costly conflicts between individuals. Therefore, standard rules of expectation formation are only optimal when conflicts are costly or provide poor information.*

Implications – *Rules that govern the formation of expectations may have served an evolutionary purpose in guiding individuals towards coordination while minimizing conflict, but these psychologically hardwired rules lead to suboptimal hierarchies.*

Originality – *This paper looks at how well empirically observed expectation-generating rules lead to group coordination by adding a game theoretic conception of interaction to the e-state structuralism model of hierarchy formation.*

Keywords: Expectation states; coordination; conflict; simulation; small groups; hierarchy

Sociological social psychologists have extensively studied how individuals in task groups form expectations about one another in the expectation states theory (EST) literature. The processes that govern expectation formation are known to reflect preexisting status differences between individuals based on status characteristics. Behavioral interaction is also known to generate expectations, often reinforcing a priori status differences. These processes generate an unequal distribution of task participation across the group. The e-state structuralism (ESS) approach has used simulation-based approaches to transform these expectation-forming processes into simple rules to demonstrate how they lead to the formation of linear hierarchies (Fararo & Skvoretz, 1986; Fararo, Skvoretz, & Kosaka, 1994; Skvoretz & Fararo, 1996).

While sociologists are (correctly) concerned with the negative consequences of hierarchical social structures, psychologists have pointed out that hierarchies in groups can be useful in solving coordination problems. When situations arise that necessitate coordinated action, hierarchical structures can help individuals quickly determine what role different individuals should take in the completion of a group task.

If we are to accept that expectation-forming rules generate hierarchy, and that hierarchy in turn improves coordination, it is a very small leap to say that the expectation-forming rules should in some way improve coordination in groups. The questions this paper asks are: How can expectation forming rules (and the way individuals behave in response to those expectations) help or hinder the coordination of groups? How efficiently do individuals in groups coordinate their actions with one another and how well does their coordination reflect the true competencies of individuals? These questions are addressed using an agent-based simulation approach, which builds upon the group modeling approach of ESS with the addition of a coordination game. In this game, two individuals simultaneously decide whether to perform the "high-importance" or "low-importance" role in a cooperative task. These roles are abbreviated by the words "lead" and "follow," respectively. (These terms are not meant to imply that the high-importance task necessarily involves one individual directing the other.) A positive payoff is received if and only if both individuals choose opposite roles. The positive payoff is correlated to the task-ability of the individual who selected the high-importance (leader) role. If both individuals choose to "lead," a "conflict" occurs: This gives an indication of the higher ability of the agent to the group, but at a cost.

The paper begins with a brief review of the rules that are thought to generate expectations in humans and animals, and how these expectations lead to the generation of hierarchical group structures. The proposed functions of hierarchy for social coordination are then discussed. Group coordination problems are then parameterized into a series of games between pairs of individuals. Standard expectation-forming rules found in the sociology, psychology, and animal behavior literature are parameterized. The expectations these rules generate then guide agent decision-making in pairwise coordination games played within a group. The ability of a group to optimally coordinate action is measured by their collective performance in said games. The presence of certain expectation-forming rules can accelerate the process of coordination, but at the expense of coordination quality. Furthermore, it is found that the costs and benefits of two individuals having conflicting expectations of who will "lead" has a large influence on which sets of expectation-forming rules are best for group coordination.

EXPECTATION FORMATION IN UNDIFFERENTIATED GROUPS

EST is a theoretical research program within the field of social psychology that is primarily concerned with how certain individuals in task groups are given more prestige and influence than others. Similarly, the question of how hierarchical social structures and pecking orders emerge in groups of animals is also of interest to scholars of animal behavior. In both cases, individuals have expectations about whether other individuals are above or below them in a social hierarchy, and individuals claim (or are given) resources and influence accordingly.

There are two main mechanisms that lead to these expectations: visible attributes and prior interactions. Visible attributes that generate hierarchy range from socially privileged status characteristics (Berger, Cohen, & Zelditch, 1972), such as gender (Ridgeway, 2015), in humans, to physical size and athletic ability in animals and adolescent humans (Morgan et al., 2000; Savin-Williams, 1979; Whiteman & Cote, 2004). Prior interactions typically take the form of an observable dominance behavior directed from one individual to another. In a task group of humans, an act of dominance may take the form of a nonverbal cue (such as eye gaze) (Ridgeway, 1987), or a direct verbal act such as an interruption of another speaker (Smith-Lovin & Brody, 1989) or even a humorous remark (Robinson & Smith-Lovin, 2001). In an animal group, an act of dominance may be a peck or a bite (Chase, 1974). This paper is focused on how prior interactions between pairs of individuals, and the reaction of other individuals to these interactions, sort and coordinate groups of individuals who have no distinguishable differences in visible attributes.

Research on both human task groups and animal hierarchies similarly find that observable interactions between pairs of individuals influence both their perceptions of others, and others' perceptions of them. This phenomenon at its most basic level has been documented in triads of chickens: The chicken who pecks another chicken first is found more likely to peck a bystanding third chicken, and the chicken who was pecked first is more likely to be pecked by the bystanding chicken (Chase, 1982). Initial acts of dominance within a group are thought to influence individuals in multiple ways: There is a winner effect, where individuals who perform acts of dominance are emboldened, a loser effect where individuals who are dominated become more submissive, and a bystander effect where a third individual witnessing an interaction is more likely to dominate the interaction's submissive member and submit to their dominant member. These effects enhance an individual's estimate of the "resource holding potential" (RHP) of themselves and others (Parker, 1974). RHP is an animal's broadly defined ability to use their physical dominance to hold onto access to food, territory, reproductive partners, etc. These effects function differently by species (Hsu, Earley, & Wolf, 2006), and the presence of different effects in a population has been shown to influence the process of group hierarchy formation (Dugatkin, 1997; Dugatkin & Earley, 2003).

Studies of animal groups tend to focus on the task of resource distribution, which is inherently more zero-sum than the types of activities studied experimentally in the literature on status characteristics. Just as animals use cues to assess their RHP and the RHP of their opponents, the actions and interactions of individuals in a task group may influence assessments of competence. A main branch of EST research concerns itself with the influence of interactions on the formation and maintenance of power and prestige orders, where evaluations and expectations work in tandem to produce high levels of inequality in group participation (Fisek, 1974; Fisek, Berger, & Norman, 1995; Wagner & Berger, 2002). Early experiments in this area demonstrated that individuals who have high initial performance expectations have greater influence over others as a group process continues (Berger & Conner, 1969). As such, an early display of dominance (such as an eye gaze, joke or interruption) or competence (display of expertise with regards to the task at hand, Ridgeway, 1987) by an individual can lead to their stable position of high influence within a group.

FROM EXPECTATION TO HIERARCHY

The importance of observable attributes and interactions for the formation of hierarchies have been considered by observers of both human and animal groups. Generally, the stability of linear hierarchies is attributed to the observability of dominant behavior by individuals and the influence it has on members of the group; whereas the position of individuals within a linear hierarchy is correlated with individual attributes. Stable linear hierarchies in cichid fish emerge as a product of social interaction, as opposed to differences in individual attributes (Chase, Tovey, Spangler-Martin, & Manfredonia, 2002). Further work on models of animal hierarchies has suggested not only that individual attributes are insufficient for hierarchy formation in small groups, but that the influence of an interaction on the two participants alone (winner effects and loser effects) are also insufficient; other individuals in the group observing interactions are necessary (Chase & Lindquist, 2016).

Within the sociological literature, a compelling synthesis of the importance of attributes and interactions, as well as accounts of animal behavior, is introduced by ESS (Fararo & Skvoretz, 1986). The ESS approach unifies the EST literature with research focused on the structure of social networks. This work also draws upon empirical studies of animal pecking order formation by Chase and his colleagues to empirically verify their theory. Work in the ESS literature uses a simulation approach to demonstrate that the probability of a linear hierarchy emerging in a group is a function of how likely a pairwise interaction is to create a dominance relation between two actors, and how likely the pairwise interaction is to have an influence on the dominance behavior between the two actors and other members of the group. Later work shows how the salience of status characteristics can improve the probability of a stable hierarchy emerging in a group (Skvoretz & Fararo, 1996).

FUNCTIONALITY OF HIERARCHY

Sociologists correctly concern themselves with how quickly and drastically structurally relevant attributes and psychological mechanisms can generate (and reproduce) differences in status (where status is the deference shown to an actor by others) and arrange individuals in a hierarchical pattern within a small group. To the extent that hierarchies create and reproduce inequality, sociologists are concerned with the consequences of hierarchy. However, the proposed functions of hierarchy should be thoroughly considered as well. Hierarchies are thought to help facilitate intra-group coordination in groups (Van Vugt, Hogan, & Kaiser, 2008). Anderson and Brown (2010) provide an excellent review of the three main functions of hierarchy in the sociological and psychological literature. First, hierarchies are thought to enhance collective decision-making in a group. Groups tend to give higher rank to members who exhibit superior abilities, thus improving the performance of the group (Berger, Rosenholtz, & Zelditch, 1980). Second, hierarchies motivate members of the group to behave pro-socially and perform the collective task to the best of their abilities, by assigning higher rewards to higher-ranking members (Berger et al., 1972). Third, hierarchy facilitates intra-group coordination given that individuals accurately perceive their position in a hierarchy. Anderson and Willer argue that this functionality persists even though it is bounded by the problem of self-interested individuals within a hierarchy, and the difficulties of correctly assigning merit to status (2014).

A linear transitive hierarchy would address the first proposed function if there is a correlation between hierarchical position (status) and the ability of individuals. The second proposed function, the motivation of high-ability individuals, is dependent on how payoffs are correlated with status. A linear hierarchy only addresses this to the extent that payoffs are associated with position. Fulfilling this second function is more dependent on how the reward distribution of the task motivates high-ability individuals to pursue status. The emergence of a linear transitive hierarchy would successfully address the third function of a hierarchy. If a coordination is considered to be a two-person interaction where one individual assumes a dominant or high-importance role and another assumes a deferential or low-importance role, and all agents are at a consensus as to who should be dominant and who should be deferential in each interaction, then all problems of coordination are solved by a perfectly linear hierarchy

Using the theoretical model proposed by the creators of ESS as a starting point, the successful coordination of a series of pairwise interactions will be used to measure the efficacy of various expectation-forming rules. By conceiving of group actions as a series of pairwise coordination games (that are observable to the group), the ability of empirically observed expectation-forming rules from studies of task groups and animal pecking orders to successfully coordinate a group can be tested via simulation.

MODEL OF GROUP COORDINATION

Whereas some social psychologists are concerned with how hierarchical structure emerges from expectations, and others are more focused on how hierarchical structure solves problems of coordination, the model of small group interaction presented is not explicitly concerned with the presence of a hierarchy. While the measured transitivity of expectations between individuals (hierarchy) is correlated with both the rules governing expectation formation and the overall levels of coordination within the group, the model presented addresses how the expectation forming rules directly influences the quantity and quality of group coordination. The measured levels of hierarchy present in the group are merely a mathematical side-effect.

The model of small group behavior outlined consists of three main components: a series of interactions between individuals, expectations that individuals hold of how they should interact with others, and rules that govern how individuals form these expectations. Expectations and expectation-forming rules have been used in the previously mentioned models of small group behavior in the ESS literature. However, where individuals in ESS models take turns directing actions of dominance at one another, individuals in the conception of small group behavior presented here engage in bidirected coordination games. This alteration turns the dependent variable of interest from the transitivity of the network of dominance relations to the quantity and quality of coordinated behavior.

This model will be explicated piece by piece, beginning with the basic structure of the game that pairs of individuals play with one another. Following this, the underlying expectations and rules that determine how individuals play each game with each other will be outlined.

Coordination "Game" with Sensitivity to Initial Attributes

Group behavior is fundamentally modeled as a series of pairwise interactions between individuals, where the other members of the group witness the outcome of each interaction. A pairwise approach to study problems of social order is far from novel. The problem of trust and cooperation in a society has been framed and examined extensively as a Prisoner's Dilemma game (Rapoport & Chammah, 1965). Whereas cooperation and trust games are primarily interested in how two individuals choose to behave altruistically or selfishly, coordination games in their purest form are interested in how actors synchronize their actions.

Earlier work in EST has framed pairwise expectations as a situation where both individuals have one of two possible expectations about one another (Berger & Snell, 1961). If each expectation translates to a different action, we can treat the problem of social coordination as a pairwise game that rewards complimentary sets of expectations. What is best for the individual is best for the pair (and in this case, the larger group).

Optimal and Suboptimal Coordination

In a simple form of a coordination game, individuals will both receive a positive payoff for correctly anticipating the action of their opponent, and no payoff otherwise. Each individual chooses between playing a "high-importance" role (which could also be referred to as a "dominating" or "leading" role) and a "low-importance" role (which could also be referred to as "deferential" or "following" role). If both individuals choose opposite roles, they will be successfully coordinated, and they will receive a positive payoff. However, not all coordinations are created equal: The payoff received will correspond to the ability of the individual in the "high-importance" role, so both individuals benefit if the higher-ability person assumes the dominant role in a successful coordination.

Miscoordination and Conflict

Miscoordinations differ as well. A situation where both individuals behave deferentially will not only result in a successfully coordinated action, but will also not result in a potentially costly struggle between two dominant individuals. Advances in ESS have allowed for the possibility that individuals may not share perceptions about who is dominant in a pair (Fararo et al., 1994). This is referred to as being in a state of conflict, which is settled in the updated ESS model by randomly drawing a tie from one individual to the other. Empirically, it has been found that cases of conflict and violence are most likely to emerge between two individuals of similar social status, whose position relative to one another is ambiguous (Gould, 2003). Similarly, experimental evidence suggests that two individuals mutually perceiving themselves to be higher in status than one another (upward disagreement) may cause those individuals to contribute less, thereby harming the group (Kilduff, Willer, & Anderson, 2016). These findings reinforce an underlying benefit of the quick formation of performance expectations and stable hierarchies: the minimization of intergroup conflict. But they also highlight the function of conflict proposed by Simmel (1904): Conflict is necessary to "remove the dualism and arrive at some form of unity." In the model presented here, conflict results in revealing information about which of the two agents has a higher ability and will therefore be superior in the high-importance role. This information will be correct between 50% and 100% of the time depending on the magnitude of the ability difference between the two agents, and a fixed parameter that alters the result of the conflict from perfectly random (a coin-flip) to perfectly indicative of superior ability.

The form of the game ultimately reached not only resembles the game of "leader," an asymmetric and nonzero-sum game which has been used as a framework for discussing problems of asymmetric coordination in groups (Rapoport & Guyer, 1978; Van Vugt, 2006), but also incorporates the costly conflict element of "Hawk-Dove" or "Chicken" games (Rapoport & Chammah, 1966). Unlike these games, however, payoffs are received at the group level and are therefore always equal for both actors. Suboptimal outcomes are due to miscoordination, not selfishness.

Broadly, there are four types of outcomes: optimal coordination, suboptimal coordination, mutual deference, and conflict. More specifically, the payoff of deference is 0, and the payoff of a coordination is in proportion to the ability of the leading agent. If conflict is the result, the payoff is a signal (of variable quality) of which agent has better leadership ability. (Conflicts may also have a cost, which is a parameter that can be varied in the overall model.)

The specific consequences of each interaction for the group are shown in Table 1. As an abbreviation, "lead" is the term used when an individual pursues the high-importance (or dominant) role in the interaction, and "follow" is the term used when an individual pursues the low-importance (or deferential) role in the interaction. Further, when an agent i takes on the high-importance role and an agent j takes on the low-importance role, it is said that i "leads" j, and j "follows" i. Table 1 differs from the payoff matrices associated with traditional games, because payoffs are presented in terms of the overall group instead of the individual members. While individually rational people may face a dilemma in terms of choosing between leading and following as an inferior agent if leaders receive a disproportionate reward, the decisions of agents in this model are determined automatically by preformed expectations, not utility maximizing calculations.

In the simulations that are conducted, one individual in each group is assigned an ability of $i/(n + 1)$, where n is the number of individuals in the group and i is an integer between 0 and $n + 1$. In a group of 6 individuals, for example,

Table 1. The Outcomes and Group Payoffs for Each Combination of "Lead" and "Follow" Behaviors for a Pair of Agents with Differing Leadership Abilities.

	Superior Agent Plays "Lead"	Superior Agent Plays "Follow"
Inferior agent plays "lead"	Outcome: Conflict Group payoff: Information on better leader, cost of conflict	Outcome: Inferior agent leads coordination Group payoff: Proportional to ability of inferior agent
Inferior agent plays "follow"	Outcome: Superior agent leads coordination Group payoff: Proportional to ability of superior agent	Outcome: Mutual deference Group payoff: None

Note: The simulations of group behavior presented are based on a series of these interactions.

agents would have abilities of 1/7, 2/7, 3/7, 4/7, 5/7 and 6/7. In a group where all individuals coordinate but there is no correlation between ability and who "leads" a coordination, the average payoff will eventually converge to 1/2 — the average individual ability. In a group that is perfectly coordinated, and where the higher-ability agent always leads, the average payoff will eventually converge to 2/3.[1]

FORMING EXPECTATIONS

The proposed model considers a small group interaction as a series of coordination games that are played between randomly selected pairs of individuals. All individuals can observe the result of every coordination, failed coordination, and conflict that they participate in with another group member, or that two other members of their group participate in. These observations and memories become the basis of their expectations for how to participate in future interactions.

This pairwise framing of a small group process resembles what is proposed in the ESS framework, where the group process is conceived as a series of directed "attacks" from one actor to another, and actors form expectations in response to said attacks (Fararo & Skvoretz, 1986).[2]

Expectations should cleanly translate into behaviors (Balkwell, 1991). An expectation, E_{ij}, can be thought of as an individual i's predisposition towards a hypothetical interaction with another individual, j. Each individual in the model harbors one of three possible expectations for a potential interaction with each other person in the model, and these expectations map onto the behaviors that individuals select for each interaction. An individual may expect that they would behave in a dominant ($E_{ij} = 1$) or deferential ($E_{ij} = -1$) manner towards an individual in an upcoming interaction, or they may not hold any expectations at all ($E_{ij} = 0$).

The extent to which individuals behave dominantly (choose to play "lead") as opposed to deferentially (choose to play "follow") when they have an unformed expectation of another individual could take on any value between 0 and 1. In order to keep the model parsimonious these values will take on the preset values of 0, 0.5, or 1. Individuals either default to deferential behavior (0), randomly decide how to behave (0.5), or default to dominant behavior (1). This parameter is referred to as "default dominance."

Interacting actors update their expectations about other actors, and other (bystanding) actors update their expectations about the interacting actors, following each specific pairwise interaction. There are three initial mechanisms parameterized for the model that are discussed in the literature on ESS and animal pecking orders (Chase, 1982; Dugatkin, 1997; Fararo & Skvoretz, 1986; Skvoretz & Fararo, 1996). Whether or not each actor either forms or updates their expectation is a function of the mechanisms discussed, and the signal given by the interaction. The three expectation forming mechanisms have different names in the literature, but are renamed here as 1st Person, 2nd Person, and 3rd Person effects:

1st Person Effect: This is a synthesis of what are referred to as "Winner Effects" and "Loser Effects" in the previous literature. The 1st Person Effect causes individuals to form expectations of how they will behave towards others after they have had an interaction with one individual. If *i* defeats *j* in a conflict, or leads *j* in a coordinated action, *i* forms a dominating orientation towards other actors with a certain probability if *i* currently holds no expectations of them. Likewise, *j* forms a deferential expectation towards other actors if *j* holds no preexisting expectations of them.

2nd Person Effect: This is referred to as the "Specific-pair Effect" in the previous literature. The 2nd person effect causes an individual to form expectations of how they will behave towards an individual with whom they have just interacted. If *i* defeats *j* in a conflict or leads *j* in an interaction, then *i* develops a dominant expectation (meaning *i* expects to be the dominant individual in future interactions) towards *j* if *i* holds no prior expectation towards *j*, and *j* develops a deferential orientation towards *i* if *j* holds no expectation towards *i*.

3rd Person Effect: This is referred to as the "Bystander Effect" in the previous literature. The 3rd Person Effect causes individuals to form expectations of others based on interactions they observe, as oppose to actions they participate in. If *i* defeats *j* in a conflict, or leads *j* in a coordinated action, each other actor forms a deferential expectation towards *i* if they previously held no expectation towards *i*. Likewise, each actor forms a dominant expectation towards *j* if they previously held no expectation towards *j*.

The three values of default dominance, and the binary presence of each of the three expectation formation effects discussed generates 24 different combinations of parameters ($3*2^3$). This is implemented by converting the parameters into lists of values that serve as instructions for how individuals should form expectations about other individuals in response to different events, and three different values for how they should play the game in accordance with different expectations. (This process draws on the automata approach used in the other studies of game theory and is explicated more thoroughly in a technical appendix for the interested reader.) A more nuanced analysis may break up one or more of these three effects into positive and negative subsets. For example, an individual may only use 1st person effects to form dominant expectations, and 3rd person effects to form deferential expectations, and 2nd person effects to form either. But even such a simple complication would demand the analysis of eight-times as many configurations. The introduction of a far greater number of more nuanced rule sets is possible, but it would lead to a less parsimonious, tractable, and theoretically grounded analysis.

RULE SET PERFORMANCE IN TWO DIFFERENT "GAMES"

Two scenarios are first considered – one scenario where conflicts are very useful in determining who is superior at task performance (the high-ability agent wins a conflict with a probability very close to 1.0), and conflicts are not costly (no

Expectations and Coordination in Small Groups 191

points are deducted from the group's final payoff) – and another scenario where conflicts do not accurately determine who is better in a task (the high-ability agent wins with a probability of 0.5), and conflicts are costly (five points per conflict are deducted from the group's final payoff). These are referred to as Scenario A and Scenario B, respectively.

For each scenario, all 24 possible rule combinations are considered. One hundred simulations of a group of six are conducted, and each group participates in 1,000 pairwise interactions. Table 2 shows the results of each rule set for both scenarios.

The best rule set for the Scenario A only includes the 2nd person effect and has a default dominance level of 1 (individuals default to "lead" when they hold no expectations about their interaction partner). The average number of conflicts is 15 exactly, which is the total number of possible pairings in each group of six. In these scenarios, each individual pair has a single conflict to determine who is the superior leader among them, and then interacts in accordance with that expectation moving forwards.

The next most successful expectation formation rule set after this incorporates 1st person, 2nd person, and 3rd person effects has a default dominance level of 1. In this case, there is an average of only 1.65 conflicts, and as a result there is imperfect information about superior agent performance. Only about two-thirds of coordinations are optimal. This is much less than the nearly perfect coordination optimization of the "2nd person only" rule set, yet it is much better than 50% that would be expected with random behavior, and is accomplished with an average of fewer than two conflicts as opposed to 15 conflicts. Furthermore, the "1st–2nd–3rd person" rule set is far more robust to lower levels of default dominance. When default dominance is set to 0.5, an average of 97.75 conflicts occur before the "2nd person only" rule set optimizes. Somewhat paradoxically, consistently defaulting to dominant behavior causes less conflict than defaulting to dominant behavior 50% of the time.

When attention is turned to Scenario B, where each conflict comes at a cost of five points to the group and provides somewhat less information, the best three rule sets all use the 1st person and 2nd person effect. The outcomes of these three rule sets are displayed in rows 2–4 of Table 2. These rule sets minimize conflict, which comes at a high cost and provides no benefit in this scenario. In Scenario A, there is a wide range of the percentage of conflicts that are optimized: from 50% to 100%. In Scenario B, almost all rule sets that facilitate coordination at all have optimized coordination levels of roughly 50%, which is what would be expected by chance.

In both scenarios, there are rule sets that fail to generate coordination entirely. Some of these are not surprising. One example is the rule set where each individual uses no expectation forming rules and defaults to deferential behavior. In this case, there would be no mechanism leading an individual to ever develop an expectation to play "lead," and no one leads in the absence of that expectation.

More interesting is the "1st–3rd" person rule set with a default dominance level of 0.0. In this case, individuals can form expectations about everyone

Table 2. Payoffs and Outcomes for 24 Different Sets of Expectation-forming Rules and Probabilities of Defaulting to Dominant Behavior in Two Different Scenarios. Rows Are Sorted by the Rule Set's Performance in Scenario A.

Rule Set	Scenario A: No-cost, High-information Conflicts				Scenario B: High Cost, No information Conflicts			
(1st Person Effect–2nd Person Effect–3rd Person Effect–Default Dominance)	Average Payoff	Total Coordination (%)	Coordinations Optimized (%)	Average Conflicts	Average Payoff	Total Coordination (%)	Coordinations Optimized (%)	Average Conflicts
0–1–0–1	654.62	98.50	98.15	15.00	409.60	98.50	48.31	15.00
1–1–1–1	571.63	99.84	66.60	1.65	498.75	99.83	52.03	1.70
1–0–1–1	557.98	99.81	62.78	1.88	499.92	99.81	52.36	1.91
1–0–1–0.5	518.78	99.89	54.64	0.52	500.01	99.89	50.93	0.54
1–1–1–0.5	513.87	95.57	58.82	11.04	374.74	94.48	52.54	22.10
1–1–1–0	426.72	81.35	55.94	180.29	−432.76	82.52	49.09	168.62
0–1–0–0.5	360.30	62.39	71.34	97.75	−153.57	63.46	52.83	95.57
0–1–0–0	334.21	66.37	50.69	316.23	−1,381.42	63.93	51.54	340.40
0–1–1–1	332.06	51.24	83.34	292.95	−1,346.34	51.08	52.49	321.91
1–0–0–1	325.01	50.12	84.44	293.71	−1,407.70	47.21	51.56	329.03
0–0–1–1	322.08	49.20	83.63	295.12	−1,335.24	48.48	50.09	316.11
1–1–0–1	314.62	50.66	82.77	314.95	−1,258.52	51.45	51.41	303.40
1–0–0–0.5	305.59	51.76	68.57	224.48	−651.72	53.93	48.43	183.29

0-1-1-0.5	291.75	51.01	67.31	243.64	-956.21	51.25	47.94	241.81
1-1-0-0.5	285.40	51.67	61.39	209.29	-828.30	51.35	47.07	215.84
1-1-0-0	282.17	53.33	54.75	247.38	-887.71	53.10	48.51	229.71
0-0-1-0.5	279.94	52.01	61.10	218.94	-793.97	53.04	51.41	212.90
0-1-1-0	264.87	51.26	54.74	224.42	-926.00	53.09	49.42	238.39
0-0-0-0.5	249.68	49.95	50.16	250.78	-993.54	50.28	49.59	248.79
0-0-0-0	0.00	0.00	—	0.00	0.00	0.00	—	0.00
0-0-0-1	0.00	0.00	—	1,000.00	-5,000.00	0.00	—	1,000.00
0-0-1-0	0.00	0.00	—	0.00	0.00	0.00	—	0.00
1-0-0-0	0.00	0.00	—	0.00	0.00	0.00	—	0.00
1-0-1-0	0.00	0.00	—	0.00	0.00	0.00	—	0.00

except the individual with whom they are directly interacting, yet the unwillingness of anyone to lead in the absence of an expectation to lead, or to form dominant expectations towards they interact with, leads to a group of people who solely play "follow."

RULE SET PERFORMANCE IN VARIABLE SCENARIOS

The two scenarios in the initial analysis are meant to provide examples of opposite situations: One where the coordination quantity is the sole driver of the overall group success, and another where the coordination quality is important. The difference between these two scenarios is encapsulated in two variables associated with the conflicts that occur between agents: The cost of the conflict and the quality of information that the conflict provides. These two dimensions can be varied to create an imaginary plane, of which Scenario A and Scenario B sit at opposite corners.

The quality of the information can be thought of as how accurately a conflict correctly identifies the agent of superior ability, which can be varied with a single parameter. Consider the following formula for how likely agent i with ability a_i is to defeat agent j with ability a_j in a conflict.

$$\frac{a_i^d}{a_i^d + a_j^d}$$

The parameter d in this model is used to manipulate the determinism of the conflict. If d is equal to 1, then the odds of an agent winning is a function of the ratio of its ability to its opponents. An agent of ability 1/2 has 4:3 odds ($p = 3/7$) of defeating an agent of ability 2/3. As d approaches 0, the probability of the better ability agent winning approaches 0.5, regardless of the size of the ability gap between the two agents. As d approaches infinity, the probability of the better ability agent winning approaches 1, regardless of the size of the ability gap.

For this second set of simulations, 11 different values (0, 0.05, 0.1, 0.2, 0.5, 1, 2, 3, 4, 5, and 10) are considered for the determinism parameter, d, and the cost of conflict, c. For each pair of values for c and d, 1,000 simulations of 1,000 interactions each are run for each of the 24 different rule sets defined in the first part of analysis. The rule set that performs best for each of these 121 different scenarios is mapped in Fig. 1. In total, only 4 of the 24 different rule sets performed optimally in at least one of these scenarios.

The rule set that only uses 2nd person effects with a default dominance of 1.0 (0–1–0–1) is dominant in the space, where conflict cost is low and conflict benefit is high. In these scenarios, the best outcome for the group is guaranteed by making sure that each pair uniquely determines who will best lead their interaction. There is an absence of any effect that occurs beyond the individual pair interacting, as neither individual in the pair forms an expectation of behavior towards anyone outside the pair, and no one outside the pair forms an expectation towards anyone inside of the pair.

Expectations and Coordination in Small Groups 195

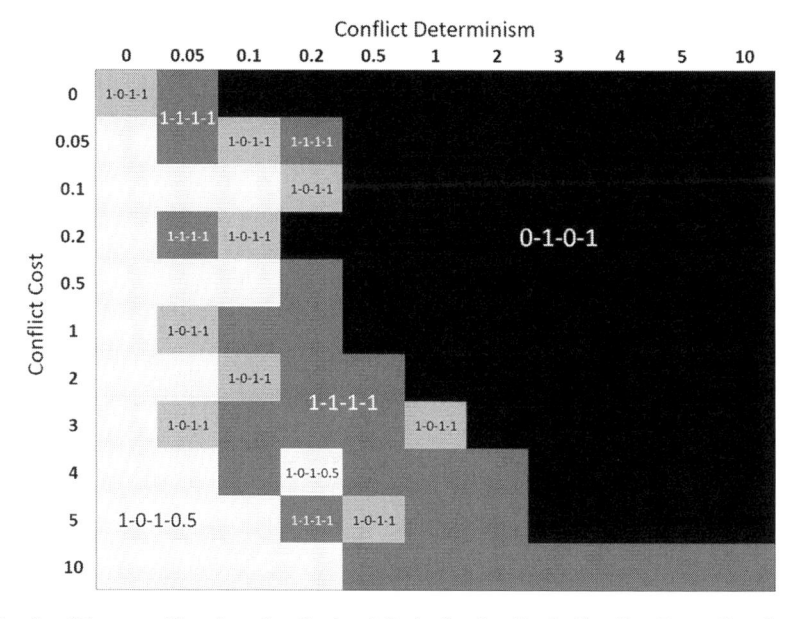

Fig. 1. Diagram Showing the Optimal Rule Set for Each Conflict Type Simulated. *Note*: Of the 24 possible rule sets, only four performed optimally in at least one scenario. Each color in the map above corresponds to a rule set, Which are spelled out as their 1st person effect, 2nd person effect, 3rd person effect, and default dominance values.

The remainder of the space is split between 3 other rule sets. Towards the far-left side and bottom-left corner of the space, the rule that dominate features 1st and 3rd person effects and a default dominance of 0.5 (1−0−1−0.5). This is the rule set that minimizes conflict: Individuals use information from other interactions to synchronize expectations − and the default dominance value of 0.5 means that the initial interaction in a simulation is a successful coordination 50% of the time, and a pointless and potentially costly conflict only 25% of the time.

In the space between the areas dominated by 0−1−0−1 and 1−0−1−0.5 is a rule set that strikes a balance between these two. In this rule set, all three expectation forming mechanisms are used, and default dominance is 1.0 (1−1−1−1). In this rule set, the information provided by possible initial conflicts is worth the cost, but guaranteeing that each individual pair is perfectly optimized is not worth the cost of the extra conflicts that would occur.

In the same area between the first two rule sets, there is another 4th rule set that is the most successful in a handful of conflict scenarios, although not nearly as frequently as the third rule set. This rule set leverages 1st person and 3rd person effects and has a default dominance parameter of 1.0 (1−0−1−1). It has a slightly higher average number of conflicts than 1−0−1−0.5, because any interactions between agents with mutually unformed expectations of one another end in conflict.

EXPECTATION FORMING RULES AS SOCIAL SORTING ALGORITHMS

The payoffs of the more successful rule sets are a function of two things. First, how few miscoordinations does it take for expectations to stabilize – or how quickly does each pair of individuals form expectations about one another? Second, how effective is the equilibrium that is reached by the agents? How many pairs of individuals have coordinated expectations, and how many of those sets of coordinated expectations are optimal?

First, the question of which rule sets can produce coordinated expectations quickly is addressed. For this round of simulations, each rule strategy is tested 100 times with conflict determinism, d, fixed at 1. (This parameter should not affect the amount of time it takes for expectations to form.) Results are summarized in Table 3. Of the 24 rule sets tested, six fail to stabilize altogether: meaning individuals fail to form expectations. Three of these rule sets are simply the rule sets where the 1st, 2nd and 3rd person effects are all absent. In addition to these "0–0–0–X" rule sets, the other three are rule sets where the 1st person and/or the 3rd person effects are present, but 2nd person effects are absent and default dominance is equal to 0.[3]

In the four rule sets where there is no 2nd person effect and default dominance is equal to 0, no individual ever behaves dominantly and every action is a mutual deferral. In the absence of expectation-forming mechanisms and with a default dominance of 0.5, individuals play either strategy 50% of the time and as such coordinate 50% of the time, and when default dominance is turned up to 1.0, individuals are in a state of perpetual conflict.

Furthermore, only four rule sets of 24 create a full set of mutually coordinated expectations across every pair 100% of the time. These are the same four rule sets that are found to perform optimally in at least one of the conflict scenarios during the prior portion of the analysis, and the same four rule sets that performed best in each scenario in the first portion of the analysis. It is now apparent that their superior performance can be attributed to the fact that they are the only combinations that lead to perfect coordination between all pairs of individuals in the group.

The percentage of pairs that are optimized by all four coordinating rule sets vary as a function of how accurately conflicts identify the higher-ability agent. Figs. 2a and 2b show their average performance in 1,000 simulations across 11 levels of conflict determinism, with regards to both the number of optimally coordinated pairs (15 being the theoretical maximum and 7.5 being the theoretical minimum) and the average payoff per coordinated action (2/3 being the theoretical maximum and 1/2 being the theoretical minimum). Table 4 summarizes the average number of conflicts and total interactions it takes for each rule set to coordinate all pairs, and their average payoff and number of optimized pairs at

Expectations and Coordination in Small Groups 197

Table 3. Table Showing the Performance of Each Rule Set With Regard To Whether or Not It Leads to the Formation of Expectations, How Long It Takes These Expectations to Form, and the Number of Complimentary Sets of Expectations (the Average Number of Pairs Who Will Have Coordinated Actions Going Forward).

Rule Set	Expectations Form	Interactions Required for Total Expectation Formation	Coordinated Pairs (Out of 15)
1−0−1−0.5	Yes	5.75	15.00
1−1−1−1	Yes	4.12	15.00
0−1−0−1	Yes	47.71	15.00
1−0−1−1	Yes	5.11	15.00
0−0−1−0.5	Yes	72.70	13.28
1−1−1−0.5	Yes	5.19	13.20
0−1−1−0	Yes	18.24	12.90
1−1−0−0	Yes	18.14	12.90
1−0−0−0.5	Yes	25.91	12.90
0−1−0−0	Yes	86.79	12.30
1−1−1−0	Yes	11.00	11.70
1−1−0−0.5	Yes	9.44	11.25
0−1−0−0.5	Yes	56.94	10.80
1−0−0−1	Yes	15.85	10.65
0−0−1−1	Yes	15.84	10.35
0−1−1−0.5	Yes	9.47	10.05
0−1−1−1	Yes	6.66	8.55
1−1−0−1	Yes	7.07	7.35
1−0−1−0	No	–	–
1−0−0−0	No	–	–
0−0−1−0	No	–	–
0−0−0−0	No	–	–
0−0−0−0.5	No	–	–
0−0−0−1	No	–	–

conflict determinism levels of 0 (no information from conflict), 1, and 10 (nearly perfect information from conflict).

The rule set "0−1−0−1," where each individual pair separately determines the best individual to lead an interaction by first engaging in a conflict, sorts out individuals almost perfectly in situations where conflicts are highly informative (conflict determinism is high). Yet, this benefit is far less pronounced when conflicts are not fully informative. Furthermore, groups using this rule set take the longest amount of time to form a complete set of expectations, and require the highest number of conflicts to do so.

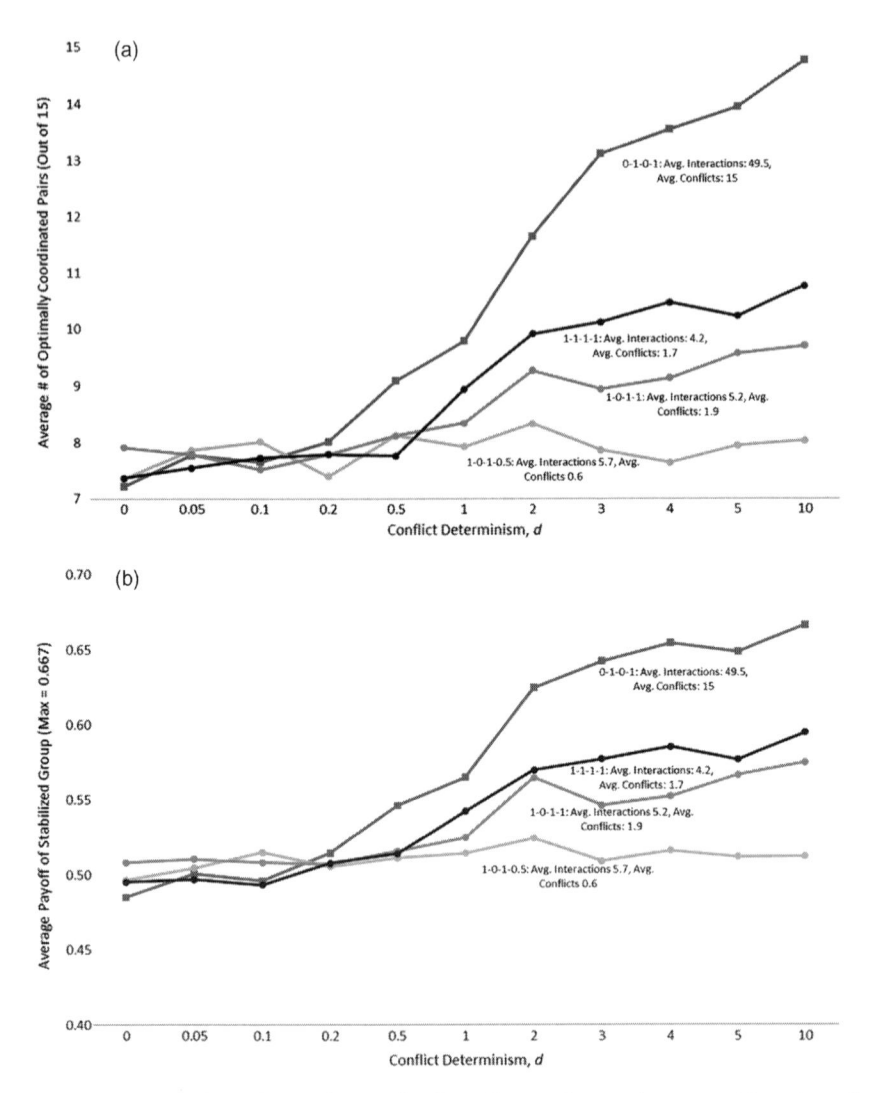

Fig. 2. How Each Rule Set Optimally Coordinates Interactions as a Function of Conflict Determinism. *Note*: Each rule set is labeled with the average number of interactions and conflicts it takes to coordinate all pairs. At low values, where conflicts are relatively uninformative, all groups perform similarly. As conflicts become more informative, rule sets that have more conflicts coordinate more efficiently, making even more costly conflicts beneficial to the group.

Expectations and Coordination in Small Groups

Table 4. Table Showing the Average Number of Conflicts and Interactions It Takes for Each Fully Coordinating Rule Set to Form Expectations, and the Quality of That Coordination (# of Optimized Pairs and Average Payoff) at Different Levels of Conflict Determinism.

Rule Set	Average # of Interactions	Average # of Conflicts	Average # of Optimized Pairs (Max = 15)			Average Payoff of Stabilized Group (Max = 2/3)		
			$d=0$	$d=1$	$d=10$	$d=0$	$d=1$	$d=10$
0–1–0–1	49.54	15.00	7.22	9.80	14.76	0.485	0.565	0.666
1–0–1–0.5	5.72	0.57	7.35	7.92	8.03	0.496	0.514	0.512
1–0–1–1	5.19	1.89	7.91	8.34	9.71	0.508	0.525	0.575
1–1–1–1	4.23	1.66	7.37	8.94	10.77	0.495	0.542	0.595

The rule set "1–0–1–0.5" minimizes the number of conflicts that is necessary to achieve full coordination, with an average of less than one conflict necessary for each group to fully coordinate. As seen earlier, this rule set is optimal for a situation where conflicts provide little to no information and are costly.

The rule sets "1–0–1–1" and "1–1–1–1" not only involve a slightly higher number of average conflicts, at 1.89 and 1.66, respectively, than "1–0–1–0.5," but they also require a smaller number of overall interactions to coordinate. Furthermore, when conflicts are informative, the average payoffs for each are roughly halfway between the expected payoff of a fully optimized group (2/3) and a group that is coordinated randomly (1/2). On average, the rule set "1–1–1–1" seems to be superior to "1–0–1–1," as it has a lower number of interactions and conflicts before a full set of expectations form, and higher expected payoffs than "1–0–1–1" in situations where conflicts are highly informative. Ultimately, the coordination game as it is defined here has three potentially optimal solutions, depending on the cost and information quality of conflict. One that works when cost is high and quality is low, another when cost is low and quality is high, and a third that performs best in between these two regions.

DISCUSSION

Social psychologists and ethologists have frequently observed how individual humans and animals are easily influenced by directed actions between other pairs of individuals, and simulation studies have shown how this can lead to the formation of transitive hierarchies. By shifting the event of analysis from hierarchical directed action to interaction, and by allowing for the possibility of a costly but informative conflict, the simulations presented here contextualize this finding. When two individuals interact with each other, it can be beneficial for others to form expectations about them, and for those two to form expectations about others, based on said interaction. Certain ways of forming expectations enable groups to perfectly synchronize their expectations with only a handful of interactions. However, quickly forming expectations comes at a cost of coordination quality. There is a tradeoff between sorting quickly and sorting correctly. When pairs of individuals can accurately compare their abilities to one another at a low cost, sorting correctly is more important than sorting quickly.

This finding has two main implications. For those interested in the evolutionary origins of power and prestige orders at either a biological or cultural level, the efficiency and effectiveness of conflict between individuals should have a profound influence on how individuals form expectations about others. For example, a species that is capable of only engaging in costly fights with one another or a culture that has a custom of determining social rank via violent conflict may quickly form judgments to fully leverage the information provided by a small number of conflicts. Meanwhile, a middle school chess team trying to determine who should be "first chair" in its upcoming meet may develop a tradition of having challenges between its members – as each conflict has lots of relevant information and comes at a relatively low cost.

For those who study industrial psychology and organizational behavior, this work implies that the ways in which groups of humans may be hardwired to determine prestige order are far from optimal. If the assumption is made that interactions between individuals reveal information about who should "lead" and who should "follow," then there may be a tendency for individuals to quickly grab a small amount of information from those interactions and form hierarchies that reflect coincidence more so than ability. If it is the natural tendency for individuals to observe interactions to determine their place in a group, then organizations may benefit from creating an environment that encourages all individuals to behave dominantly in the early stages of a group task. From the perspective of the group, coordination will always be improved when two things occur: High-ability actors are given status, and status without ability does not beget more status. (Status is defined here as being given the opportunity to take on high-importance roles in group interaction.) Teaching those who facilitate group work to limit the tendency to sort quickly in situations where a more thorough sorting process is optimal could be beneficial.

The model of small group behavior presented is clipped in several ways in order to make the analysis presented tractable. While general patterns should still hold, altering the number of individuals in a group, or the number of interactions that occur in a simulation, could easily shift the spaces where some rule sets are more beneficial than others. Furthermore, the total number of rule sets analyzed is limited to 24 rule sets that are based on empirically observed patterns in other papers. The four numbers in each rule set are translated into over 70 different instructions for agents to observe when translating prior interactions in to expectations. The total number of rule sets that can be employed using an automata approach as it is outlined here is staggeringly large (and is discussed further in the Appendix). More nuanced rule sets that produce optimal results in certain scenarios likely exist.

The approach outlined in the model presented lends itself to the exploration of several other interesting facets of group coordination. The tension between the individual and the group could be explored by giving individuals differential payoffs based on whether they have played the "lead" or "follow" role: In this case, rule sets that benefit the individual may not be the same as those that benefit the group. Furthermore, while the creation of an ability-based hierarchy is ideal in the model of group behavior here, other scholars have focused on the fact that hierarchies have their roots in both prestige – where rewards are heaped on those who can contribute to the group – and dominance – where rewards are given to the most feared (Cheng, Tracy, Foulsham, Kingstone, & Henrich, 2013). An analysis of a scenario where each agent has two ability variables, one that determines success in conflict and another that determines success in leading coordinated activities, could explore this parallel process of hierarchy formation further. Additionally, just as the models of hierarchy formation provided by the ESS perspective have been integrated with diffuse status characteristics (Skvoretz & Fararo, 1996), a parallel extension could model the influence of intra group variation in race and gender on group coordination. Finally, status characteristics theory dictates that high-status individuals are more likely to participate in group interactions, while this paper uses random pair selection to determine who will participate in each interaction within the larger group task being modeled, the tendency for individuals to participate more (less) as their status in the group increases (decreases) could also be incorporated in future work.

CONCLUSION

The formation of expectations based on observed interactions has been well documented in research on both animal and human behavior. As predicted, which rules are used to form expectations have a large influence on the overall tendency of the group to the coordinate. The costs and benefits of each individual interaction (particularly conflicts) determine which type of coordination, quick and hasty or slow and thorough, is better for the group, and consequently which expectation-forming rules are better for the group. The tendency of individuals to form expectations of individuals who they have not interacted with is only beneficial when pairwise competitions between individuals are costly or uninformative.

NOTES

1. In a group of n individuals, there are a total of $\binom{n}{2} = \frac{n(n-1)}{2}$ possible pairs of individuals that should each occur with equal probability. A group of n agents have abilities of $\frac{1}{n+1}, \frac{2}{n+1}, \ldots, \frac{n}{n+1}$. These abilities correspond to the payoff received by the group for an interaction led by an agent. An agent with ability $\frac{i}{n+1}$ could be expected to lead a total of $i - 1$ pairwise interactions in a perfectly optimal system, one for each other agent with lesser ability. This means that in an optimal system $n - 1$ out of $\binom{n}{2}$ possible interactions will have a payoff of $\frac{n}{n+1}$ and $n - 2$ out of $\binom{n}{2}$ possible interactions will have a

payoff of $\frac{n-1}{n+1}$, and so on. This means the expected value of an interaction in an optimal system can be expressed by the following sum, the sum of the products of each agent's probability of leading an interaction multiplied by the payoff of an interaction led by them:

$$\sum_{i=1}^{n} \frac{(i-1)}{\binom{n}{2}} \frac{i}{(n+1)}$$

Mathematically, this sum can be shown to be equal to $\frac{2}{3}$, regardless of the value of n:

$$= \sum_{i=1}^{n} \frac{(i-1)}{\frac{(n)(n-1)}{2}} \frac{i}{(n+1)}$$

$$= \frac{2}{n(n-1)(n+1)} \sum_{i=1}^{n} (i-1)i$$

$$= \frac{2}{n(n-1)(n+1)} \left[\sum_{i=1}^{n} i^2 - \sum_{i=1}^{n} i \right]$$

The two sums on the right of this equation have known solutions in terms of n that can be substituted in:

$$= \frac{2}{n(n-1)(n+1)} \left[\frac{n(n+1)(2n+1)}{6} - \frac{n(n+1)}{2} \right]$$

From here, an algebraic solution can be found:

$$= \frac{2}{n(n-1)} \left[\frac{n(2n+1)}{6} - \frac{n}{2} \right]$$

$$= \frac{2}{(n-1)} \left[\frac{(2n+1)}{6} - \frac{1}{2} \right]$$

$$= \frac{2}{(n-1)} \left[\frac{(2n+1) - 3}{6} \right]$$

$$= \frac{2}{(n-1)} \left[\frac{2n-2}{6} \right]$$

$$= \frac{2}{3}.$$

2. In the axioms presented by Fararo and Skvoretz (1986): (1) there are no initial expectations between actors, (2) with a certain probability if X attacks Y, then a dominance expectation forms where X expects to dominate Y and Y expects to defer to X, (3) once an expectation has formed, it cannot be undone, (4) an actor cannot attack an actor who (s)he has a deferential state towards, (5) bystanders with a certain probability will form a deferential status towards actors they observe attacking, and a dominant status toward actors they observe being attacked, and (6) all possible attacks are equally likely.

3. Using pseudo-logical notation, we can say that a complete set of expectations will form in the following conditions:

2nd Person OR ((Default Dominance > 0) AND (1st Person OR 3rd Person)).

ACKNOWLEDGMENTS

Earlier versions of this work were presented at the 2016 Graduate Workshop in Complexity and Computational Social Science at the Santa Fe Institute, the 2017 Cornell Sociology Research Symposium in Ithaca, NY, the 12th Conference of the Interdisciplinary Network for Group Research in St. Louis, MO, and the 2017 Group Processes Conference in Montreal, QC. Thanks to George Berry, Junius Brown, Ed Lawler, and John Miller for their thoughtful comments and suggestions.

REFERENCES

Anderson, C., & Brown, C. E. (2010). The functions and dysfunctions of hierarchy. *Research in Organizational Behavior*, 30, 55–89.

Anderson, C., & Willer, R. (2014). Do status hierarchies benefit groups? A bounded functionalist account of status. In J. T. Cheng, J. L. Tracy, & C. Anderson (Eds.), *The psychology of social status* (pp. 47–70). New York, NY: Springer.

Axelrod, R. M. (1997). *The complexity of cooperation: Agent-based models of competition and collaboration.* Princeton, NJ: Princeton University Press.

Balkwell, J. W. (1991). From expectations to behavior: An improved postulate for expectation states theory. *American Sociological Review*, 56(3), 355–369.

Berger, J., Cohen, B. P., & Zelditch, Jr M. (1972). Status characteristics and social interaction. *American Sociological Review*, 37(3), 241–255.

Berger, J., & Conner, T. L. (1969). Performance expectations and behavior in small groups. *Acta Sociologica*, 12(4), 186–198.

Berger, J., Rosenholtz, S. J., & Zelditch, Jr M. (1980). Status organizing processes. *Annual Review of Sociology*, 6(1), 479–508.

Berger, J., & Snell, J. L. (1961). *A stochastic theory for self-other expectations.* Technical Report No. 1. Stanford University, Stanford, CA, USA.

Binmore, K. G., & Samuelson, L. (1992). Evolutionary stability in repeated games played by finite automata. *Journal of Economic Theory*, 57(2), 278–305.

Chase, I. D. (1974). Models of hierarchy formation in animal societies. *Systems Research and Behavioral Science*, 19(6), 374–382.

Chase, I. D. (1982). Dynamics of hierarchy formation: The sequential development of dominance relationships. *Behaviour*, 80(3), 218–239.

Chase, I. D., & Lindquist, W. B. (2016). The fragility of individual-based explanations of social hierarchies: A test using animal pecking orders. *PloS One*, 11(7), e0158900.

Chase, I. D., Tovey, C., Spangler-Martin, D., & Manfredonia, M. (2002). Individual differences versus social dynamics in the formation of animal dominance hierarchies. *Proceedings of the National Academy of Sciences*, 99(8), 5744–5749.

Cheng, J. T., Tracy, J. L., Foulsham, T., Kingstone, A., & Henrich, J. (2013). Two ways to the top: Evidence that dominance and prestige are distinct yet viable avenues to social rank and influence. *Journal of Personality and Social Psychology*, 104(1), 103–125.

Dugatkin, L. A. (1997). Winner and loser effects and the structure of dominance hierarchies. *Behavioral Ecology*, 8(6), 583–587.

Dugatkin, L. A., & Earley, R. L. (2003). Group fusion: The impact of winner, loser, and bystander effects on hierarchy formation in large groups. *Behavioral Ecology*, 14(3), 367–373.

Fararo, T. J., & Skvoretz, J. (1986). E-state structuralism: A theoretical method. *American Sociological Review*, 51(5), 591–602.

Fararo, T. J., Skvoretz, J., & Kosaka, K. (1994). Advances in E-state structuralism: Further studies in dominance structure formation. *Social Networks*, 16(3), 233–265.

Fisek, M. H. (1974). A model for the evolution of status structures in task-oriented discussion groups. In J. Berger, T. L. Conner, & M. H. Fisek (Eds.), *Expectation states theory: A theoretical research program* (pp. 53–83). Cambridge, MA: Winthrop Publishers, Inc.

Fisek, M. H., Berger, J., & Norman, R. Z. (1995). Evaluations and the formation of expectations. *American Journal of Sociology*, *101*(3), 721–746.
Gould, R. V. (2003). *Collision of wills: How ambiguity about social rank breeds conflict*. Chicago, IL: University of Chicago Press.
Hsu, Y., Earley, R. L., & Wolf, L. L. (2006). Modulation of aggressive behaviour by fighting experience: mechanisms and contest outcomes. *Biological Reviews*, *81*(1), 33–74.
Kilduff, G. J., Willer, R., & Anderson, C. (2016). Hierarchy and its discontents: Status disagreement leads to withdrawal of contribution and lower group performance. *Organization Science*, *27*(2), 373–390.
Miller, J. H. (1996). The coevolution of automata in the repeated prisoner's dilemma. *Journal of Economic Behavior & Organization*, *29*(1), 87–112.
Morgan, D., Grant, K. A., Prioleau, O. A., Nader, S. H., Kaplan, J. R., & Nader, M. A. (2000). Predictors of social status in cynomolgus monkeys (Macaca fascicularis) after group formation. *American Journal of Primatology*, *52*(3), 115–131.
Parker, G. A. (1974). Assessment strategy and the evolution of fighting behaviour. *Journal of Theoretical Biology*, *47*(1), 223–243.
Rapoport, A., & Chammah, A. M. (1965). *Prisoner's dilemma: A study in conflict and cooperation* (Vol. 165). Ann Arbor, MI: University of Michigan Press.
Rapoport, A., & Chammah, A. M. (1966). The game of chicken. *American Behavioral Scientist*, *10*(3), 10–28.
Rapoport, A., & Guyer, M. (1978). A taxonomy of 2 × 2 games. *General Systems*, *23*, 125–136.
Ridgeway, C. L. (1987). Nonverbal behavior, dominance, and the basis of status in task groups. *American Sociological Review*, *52*(5), 683–694.
Ridgeway, C. L. (2015). The gender frame and social order. In E. J. Lawler, S. R. Thye, & J. Yoon (Eds.), *Order on the edge of chaos: Social psychology and the problem of social order* (pp. 189–207). New York, NY: Cambridge University Press.
Robinson, D. T., & Smith-Lovin, L. (2001). Getting a laugh: Gender, status, and humor in task discussions. *Social Forces*, *80*(1), 123–158.
Savin-Williams, R. C. (1979). Dominance hierarchies in groups of early adolescents. *Child Development*, *50*(4), 923–935.
Simmel, G. (1904). The sociology of conflict. I. *American Journal of Sociology*, *9*(4), 490–525.
Skvoretz, J., & Fararo, T. J. (1996). Status and participation in task groups: A dynamic network model. *American Journal of Sociology*, *101*(5), 1366–1414.
Smith-Lovin, L., & Brody, C. (1989). Interruptions in group discussions: The effects of gender and group composition. *American Sociological Review*, *54*(3), 424–435.
Van Vugt, M. (2006). Evolutionary origins of leadership and followership. *Personality and Social Psychology Review*, *10*(4), 354–371.
Van Vugt, M., Hogan, R., & Kaiser, R. B. (2008). Leadership, followership, and evolution: Some lessons from the past. *American Psychologist*, *63*(3), 182.
Wagner, D. G., & Berger, J. (2002). Expectation states theory: An evolving research program. In J. Berger & M. Zelditch Jr (Eds.), *New directions in contemporary sociological theory* (pp. 41–76). Lanham, MD: Rowman & Littlefield.
Whiteman, E. A., & Cote, I. M. (2004). Dominance hierarchies in group-living cleaning gobies: Causes and foraging consequences. *Animal Behaviour*, *67*(2), 239–247.

APPENDIX: MODELING INTERACTIONS IN A GROUP WITH FINITE STATE AUTOMATA

Finite state automata (FSA) have been used to explore optimal strategies in repeated games between two players. In these repeated games, a player's decision on how to play the game next in the next round is determined by what "state" it is in. The state that the player is in is a function of what state the player was in during the previous round and the decision its opponent made in the previous round. This can be contrasted to a "pure strategy," where an individual makes the same decision each time, or a "mixed strategy" where individuals select each strategy with a fixed probability, or a predetermined sequence of strategies that are made regardless of the decisions of their opponent.

This framework has often been used to study the repeated "Prisoner's Dilemma" game. Two well-known strategies for this game that can be expressed as an FSA are "tit-for-tat," where players begin with "cooperate" and then copy the decision of their opponent in the previous round, or "grim trigger," where players begin at "cooperate" and then "defect" indefinitely as soon as their opponent plays defect. FSA can be displayed visually as network diagrams (Binmore & Samuelson, 1992), and the examples for these two strategies are shown in Fig. A1. An advantage of the FSA approach is that it allows for all strategies to be expressed as a string of numbers (typically a bit string of "1"s and "0"s). The length of the string is a function of the number of states (which map onto different strategies, not necessarily in a 1-to-1 manner), and the number of different choices an individual player can make each round (or the number of different outcomes for each round). Expressing these strategies as FSAs and bit-strings allows the systematic exploration of all possible strategies for FSAs with a small number of states and strategies, and for genetic algorithms to be used to find high-performing FSAs regardless of the number of states (for examples see Miller 1996 or Axelrod 1997).

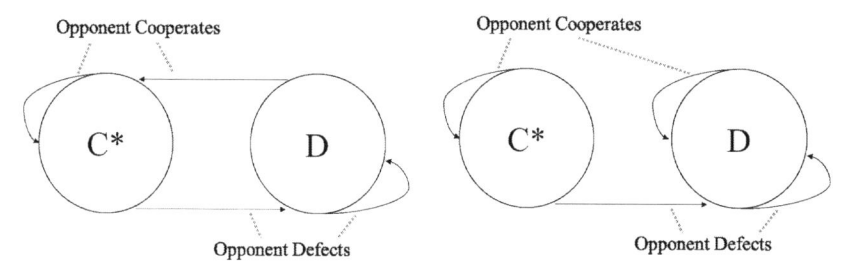

Fig. A1. A Diagram of How Players Update Their Upcoming "Move" in a Prisoner's Dilemma Game Using the "Tit-for-tat" and "Grim Trigger" Strategies, Each of Which Can Be Conceived as a Finite State Automaton That Can Be Represented by a Network Diagram. *Note:* "*" Indicates the automaton's initial state.

The approach used in this paper builds on this. Each FSA in the model has three states, one that corresponds to each of three expectations: dominant, deferential, and unformed. However, the FSA approach for several individuals introduces several complications. First, each agent has an identical FSA for each other individual in the group: The same decision-making rules are used for each other person, but individual FSAs may be in different states at each point in time. Second, individuals must not only react to the specific decision of their opponent, but must also react to the specific outcome of a conflict when both individuals play "lead." Third, individuals may update their expectation states of individuals with whom they are not directly interacting. Fourth, certain elements of the model are stochastic: individuals may update their states probabilistically instead of deterministically in certain situations, and each state may correspond to "lead" or "follow" with a certain probability.

In the scenario modeled in this paper, an individual's expectations about another can be in one of three states, each of those three states corresponds to "lead" or "follow" with a certain probability. Each interaction has one of five outcomes (conflict with one of two possible winners, coordination with one of two possible "leaders," and mutual deference), and distinct rules about how to update expectations towards (1) an individual with whom they just interacted, (2) individuals who were not involved in their interaction, and (3) other pairs of individuals interacting separately.

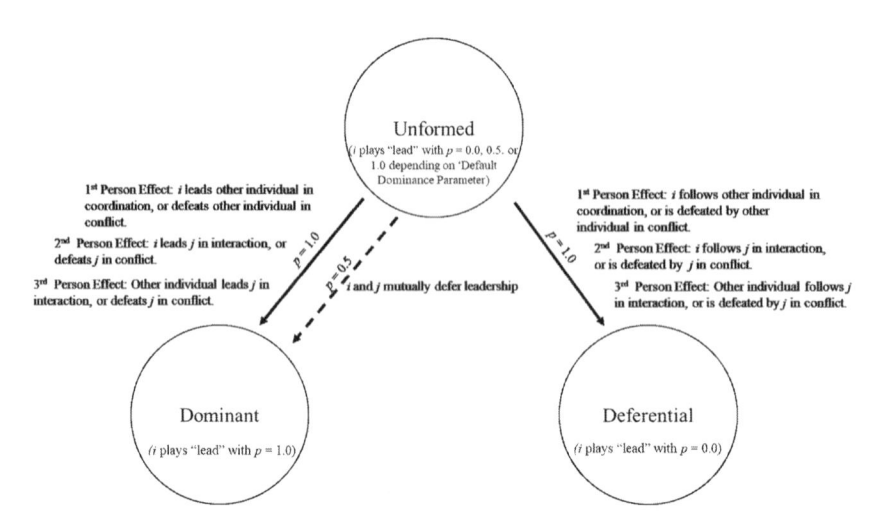

Fig. A2. Figure Showing an Example Finite State Automaton Corresponding to an Agent *i*'s Expectation toward Agent *j*. State Transitions That Are Dependent on the Presence of 1st Person, 2nd Person, and 3rd Person Effects and Behavior That Is Dependent on Default Dominance Are Both Labeled Accordingly.

The number of possible combinations is overwhelming and reducing the number of candidate FSAs to 24 involved several decisions. First, rules about updating expectations were based on the three sets of effects identified in the paper, each of these three sets is either "on" (1) or "off" (0). Second, individuals are only allowed to update an "unformed" expectation – dominant (lead) and deferential (follow) expectations are "absorbing." Third, dominant expectations always cause an individual to play "lead," and deferential expectations always cause an individual to play "follow," only the unformed expectation can vary. Fourth, mutual deference between individuals with unformed expectations about one another leads them to forming dominant expectations about one another with a probability of 0.5. A network diagram showing the FSA used by all agents, and the portions of it that are subject to variation, are shown in Fig. A2. Each individual agent in a simulation possesses identical copies of this machine for each other agent in the simulation.

The entire model of small group behavior can be reduced to three parts: the interaction between individuals (the "game"), the way in which those interactions influence an individual's expectations of others (expectation-forming rules), and the way in which those expectations map onto the way an individual interacts with others – which here is referred to as the "personality" of an agent. An overall diagram of how these elements map onto one another in the simulation is shown in Fig. A3. (Code for the simulation is available upon request.)

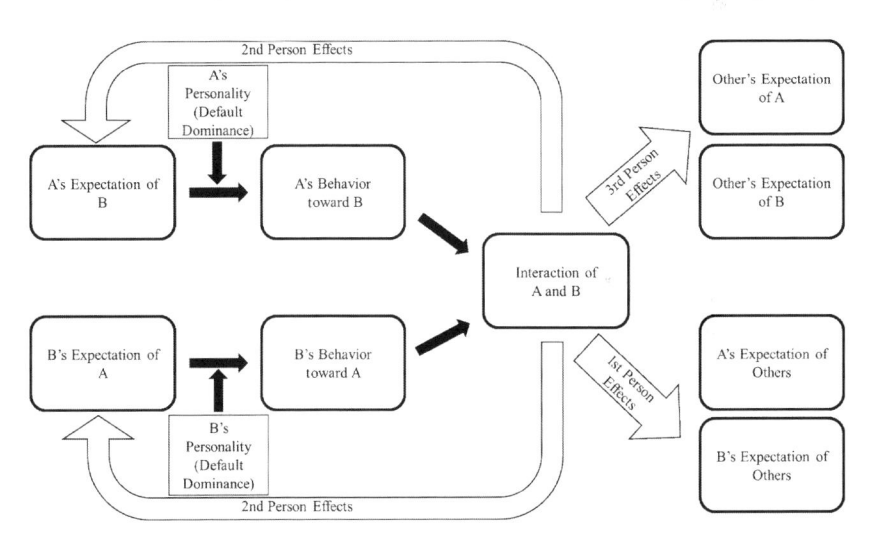

Fig. A3. A Diagram Showing the Core Components of the Model Presented: Interactions, Expectations, and the Translations of Expectations to Behaviors.

INDEX

Accelerometers
  classifications and dimensions of aggression, 32–33
  definition, 30
  research using, 31–32
  types, 31
  use of, 41
  measure of emotion, 40
Affect control theory (ACT), 104, 108–109, 121
  interact simulation between physician and client, 108–109
Aggression measurement using accelerometers, study of
  correlation and multiple regression analyses, 38
  data collection and analysis, 35
  dominant and nondominant-hand average peak acceleration, 35–36, 38, 40–41
  equipment and method, 34
  masculinity threat, 38–40
  peak acceleration, 35–36
  physical aggression, measure of, 36
  procedure, 34–35, 37–39
  relationship between BPAQ and behavioral measures of aggression, 36–37
  stability and representative reliability, 35–36
Amazon Mechanical Turk (AMT), 9
Anti-White bias, study of, 131, 137–138
  method
    analytical strategy, 141
    control variables, 140–141
    data and sample, 138–139
    dependent variables, 139
    independent variables, 139–140
    measures, 139–141
    odds ratios (ORs), 141
  results
    binary logistic regressions of status characteristics on resource reallocation, 141–146
    effects of whiteness and White privilege, 151
    predicted probabilities of perceived personal encounters, 148, 149
    probit regressions of status characteristics on resource reallocation, 148–149
  status dissonance theory
    framework, 138, 150–151
    association between social class and status dissonance, 150
    reverse discrimination, 148, 149–151

Behavioral interaction, 182
Bem Sex Role Inventory (BSRI), 39

Cognitive function of accommodation, 60
Communication accommodation theory (CAT), 59–61
Criminality score, perceptions of, 109–113

De Beers, 7–8
Diamond jewelry, 3
  diamond rings, 7
Diamonds

209

4Cs of, 7
features of, 7
gem-quality, 8
lab-created, 8–9
mined, 7–8
pipeline, 7–8
polished, 8
production processes of, 3, 8–9
  high pressure-high temperature (HPHT) method, 8
  non-traditional, 9–12
  technological innovation in, 8–9
  See also Gift-giving behavior, study of effect of high-stakes rituals on; Ritual
Diamond trading company (DTC), 8

Engagement rings, 3, 7
E-state structuralism (ESS), 182, 184–185
Expectation-forming rules, 182, 200
  expectation forming mechanisms, 189–190
  functions of hierarchy, 185–186
  group coordination and, 186–189, 200
  in animal groups, 183–185
  miscoordination and conflict, 187–188
  optimal and suboptimal coordination, 187
  prior interactions, 183
  sensitivity to initial attributes, 186–187
  types of outcomes, 188–189
  visible attributes, 183
  in hierarchical pattern, 184–185
  resource holding potential (RHP), 184
  rule combinations, 190–194
  rule set performance in variable scenarios, 194–196, 200
  as social sorting algorithms, 196–199
  in undifferentiated groups, 183–184
Expectation states theory (EST), 182–184, 187
Expressive legitimacy cues, 62

Gender Identity Test, 39
Gift-giving behavior, study of effect of high-stakes rituals on
  method, 12–13
  post hoc analyses, 14–18
    lab-created diamonds, likelihood of choosing, 15
    logistic regression analysis, 15–16
    mined diamonds, likelihood of choosing, 15, 20
    multinomial regression analysis, 17
  testing of, 13–14
Group coordination problems, 183
  See also Expectation-forming rules

Hierarchy
  ability-based, 201
  expectation-forming rules and, 184–185
  functions of, 185–186
  linear, 184–185
  See also Expectation-forming rules
High pressure-high temperature (HPHT) method, 8

Identity theory, 76–77, 99n1
  differences between programs of, 79–80
  integration of programs of, 80–81, 97
  perceptual control program of, 79
  structural program of, 78–79
  unified, 77
Institutionalizing process, 23

Kimberlite, 8

Lab-created diamonds, 3, 8–9, 23

Micro–macro problem, 76–77, 98
Moissanite, 9

Nintendo Wii, 34
Normative identities *vs* counter-normative identities, study
  data, 84–85
  descriptive statistics of identities and conditions, 87
  limitations and future research, 98–99
  nonverification effects, 92, 95–98
    on authenticity, 95–96
    on efficacy, 95
    on salience, 95
    on worth, 92
  participants, 85
  particular combinations of identities, 85
  positive effect of prominence
    on authenticity, 95–96
    on efficacy, 95
    on salience, 95
    on worth, 92
  results
    goodness of fit statistics, 92
    structural equation model, 90–94
    zero-order correlation coefficients, 89–90
  variables and measures
    identity prominence, 85–86
    identity salience, 86
    nonverification, 86
    role-specific authenticity, 88–89
    role-specific efficacy, 88
    role-specific worth, 88

Occupational status on sentencing decisions, vignette experiment, 107, 110–113
  crime word on sentencing recommendations, 113

criminality score, perceptions of experiment design, 114–115
  mediation hypotheses, 117
  participant attributes, 117
  recommended sentence, 115
  sample, 114
criminal perceptions of offender, 109, 113
findings, 122–124
impression formation hypotheses, 110–113
impressions of criminality hypotheses, 120
noncriminal perceptions of offender, 113
OLS regressions of recommended sentence, 117–121

People's behavior and attitudes, studies of social influence on, 160–161
  "accurate" and "inaccurate" perceptions of influence, 174
  attribution to self, 171–173
    egocentric biases and, 171–172
    influencer's motivations, 172–173
    spotlight effect, 171–172
  conditions for takes or forsakes, 160–162
  cumulative influence, 174
  determining responsibility, 163–164
  external forces, impact on attitude or behavior
    cognitive biases and dispositional attributions, 169–170
    target qualities and, 170
  identifying change in attitude or behavior, 164–169
    influencer qualities, 166
    influencer's attention and memory, 168

influencer's knowledge of person's behavioral inclination, 168
influencer–target relationship, 166–167
motivated cognition, 169
signal strength and target's response to it, 164–167
target qualities, 167
modes and outcomes of influence, 173–174
taking responsibility for outcomes, 162–163
Perceptual control processes, 77
Perceptual control program of identity theory, 79
Prisoner's Dilemma game, 186
Production process conservatism, 2, 6, 22–23
ritual effect in, 18–21

Racial discrimination, 130
Racial equality, 130
Resource holding potential (RHP), 184
Ritual
artifacts or commodities, 4
defined, 2
effect, 6
effect, study of perceived risks associated with
goals, 18
mediating effect, 20–21
method, 19
OLS regression analysis, 19–20
high-stakes nature of, 3, 6–7, 12
outcome of, 3
performers, 4–5
production process conservatism and, 12–21
rationale for, 3–5
rules, 5–7
implicit, 5–7
production processes as dimension of, 6

symbols of, 2–3
See also Gift-giving behavior, study of effect of high-stakes rituals on

Self-esteem, 81–82
authenticity component of, 83, 96
efficacy component of, 82–83, 96
moderation effects of prominence and salience on, 83–84
normative identities *vs* counter-normative identities, 84, 96–98
worth component of, 82, 96
Sentencing decisions
effect of occupational status on, 106–107
focal concerns perspective, 104–106
uncertainty avoidance perspective, 104–106
Social behavior, 31
Status construction theory, 131–133
Status dissonance theory, 134–138, 150–151
broadcast processes of cultural diffusion, 136
differential roles of status characteristics, 134–135
justice perceptions, 136–137
in lower class, 150
nomological depiction of, 137
referential structures, 135–136
status dissonance and positional lens, 137–138
See also Anti-White bias
Status generalizations, 133–134
Structural and perceptual control concepts, 77
Structural program of identity theory, 78–79
Synthetic diamonds, 3

Thanksgiving dinner, 5

Index

Vehicular acceleration, 31
Vocal accommodation
  differences between convergence and, 59–60
  fast Fourier transform (FFT) analysis, 56–58, 66–67
  group structure and, relationship between, 63–65, 71
  modeling, 68–69
  paraverbal frequencies and, 58–59, 61
  in presidential debates, 62
  prestige and, relationship between, 63
  procedures for measuring, 65–70
    acoustic analysis result (AAR) scores, 68–69
    acoustic expectation standing (AES) scores, 69–70
    data preparation and analysis, 68
    equipments and data-acquisition software, 67
    fast Fourier transform (FFT) analysis, 66–68
    recordings of discussion groups or interviews, 66
  process of, 53
  research, 52–53
  rhythm and musicality of interaction, 53–54
  speech convergence and, 56–65
  status and dominance perceptions and, relationship between, 59–62, 64–65, 71
  synchronizing behaviors, 54–56
    between actual conversation partners and virtual partners, 58, 71n1
    children's playground behaviors, 53–54
    interactions between neonates and parents and caretakers, 55
    inward interactional synchrony, 55–56
    outward interactional synchrony, 54–55
    self-synchrony, 54
  vocal patterns in different phases of interaction, 58–59

Western Christian culture, 4
Wii avatars, 34

Zirconium, 9